Sabert Basescu

RELATIONAL PERSPECTIVES BOOK SERIES

Volume 42

RELATIONAL PERSPECTIVES BOOK SERIES
LEWIS ARON & ADRIENNE HARRIS
Series Editors

The Relational Perspectives Book Series (RPBS) publishes books that grow out of or contribute to the relational tradition in contemporary psychoanalysis. The term "relational psychoanalysis" was first used by Greenberg and Mitchell (1983) to bridge the traditions of interpersonal relations, as developed within interpersonal psychoanalysis, and object relations, as developed within contemporary British theory. But under the seminal work of the late Stephen Mitchell, the term "relational psychoanalysis" grew and began to accrue to itself many other influences and developments. Various tributaries—interpersonal psychoanalysis, object relations theory, self psychology, empirical infancy research, and elements of contemporary Freudian and Kleinian thought—flow into this tradition, which understands relational configurations between self and others, both real and fantasied, as the primary subject of psychoanalytic investigation.

We refer to the relational tradition, rather than to a relational school, to highlight that we are identifying a trend, a tendency within contemporary psychoanalysis, not a more formally organized or coherent school or system of beliefs. Our use of the term "relational" signifies a dimension of theory and practice that has become salient across the wide spectrum of contemporary psychoanalysis. Now under the editorial supervision of Lewis Aron and Adrienne Harris, the Relational Perspectives Book Series originated in 1990 under the editorial eye of the late Stephen A. Mitchell. Mitchell was the most prolific and influential of the originators of the relational tradition. He was committed to dialogue among psychoanalysts and abhorred the authoritarianism that dictated adherence to a rigid set of beliefs or technical restrictions. He championed open discussion as well as comparative and integrative approaches, and he promoted new voices across the generations.

Included in the Relational Perspectives Book Series are authors and works that come from within the relational tradition and extend and develop the tradition, as well as works that critique relational approaches or compare and contrast them with alternative points of view. The series includes our most distinguished senior psychoanalysts along with younger contributors who bring fresh vision.

RELATIONAL PERSPECTIVES BOOK SERIES
LEWIS ARON & ADRIENNE HARRIS
Series Editors

Vol. 19
Who Is the Dreamer, Who Dreams the Dream?
A Study of Psychic Presences
James S. Grotstein

Vol. 18
Objects of Hope:
Exploring Possibility and Limit in
Psychoanalysis
Steven H. Cooper

Vol. 17
The Reproduction of Evil:
A Clinical and Cultural Perspective
Sue Grand

Vol. 16
Psychoanalytic Participation:
Action, Interaction, and Integration
Kenneth A. Frank

Vol. 15
The Collapse of the Self and Its Therapeutic
Restoration
Rochelle G. K. Kainer

Vol. 14
Relational Psychoanalysis:
The Emergence of a Tradition
Stephen A. Mitchell & Lewis Aron (eds.)

Vol. 13
Seduction, Surrender, and Transformation:
Emotional Engagement in the Analytic Process
Karen Maroda

Vol. 12
Relational Perspectives on the Body
Lewis Aron & Frances Sommer Anderson
(eds.)

Vol. 11
Building Bridges:
Negotiation of Paradox in Psychoanalysis
Stuart A. Pizer

Vol. 10
Fairbairn, Then and Now
Neil J. Skolnick and David E. Scharff (eds.)

Vol. 9
Influence and Autonomy in Psychoanalysis
Stephen A. Mitchell

Vol. 8
Unformulated Experience:
From Dissociation to Imagination in
Psychoanalysis
Donnel B. Stern

Vol. 7
Soul on the Couch:
Spirituality, Religion, and Morality
in Contemporary Psychoanalysis
Charles Spezzano & Gerald J. Gargiulo (eds.)

Vol. 6
The Therapist as a Person:
Life Crises, Life Choices, Life Experiences,
and Their Effects on Treatment
Barbara Gerson (ed.)

Vol. 5
Holding and Psychoanalysis:
A Relational Perspective
Joyce A. Slochower

Vol. 4
A Meeting of Minds:
Mutuality in Psychoanalysis
Lewis Aron

Vol. 3
The Analyst in the Inner City:
Race, Class, and Culture Through a
Psychoanalytic Lens
Neil Altman

Vol. 2
Affect in Psychoanalysis:
A Clinical Synthesis
Charles Spezzano

Vol. 1
Conversing With Uncertainty:
Practicing Psychotherapy in a Hospital Setting
Rita Wiley McCleary

Sabert Basescu

*Selected Papers
on Human Nature
and Psychoanalysis*

Edited by
George Goldstein and Helen Golden

Routledge
Taylor & Francis Group
New York   London

Routledge
Taylor & Francis Group
270 Madison Avenue
New York, NY 10016

Routledge
Taylor & Francis Group
27 Church Road
Hove, East Sussex BN3 2FA

© 2010 by Taylor and Francis Group, LLC
Routledge is an imprint of Taylor & Francis Group, an Informa business

Printed in the United States of America on acid-free paper
10 9 8 7 6 5 4 3 2 1

International Standard Book Number: 978-0-415-87167-9 (Hardback) 978-0-415-87168-6 (Paperback)

Library of Congress Cataloging-in-Publication Data

Basescu, Sabert.
    Sabert Basescu : selected papers on human nature and psychoanalysis / edited
by George Goldstein, Helen Golden.
        p. cm. -- (Relational persectives ; . 42)
    Includes bibliographical references and index.
    ISBN 978-0-415-87167-9 (hardcover : acid-free paper) -- ISBN
    978-0-415-87168-6 (pbk. : acid-free paper) -- ISBN 978-0-203-86866-9
    (e-book)
    1. Psychoanalysis. 2. Self-disclosure. 3. Psychoanalysts. 4. Basescu, Sabert. I.
Goldstein, George. II. Golden, Helen. III. Title.

BF175.B327 2010
150.19'5092--dc22   2009024912

Visit the Taylor & Francis Web site at
http://www.taylorandfrancis.com

and the Routledge Web site at
http://www.routledgementalhealth.com

CONTENTS

CONTRIBUTORS

Elliot Adler, PhD, ABPP, is the former director of the Westchester Center for the Study of Psychoanalysis and Psychotherapy and was president of Section One of Division 39 (Psychoanalysis) of the American Psychological Association. He is also faculty and supervisor at the Institute for the Psychoanalytic Study of Subjectivity and the National Training Program in Contemporary Psychoanalysis.

Lewis Aron, PhD, is director of the New York University Postdoctoral Program in Psychotherapy and Psychoanalysis, cochair of the Sándor Ferenczi Center at the New School for Social Research, and an honorary member of the William Alanson White Psychoanalytic Society. Dr. Aron is coeditor of the Relational Perspectives book series for Routledge and author of *A Meeting of Minds: Mutuality in Psychoanalysis* (Analytic Press, 1996).

Sabert Basescu, PhD, is professor emeritus at the New York University Postdoctoral Program in Psychotherapy and Psychoanalysis, where he taught and supervised from the program's inception until the day of his accident in 2006. He was one of the founders of the Westchester Center for Psychoanalysis and the last of the founders to be still teaching and supervising. He received his BA from Dartmouth, where he majored in philosophy, and his PhD in clinical psychology from Princeton. At Princeton he was a protégé of Dr. Sylvan Tomkins. He received his analytic training from the Postgraduate Center for Mental Health in New York City and proudly served in the U.S. Navy during

World War II. He has three children, seven grandchildren, and was married for 50 years to Elinor Basescu, who died in 2001. He married Dr. Stefanie Solow Glennon in 2003 after a 28-year friendship and professional relationship.

Barry Farber, PhD, received his degree in clinical psychology from Yale University. He has been a full-time faculty member in the clinical psychology program at Teachers College, Columbia University, since 1979 and has been a full professor since 1991. He has twice served as chairperson of the Counseling and Clinical Department, and he has been the program coordinator and director of clinical training since 1990. Dr. Farber serves on the editorial boards of several journals, including *Psychotherapy Research*, and maintains a part-time private practice in Mamaroneck, New York. He is also the author of four books, the most recent of which are *Self-Disclosure in Psychotherapy* (Guilford, 2006) and *Rock 'n' Roll Wisdom: What Psychologically Astute Lyrics Teach About Life and Love* (Praeger, 2007).

Stefanie Solow Glennon, PhD, is a supervisor at the New York University Postdoctoral Program in Psychotherapy and Psychoanalysis, faculty and supervisor at the Institute for Contemporary Psychotherapy, and faculty at the Stephen Mitchell Center for Relational Psychoanalysis. As a member of the editorial board of *Psychoanalytic Dialogues*, she has written in the areas of immediate experience, obesity, therapeutic action, mourning, artistic expression, and termination. Dr. Glennon maintains a private practice in New York City.

Helen Golden, PhD (editor), was a psychoanalyst with a practice in her home in Larchmont. She was a graduate of the Westchester Center for the Study of Psychoanalysis and Psychotherapy, where she was a faculty member and supervisor until her death in 2008. Dr. Golden was on the editorial board of *Psychoanalytic Psychology*, was an affiliate clinical professor of psychology at St. John's University, and had served as faculty and supervisor in the Albert Einstein Postgraduate Psychotherapy Training Program. She was the founding editor of *The Round Robin*, the psychoanalyst/psychologist newsletter of the American Psychological Association. Dr. Golden also served as treasurer for the Division of Psychoanalysis of the APA.

George Goldstein, PhD (editor), is on the faculties of the New York University Postdoctoral Program in Psychotherapy and Psychoanalysis, the Gordon Derner Institute of Advanced Psychological Studies,

Adelphi University, and the Suffolk Institute for Psychotherapy and Psychoanalysis. Dr. Goldstein is the former director of the Westchester Center for the Study of Psychoanalysis and Psychotherapy and has a private practice in Larchmont and Great Neck, New York.

Irwin Hirsch, PhD, is distinguished visiting faculty at the William Alanson White Institute, faculty and supervisor at the Manhattan Institute for Psychoanalysis, and adjunct professor and supervisor at the New York University Postdoctoral Program in Psychotherapy and Psychoanalysis. Dr. Hirsch serves on the editorial boards of *Contemporary Psychoanalysis, Psychoanalytic Dialogues,* and *Psychoanalytic Perspectives,* and is the author of more than 70 papers and reviews, as well as *Coasting in the Countertransference: Conflicts of Self Interest Between Analyst and Patient* (Analytic Press, 2008).

Irwin Z. Hoffman, PhD, is faculty and supervising analyst at the Chicago Center for Psychoanalysis and a lecturer in psychiatry at the College of Medicine, University of Illinois. He is on the editorial board of the *International Journal of Psychoanalysis* and *Psychoanalytic Dialogues* and is an editorial reader for the *Psychoanalytic Quarterly.* In addition, he is the author of *Ritual and Spontaneity in the Psychoanalytic Process: A Dialectical-Constructivist View* (Analytic Press, 1998).

Robert J. Katz, PhD, is faculty at the New York University Postdoctoral Program for the Study of Psychotherapy and Psychoanalysis and Westchester Center for the Study of Psychoanalysis and Psychotherapy. He is also visiting faculty at the Manhattan Institute for Psychoanalysis and supervisor at the Institute for Contemporary Psychotherapy. Dr. Katz maintains a private practice in Manhattan and Westchester, New York.

Elsa Menaker, PhD, is a clinical psychologist and a faculty member at the Westchester Center for the Study of Psychoanalysis and Psychotherapy, where she teaches attachment theory with her husband, Thomas Menaker. She has a private practice in New City, New York.

Spyros D. Orfanos, PhD, ABPP, is clinic director of the New York University Postdoctoral Program in Psychotherapy and Psychoanalysis and is on the board of directors at the Stephen A. Mitchell Center for Relational Studies. He has an independent practice of psychotherapy and psychoanalysis in Montclair, New Jersey, and New York City.

Neil Skolnick, Ph.D., is currently cochair of the relational track at the New York University Postdoctoral Program in Psychotherapy and Psychoanalysis, where he is also a supervisor and faculty member. Dr. Skolnick is also on the board of directors and faculty of the National Institute of the Psychotherapies and its two affiliated psychoanalytic training programs: the Institute for the Psychoanalytic Study of the Self and the National Training Program and the Westchester Center for the Study of Psychoanalysis and Psychoanalytic Psychotherapy. He has been active in promoting regional contemporary psychoanalytic training programs throughout the country, including Kansas City, Minneapolis, and Sacramento. He has coedited two books, *Relational Perspectives in Psychoanalysis* (1992) and *Fairbairn, Then and Now* (1998), both with Analytic Press. Dr. Skolnick maintains a practice in psychoanalysis in New York City.

Donnel B. Stern, PhD, is a training and supervising analyst and faculty member at the William Alanson White Institute as well as faculty and supervisor at the New York University Postdoctoral Program in Psychotherapy and Psychoanalysis. A past editor of *Contemporary Psychoanalysis*, Dr. Stern is currently editor of the Psychoanalysis in a New Key book series for Routledge and author of two books, *Unformulated Experience: From Dissociation to Imagination in Psychoanalysis* (Analytic Press, 1997) and *Partners in Thought: Working With Unformulated Experience, Dissociation, and Enactment* (Routledge, 2009).

George Whitson, PhD, is teaching faculty and supervisor at the Manhattan Institute for Psychoanalysis and the Derner Institute for Advanced Psychological Studies, Adelphi University. He is the cofounder of the Suffolk Institute for Psychotherapy and Psychoanalysis, where he currently serves on the board of trustees. Dr. Whitson has a private practice in Rockville Centre, New York.

PREFACE: FRIEND OF THE FAMILY

Whatever one thinks about the paradigm shifts that have taken place in our field over the last thirty years, these shifts have been transformational in both theory and practice. All current analytic traditions have contributed their own particular influences and they, themselves, have been influenced in return. Yet the important perspectives of existentialism and phenomenology, especially in clinical practice, are often overlooked or merely referenced in a passing footnote. This collection of articles is an attempt to document the work of one beloved existentialist/phenomenologist, Sabert Basescu—writer, teacher, supervisor, and analyst—and his influence on his psychoanalytic colleagues.

Sabert Basescu was a pillar of the New York area psychoanalytic scene for more than 50 years. He was a widely published writer and speaker. He was on the faculties at the New York University (NYU) Postdoctoral Program in Psychotherapy and Psychoanalysis, the Derner Institute of Advanced Psychological Studies at Adelphi University, and the Psychoanalytic Institute of the Postgraduate Center for Mental Health in New York City. Sabe was also a cofounder of the Westchester Center for the Study of Psychoanalysis and Psychotherapy.

Sabe, himself an analysand of Rollo May and Irwin Singer, maintained that it was never theory that distinguished effective psychotherapists from run-of-the-mill ones. He always believed that well-qualified and experienced psychotherapists of different schools were more alike in their clinical work than therapists with the same theoretical training but differing degrees of talent and experience. He was convinced that the important thing about psychoanalysis was not the theory itself but rather an authentic and subjectively compelling relationship with the analyst, the context in which a patient can begin to let go of the constricting defenses constructed over a lifetime of self-protection. Yet he himself was deeply committed to an existential and phenomenological view of psychotherapy.

In a paper from 1961b, Sabe remarks that

> existential psychotherapy does not in itself constitute a self-contained depth therapy that is counter to Freudian psychoanalytic psychotherapy. Nor does it refer to a body of special techniques or procedures. It would be more accurate to speak of the existential attitude toward, or context of, psychotherapy, since existentialists have thus far focused their attention on the presuppositions underlying all psychotherapies. (p. 75)

Sabe goes on to describe three elements that are essential to an existential approach. "The first attribute may be described as observation in the phenomenological mode. That is, the therapist must learn to perceive the patient in terms of his [the patient's] phenomenal reality and not in terms of the therapist's theoretical models. The second attribute is the experiential mode of knowing" (pp. 75–76). Sabe is referring here to the idea that the analyst might emphasize the patient's direct experience in the failure to realize his or her full humanity.

> This experiential mode applies to the therapist as well. An aspect of his "presence" in the "encounter" with the patient is his experiencing the patient's communications on many different levels of his own being. And finally the third attribute, which requires a primary emphasis on the "here and now," in priority to the "there and then." (p. 76)

For many years Sabe served as the director of one of the departments within the New York University Postdoctoral Program. His tenure coincided with the creative fervor, turmoil, intense conflicts, and multiplicity of voices beginning to emerge in our field. He was there at the birth of relational psychoanalysis, as it has become known, as well as for the further development of the interpersonal tradition. Sabe knew all the central figures and the issues they were championing, and they knew him and his work as well. These were very heady times indeed, and he was there at the center of the storm.

This book is not intended to be a history of those times nor a text on existentialism, but rather a look back at his work during those years. We hope this volume will document his prescient sense of the essential elements of the work, the transitions taking place in the field, and the ways in which he both was influenced by those times and was a contributor to them.

Here we have included seven of Sabe's own papers, each prefaced by an introductory discussion by a psychoanalyst who has a deep knowledge of Sabe's work, has shared a similar interest, or has been a student, supervisee, or analysand. In all cases the discussions emerge from some substantive or intimate contact with Sabe; we felt this would offer the reader unique insights into the themes being addressed as well as into Sabe himself.

The final article, "Tools of the Trade: The Use of the Self in Psychotherapy," was written almost 20 years ago and provides us with an opportunity to frame a vital and very contemporary debate on the impact of the therapist's personality on the patient and the work. Therefore, we have invited commentary from four authors representing the relational, interpersonal, classical, and research perspectives to enrich the conversation and highlight the relevant issues. We are grateful for the efforts of Neil Skolnick, George Whitson, Elliot Adler, and Barry Farber, respectively. Many of these authors were themselves part of the scene at NYU and have gone on to become central voices of considerable reputation in the analytic and academic landscape. We felt that surrounding the issues raised in this very forward-thinking article with commentary from varying theoretical perspectives allows readers to discern the essential themes and nuances inherent in this debate.

The introduction to the book should serve to familiarize the reader with some of the basic concepts of Sabe's work and the intellectual heritage that has framed it. Sabe was a lifelong student of philosophy and was exceedingly well read in the field. Bob Katz, a colleague at NYU, provides us with an in-depth treatment of the essential themes of the existential and phenomenological traditions within the field of psychoanalysis. It will be an important guide in following both Sabe's articles and the discussions that accompany them.

Lewis Aron was for many years a colleague of Sabe's at NYU, where Lew became one of the founders of the relational tradition and now serves as the director of the entire NYU Postdoctoral Program. Lew is very familiar with Sabe's professional writings as well as his more informal thinking and clinical practice, a result of many opportunities to discuss each other's ideas. We know these contacts have resulted in a deep and mutual respect and appreciation.

Irwin Hirsch, a widely published and central spokesman for the interpersonal tradition, shared a personal connection with Sabe as well as a professional one. Their contact dates back to Irwin's early days at NYU, when Sabe was one of Irwin's first instructors. Irwin credits Sabe as one of his major theoretical influences and a profound teacher in the clinical application of psychoanalytic ideas. In later years they came to influence each other in a complex reciprocity.

By contrast, Irwin Hoffman became aware of Sabe's contributions only recently and never knew him personally. His article speaks to the excitement of discovering a fellow traveler on his own theoretical journey. Irwin's generous treatment of Sabe's legacy and his appreciation of the history and tradition Sabe helped to create illuminates the existential/phenomenological tradition's rightful place in psychoanalytic history, and especially its place in the recent developments in all aspects of the two-person model of psychoanalysis.

Donnel Stern had never met Sabe until he presented a paper at the Westchester Center, but Sabe was familiar with Donnel's work and said so. Donnel describes this first meeting in his article and comments on the kind of personal and intellectual impact Sabe was to have on many who passed his way. Donnel and Sabe also shared a lifelong interest in philosophy, and that makes Donnel particularly suited to comment on Sabe's article "Human Nature and Psychotherapy."

We felt we might offer readers a unique glimpse into the clinical situation from one of Sabe's analysands, who has gone on to have her own career and find her own very different voice. Elsa Menaker not only was a student, supervisee, and analysand, but also later became a colleague of Sabe's at the Westchester Center. Her discussion is deeply personal and sheds light on Sabe's presence from inside the analytic relationship.

It is not common to find psychoanalytic articles on the creative process, although they do exist. We felt that Sabe's unique thinking on creativity was worth taking a look at. Sabe, of course, comes at the subject at his own idiosyncratic angle and here is commented on by Spyros Orfanos, who has a long-standing interest in the field of creative process. Spyros also had a long and close relationship with Sabe at NYU.

Finally, the afterword is offered by Stefanie Glennon, a colleague at NYU and Sabe's current wife. Stefanie is deeply familiar with all the contributors to this book and was on the scene during the creative years at NYU. Her depth of knowledge of Sabe's work and life informs her own unique observations.

We want to thank all the authors for their time and their devotion to this project. We wish we did not have to limit ourselves to so few invitations. Sabe's career touched the professional lives of so many of his colleagues that it was painful not to be able to include more of them explicitly in this project. Many of them contributed implicitly, however, and our thanks and appreciation to all those who did are heartfelt and sincere.

We hope that this book may serve to familiarize analysts of all meta-psychologies with Sabe's work and to allow them to recognize his role in building a vibrant, nuanced modern psychoanalysis. We also want to recognize how Sabe encouraged the growth of colleagues who could move beyond his ideas and find their own way to enrich our professional lives and the way we approach our work. Sabe, while clearly adhering to a particular way of thinking about his work, was never an ideologue. In fact, Sabe's support has encouraged the careers of analysts of widely divergent views. He never thought theory should be used as dogma and has managed to convey that open curiosity to his many students and colleagues.

It is a remarkable process in some ways to review a body of work in this manner, especially through the unique lens of such intelligent and thoughtful commentators. Each is able to find some nugget to turn over in a novel and illuminating way, thereby highlighting overlooked ideas or underappreciated clinical vignettes. We are personally grateful to these authors for their creative and thoughtful insights.

Sabe understood his role in helping us all set aside our day-to-day concerns and pay heightened attention to our patients' human condition as well as our own. What a numbing shock, then, when in May 2006 Sabe, at the height of his mature powers, was brought down in a near-fatal collision while biking through Central Park; he never made a full recovery. With a profound sense of irony and prescience, Sabe (1961b) said, "Awareness of one's being in the natural world demands an immediate awareness of possible and eventual non-being. With neither a fixed nature to unfold instinctually, nor a clear-cut transcendentally imposed destiny, man becomes what he makes of himself."

We hope this collection of articles and discussion may serve to remind us to stay ever-vigilant about our own humanity. It is the center from which we operate in this most human of endeavors.

George Goldstein
Helen Golden

REFERENCES

Basescu, S. (1961a). Human nature and psychotherapy: An existential view. *Review of Existential Psychology and Psychiatry, 2*(2), 149–157.

Basescu, S. (1961b). Phenomenology and existential analysis. In E. Lawrence (Ed.), *Progress in clinical psychology, vol. 6* (pp. 67–78). New York: Grune & Stratton.

INTRODUCTION: EXISTENTIALISM AND PHENOMENOLOGY*

Robert J. Katz

Often just the mere thought of existentialism brings to mind haunting images of an alienated figure such as Camus' *The Stranger*, who, while dwelling in a state of despair, makes futile attempts to come to terms with the sense of insignificance, finiteness, and meaninglessness that seems to inhere in the tragic shadow cast over life by death.† Throughout this struggle, there exists a profound sense of separateness and aloneness that pervades all aspects of his being. All of his existence is branded with an empty, hollow, depressive tone that silently screams out into a vacuous space in which meaningful relation is absent. It is the disconnection from both his self and others that most aptly colors this portrayal of the pathos of modern man.

Although existential philosophy does maintain a profound understanding of and relationship to the basic conditions of life into which we are all born (or thrown), existentialism actually has its origins in the struggle against the type of alienation and despair that Camus captured in such a masterly way. In fact, as will be seen momentarily, the Dutch philosopher Søren Kierkegaard (1813–1855), credited with being the founder of existential philosophy, was driven by the need to correct for the alienation, fragmentation, and lack of passionate

---

* This article was written to honor the contribution of the work of Dr. Sabert Basescu to the field of psychoanalysis. The intent of this introduction is to provide the reader with a strong sense of the "flavor" of existential thinking. It is by no means intended as a comprehensive reading of existential theory, but may provide an understanding of the rich potential of the existential/phenomenological perspective that graciously informed Dr. Basescu's work.
† The author wishes to thank George Goldstein, the editor of this volume, for his helpful suggestions and ideas.

relation that were beginning to characterize psychic life in Europe in the mid-nineteenth century. By analyzing himself, Kierkegaard came to see that the deepest anxieties of his time were actually emanating from the alienation and fragmentation he was witnessing. As a result, he set out to combat the pathological conditions that were at the root of this societal problem.

In the era in which Kierkegaard lived, a confluence of cultural forces was contributing to the fragmentation of psychic experience that became the focus of his concern. These deleterious factors had one effect in common: In one way or another, they all tended to treat man as an object. In philosophy, this phenomenon could be seen in Hegel's elevation of abstract reasoning to the source of truth ("totalitarianism of reason"), thereby making rational thought the primary determinant of the relationship to reality (Husserl, 1965). In fact, Hegel's emphasis on rational thinking spoke to the specific way in which Victorians were becoming overly reliant on a type of logical reasoning that compartmentalized their psychic experience. Here, the "child" within was separated from the overly rational "adult," and emotions were being controlled by and subjugated to a conscious willing ruled by logic. All of this served to elevate rationality to new heights and had the effect of separating the Victorians from the richness and vitality that reside in the more irrational and subjective aspects of experience. Furthermore, the industrial revolution was proceeding at a rapid rate and was increasingly becoming one of the strongest social currents shaping psychosocial experience. As a result, Victorian man was being reduced to a means to an end, an insignificant cog on the wheel of the means of production—in short, just another object on the assembly line.

All of the cultural conditions described above represent instances in which the subjective aspects of experience are cut off, separated, or diminished in importance. Each in its own way pulls for an almost exclusive focus on the more conscious, objective aspects of experience. The existentialists firmly and fundamentally believe that wherever objectifying conditions prevail, the importance of subjectivity potentially is either diminished or demeaned, with the dehumanization of experience being the inevitable result. In fact, Kierkegaard's campaign against the objectification of experience has remained at the core of both the spirit and conception of existentialism.

In that the objectification of experience is germane to both the development of the field of psychoanalysis and the issues with which contemporary analysts struggle daily, this theme will be a central focus throughout. Although it may not be evident at the moment, the conceptual development of psychoanalysis over the last fifty years has actually followed a trajectory that is consistent with the basic existential thrust of coming to terms with the philosophical issues surrounding the undoing of what philosophers call the *subject/object split*. Hence, a thorough understanding of this concept is essential to understanding much of what is to follow.

In the field of philosophy, a split between subject and object refers to a particular way of perceiving reality in which the observer and that which is being observed are considered to be entirely separate. This way of organizing the relationship to our perception of reality is the basic structure of the way in which Western consciousness is constituted. Maintaining a state of objectivity is the mode in which Western man attempts to comprehend his world. Of course, the most extreme manifestation of this type of objective thinking is found in modern science. Here, the goal is to achieve a state of absolute or pure objectivity by eliminating the contaminating influences that could potentially stem from the scientist's subjectivity. Generally, the requirement of objectivity goes hand in hand with a valuing of rationality and an implicit devaluation of the more irrational aspects of experience.

RELATIONAL TRUTH

According to the existentialists, attaining knowledge when the subject is separated from the object results in a "truth" that is basically hollow and of little use if one is genuinely interested in understanding human experience. It is devoid of the vitality and meaning that come into being when the whole person is more fully included in the equation. For the existentialists, objectively derived truth is an isolated phenomenon since it was derived without the benefit of the full engagement of the individual; such truth is like an object in that it is completely separated from the observer's subjectivity. Existentialists believe a distinct indivisibility exists between truth and the person seeking the truth. In simple terms, more familiar to contemporary analysts, truth is found in and derives its meaning from the relationship.

Writing with great clarity, Basescu (1961a) distinguishes the existential version of truth from the kind of knowledge that is derived when the observer is separated from the object being observed. He states:

> Existential truth is neither the truth of abstract propositions nor the objective facts of reality. It is concerned with the nature of a person's relation to objective fact or subjective reality, their meaning to the individual. Existential truth exists only as a person produces it in action, only as it is lived. Similarly, existential

knowledge is not familiarity with facts about someone or some-thing, but rather direct experience through meaningful participa-tion. . . . To explain human behavior, it must first be understood in terms of its meaning to the experiencing person, in a sense by participating in his world. (p. 153)

Espousing this view of *relational truth* or *truth-in-relation* was one of the ways in which Kierkegaard was attempting to correct for the objectifying forces described above. By doing so, Kierkegaard was affirming the idea that truth is individualized—it is rooted in the indi-vidual's unique subjectivity and begins with the self-awareness of the alive and active participant. This notion of truth bears some resem-blance to the psychoanalytic concept of *psychic reality*, where a fantasy can carry as much meaning as an actual traumatic event. The main difference is that the intent of the existentialists is to convey the notion that the individual (Kierkegaard's "single one") is the participant who actively relates and is responsible for the carving out of the truth that ultimately emerges and matters. Without this individualized sense of relation, truth is separated out from the individual's subjectivity to such an extent as to result in the loss of being or existence itself. In other words, the more man categorizes himself in objective terms, the more separate or distant he becomes from his own subjectivity. As the importance of his subjectivity continues to recede, the insidious loss of the sense of being or existence naturally ensues. This is one of the most fundamental tenets of existential thought and is certainly the one that is most relevant to psychoanalysis.

Once the relational nature of the existential view of truth is under-stood, the reader can begin to understand the ways in which the undoing of the subject/object split characterizes existential thought. Primarily it accomplishes this by making the subjectivity of the experiencing per-son the central concern as a way of avoiding the dehumanization and loss of being that ensue whenever and wherever the objectification of experience rears its head. The existentialists posit an indivisible unity between man and his world and always maintain an eye on the way in which the individual brings his unique subjective experience into relation, thereby avoiding the pitfalls that arise when experience is separated out from the experiencing subject or person and in this way becomes objectified.

Most germane to the practice of psychoanalysis is the fact that the concern with the objectification of experience addresses many facets of the therapeutic process in a way that attempts to both enhance and protect the integrity of the patient's subjective experience. More will be said about this later; for now, it is sufficient to note that problems emanating directly from issues surrounding the subject/object split are still at the root of many of the thorny issues that contemporary psychoanalysts struggle with. Furthermore, the major shift from a one-person paradigm to a two-person paradigm had much to do with undoing the objectivity that emanated from the Freudian conception of the analyst as a neutral observer who in good scientific fashion was required to sequester his subjectivity for the sake of making observations that could be considered "scientific" or purely objective. This stance has been replaced by two-person models that in one way or another can be considered as variations on the intersubjective connection that exists between patient and analyst. Representing an instance of the undoing of the subject/object split, this change has deepened the appreciation of the integrity of subjective experience and has done much to humanize the psychoanalytic endeavor by undoing the steely, technical-scientific quality that always tainted the image of classical analysis. In short, being consistent with the spirit of existentialism, the neutrality and objectivity of the "blank screen" has been replaced by the highly personal nature of the intersubjectivity that defines the two-person model.

Demonstrating the immense importance of the issue of the subject/object split, Swiss psychiatrist Ludwig Binswanger refers to the split as being "the cancer of all psychology." By this he meant to convey that most theorizing in the field (including the psychoanalysis of his era) was done with the split between subject and object intact. As a result, Binswanger felt, the essential nature of man was missed, since the type of truth derived by this way of relating to reality is devoid of a necessary ingredient: the person's relationship to the aspect of his psychology that is being studied.

Accordingly, Rollo May et al. (1959) define existentialism as "the endeavor to understand man by cutting below the cleavage between subject and object which has bedeviled Western thought and science since shortly after the Renaissance" (p. 11). Note that existentialism was never intended to be a complete philosophy. Instead, it was meant to be a way of relating to reality that attempts to expand human consciousness by including the fact of existence itself as a constant backdrop, influencing the awareness of how any particular individual relates to the world. The incorporation of being takes Western man out of his usual way of perceiving by eliminating the separation of subject and object.

What does it mean to "cut below the cleavage between subject and object"? This question could be and has been answered academically. However, a purely intellectual explanation would serve only to keep the reader trapped in the usual mode of conscious understanding, where the subject/object split is maintained. In fact, the difficulty in understanding this concept stands as an example of the way in which Western consciousness has difficulty transcending the objective mode of perception. The reader is going to be asked to indulge in an experiment that I hope will explain this concept in a more experiential way. For obvious reasons, this would be more consistent with the experiential thrust of all existential thinking.

Up to this point, the reader has most probably been attempting to comprehend this material in the normative academic manner. Mostly this involves a conscious focus on the material with the intent of comprehending what is being offered by assimilating the new material into cognitive categories established in the past. In this instance, subject and object are split as described above and the material is being related to primarily by a reliance on conscious, cognitive processing.

Now, in order to begin to move past the subject/object split, the reader is asked to first change focus from the conscious, purely cognitive mode, in which logic and rational thinking prevail, to a more inwardly directed awareness of being the subject, the "I," who is doing the understanding. Focusing on this aspect of the experience will bring the reader into an awareness of a more experiential state that is completely separate from the contents—this focus automatically eliminates the external, objective component (the conception) and immediately brings an essential aspect of subjectivity into awareness. This is the self aware of itself as the being that is choosing to engage in the attempt to understand the material at hand.

Actually, there are two aspects to this experience, which will further exemplify the dynamics that constantly swirl around the subject/object split. Even within this subjective realm, the experiencing individual can focus on himself as an object as if he were looking at himself from the outside in, thereby reintroducing a small measure of objectivity into this subjective realm. This would be in the form of "I am that individual who is trying to understand the material being presented." Note that this way of experiencing still involves a conception, although to a lesser extent. It should be noted that the formulation of any conception involves some degree of conscious, cognitive processing that invokes the object side of the subject/object split.

However, it is possible to go further into the subjective mode, to a point where the separation between subject and object entirely dissipates. This can be accomplished by attempting to give up all cognitive processing, increasing focal awareness on the immediacy of the experience of being engaged in the effort to understand. If a person is successful in doing this, a state of pure subjectivity or pure being can be approached.

Although it is always difficult for the Western mind to surrender the impulse to objectify and conceptualize, it is possible to significantly enhance the experience in the subjective mode by changing focus, as described here. In fact, most forms of insight-oriented psychotherapy, especially psychoanalysis, attempt to avoid intellectualizing by targeting this area of experience. However, even states of pure subjectivity do not get us to the cleavage below subject and object that is the very foundation of existential thought. To move into this realm experientially is much more difficult. It probably requires some type of dissolution or suspension of the ego that is similar to what occurs in Eastern meditative states. Nonetheless, the reader is invited to try to experientially imagine this state of pure being. Perhaps the most volitional route to reach this state is to surrender all intentionality and conceptual awareness. Doing so takes one further into a more purely subjective state than that described above, since the conceptual component and all ego functioning are entirely dissolved. Note that if an attempt is made at this point to articulate what is going on by employing words and creating conceptual categories to describe the experience, then conception and objectification would be reintroduced and the state of pure being would be seriously disrupted. In short, the state of pure being or existence lacks any self-definition whatsoever. Instead, it can be considered a state of unadulterated potentiality awaiting the invocation of committed, conscious, willing choice to bring the individual from this state of pure being into relation to the worlds of external reality, social relations, and the self.

Understanding this allows us to begin to look more closely at the existential portrait of the individual. Standing alone, squarely in the center of his own personhood, and starting from a point of pure being, he actively carves out an existence from within the grounding of his own subjective awareness. This awareness includes a sense of himself as having been arbitrarily thrown into the world at a particular point in time. Also, it includes an awareness of the self as being an active, responsible agent within a specific time period demarcated by birth at one end and death at the other. Within this time-bound context, he emerges from the state of pure being and actualizes his potential. Hence, existential man is always seen as being in a state of motion that the existentialists call *becoming*. By actively and intentionally choosing to structure and forge his subjective experience, man's relationship to the world comes into being. This is what the existentialists mean when they speak about *constituting a world*. It is by volitionally organizing and moving experience in a specific direction that the individual can be said to be choosing "to be," that is to say, choosing to exist.

BEING (*DASEIN*)

By this point, it should be apparent that the predominant thrust of existential thinking remains consistent with Kierkegaard's original intent of countering the objectification of experience wherever it rears its head so that the sense of existence itself can be preserved and the concomitant effects of dehumanization can be avoided. As noted above, the existentialists fundamentally feel that the Western mind is overly reliant on the type of categorizing and objectifying of experience that finds its ultimate expression in technological-scientific thinking. However, it appears to be easier to understand the process of objectifying experience than it is to comprehend precisely what the existentialists mean by the concept of existence itself. Again, the difficulty in comprehending this serves as an example of the way in which the sense of existence has been interfered with by the normative way in which the Western mind constructs experience.

To begin with, the term *existence* comes from the Latin root *existere*, meaning "to stand out," "to emerge." Here, the emphasis is on active choosing in that humans are not static entities that can be reduced to factors such as drives, chemical processes, or neurobiological functions. Instead, man is viewed more holistically as being forever engaged in the process of becoming—to exist is to become. Rollo May and colleagues (1959) put it this way:

> For no matter how true . . . it is that I am composed of such and such chemicals or act by such mechanisms . . . the crucial question is always that I happen to exist at this given moment in time and space, and my problem is how I am to be aware of that fact and what to do about it. (p. 12)

The way in which any particular individual answers the questions in May's quote determines that person's unique way of becoming, and according to the existentialists, this becoming constitutes the fundamental structure of human existence. To exist (to be) is to become, and the term *being* is understood as a verb connoting the fact that man is always in process and is not to be understood as a static entity that becomes fair game for reified definitions of his experience. Kierkegaard made the same point by posing man's mission as being framed by the question "How can I become an individual?" (May, 1960). Translated into the language of psychoanalysis, Kierkegaard is asking, "How can one integrate one's subjective experience in a way that brings the person into full relation to the world while preserving one's sense of identity?"

As will be seen in greater depth shortly, this view of man as becoming leads to a radical notion of self-responsibility. The individual not only is charged with the task of constantly being aware of existence but also must use this awareness to engage in and be responsible for the creation of the self and the direction that it assumes in life. From a historical perspective, the counterpoint to the existential notion of self-responsibility was found in religious doctrines that basically promulgated the idea that God holds the ultimate responsibility for what happens in the world. When Nietzsche declared that "God is dead" he removed the idea of religious determinism and thus freed man, giving him the responsibility for self-determination. Succinctly capturing the paradoxical flavor of man's plight, Sartre (1970) ironically describes this state as being "condemned to freedom." Further commenting on the radical sense of responsibility being discussed, Sartre writes, "Condemned, because he did not create himself, yet, in other respects is free; because, once thrown into the world, he is responsible for *everything* he does" (p. 23, italics added).

Additionally, the existential notion of radical freedom and responsibility is grounded in Sartre's well-known saying that "existence precedes essence." This idea has become a hallmark of existential thought. Sartre calls this idea "atheistic existentialism." It refers to the notion that since God is considered to be nonexistent, then man is the being that exists before he is defined and therefore must define himself. In effect, this is just another way of saying that the meaning in life is derived from the way an individual crafts his relationship to the world. Here, there are no a priori meanings or essences. As reflected in the questions in May's quote above, man is thrown into the world, becomes aware of his existence, and then sets out to determine what his existence will be, all the while bearing the tremendous burden of the outcome.

The idea that existence precedes essence further establishes and reflects the powerful and all-pervasive commitment that existentialists have to the importance of subjective experience. It can easily be seen that without essences, there are no universal categories that can be applied to the understanding of man's nature on an a priori basis. In effect, there is nothing to objectify. This is in full accord with Sartre's (1970) belief that "subjectivity must be the starting point" for the understanding of existence (p. 13). Hence, there is an inherent incompatibility between the open-ended nature of existence as existentially defined and any methodology that sets out to reductively understand it on an objective basis. It should be noted that the existentialists do not deny the reality or utility of objectively derived facts. However, given the static and isolated nature of these facts, they can never fully or accurately capture the true quality of life as it is actually lived—existence is always more than the sum of the accumulation of objectively derived knowledge. To reiterate what was said earlier, a fuller understanding always requires a knowledge of the way in which each individual brings his unique subjectivity into relation to whatever it is that is being understood. Objective methods of inquiry compartmentalize experience and separate out the component that is being studied from the person who is the object of the inquiry in question, thereby eliminating being from the picture. A psychiatric view of a patient based entirely on standardized diagnostic considerations serves as an example of an approach where the subjective experience of the patient is for all intents and purpose eliminated as an essential consideration.

Exactly what the existentialists mean by the concepts of existence and being can be hard to grasp in today's world, where the scientific model has become the preeminent force in the creation of the cultural aesthetic. At present, the idealization of science and the extent to which contemporary life has become entwined with and dependent on digital technology continue the kind of objectification and fragmentation that Kierkegaard was responding to in the mid-1800s. Note that the field of mental health itself is dominated by a neurochemical view of psychic experience where the idea of "mind" becomes an epiphenomenon that is subsumed by the concept of the brain. Making matters worse, the brain itself is considered to be analogous to a highly complex computer, an inert object. In short, the field of mental health has been almost entirely brought into the objective realm. Today, in proportions that would have seemed unimaginable to Kierkegaard and the other early existentialists, the importance of subjective experience has been greatly diminished if not outright annihilated by the scientific-technological zeitgeist. The decline in the popularity of psychoanalysis is in perfect accord with the way in which subjectivity is currently being treated and demeaned by Western culture. In effect, this speaks to the cultural relevance of restoring a more humanistic approach, where the existential emphasis on the immense importance of subjective experience and the awareness of being is considered to be more central than is presently the case.

An unquestioned belief in a technological-scientific view of man perpetuates the idea that what is most real can be reduced to mathematical formulas or other abstractions. Note that ultimately this returns us to the view that man has an essential nature that can be understood by scientifically breaking down his physical structure into component parts.

For example, psychological experience can be examined and dissected from an almost infinite number of perspectives, all having a scientifically ordained reality and varying degrees of pragmatic value (e.g., neuro-chemical, drives, instincts, genetics, etc.). Although this way of proceeding may generate many interesting and useful ideas, it always misses, and it frequently does violence to the integrity of subjective experience and the totality of the individual. In short, it sees the biochemistry of the brain but completely misses the mind, the person, and the sense of being.

Being enters the picture precisely where the scientific model comes to a dead end. By cutting below the subject/object split, the objective constituent is eliminated, and in turn the subjectivity of the person is brought to life and taken to its ultimate conclusion as the foundation of experience. It is this dimension of experience that existentially defines and demarcates being. With pure subjectivity, it can be said that there is an existence without an essence that exists as raw potential, awaiting structuring by an active, willing agent. This is where the person can be seen as transcending inert, objectified description by becoming a more vital participant in his own life, actively choosing to be aware of his own awareness and utilizing this awareness for the purpose of relation to the world.

Existentialists call the study of this category of experience *ontology* (the study of being) and, following Martin Heidegger, call the distinctive human capacity just described *Dasein*. In making what Heidegger meant by *Dasein* comprehensible, Sabert Basescu (1961b) sums up much of the above by stating:

> Without becoming overly involved in the intricacies of Heidegger's thought, we may say that he directs himself to seeking the necessary preconditions of all activity and function in man. He refers to man by the term *Dasein* (being there, i.e., the being who is there in his world) in order to convey that "man" and "world" are not separate entities, but that in his essential nature man is "being-in-the-world." (p. 70)

Actually, by employing the term *Dasein*, Heidegger was attempting to convey the idea that the human is the only entity that cares about the meaning of its own being and that of the world, that is, for whom being is itself an issue. Heidegger felt that it was in the nature of *Dasein* to follow a particular trajectory from the condition of "thrownness" to a state of greater self-actualization that he referred to as "authenticity." He described this state as movement "towards its being as its ownmost possibility." Hence, *Dasein* is conceived of as a special form of being that is never exhausted by any set of particular conditions. It always emerges into a set of new possibilities, so in any given moment it is simultaneously "what it is, what it has been and what it may yet become" (Seigel, 2005, p. 571).

In sum, the primary difficulty in understanding the concept of *Dasein* lies in capturing the nature of the movement just described. This is due to the fact that any conceptualization inevitably involves the use of categorization, which implicitly brings some measure of reification and objectification into the picture. In general, this objectification, even in those instances where it is minute, still reduces whatever is being described to a static state, even if the language itself is geared toward describing process. This is because language is not the phenomenon itself but a concretized abstraction of it. Magritte seemed to have understood this distinction when he wrote the words "This is not a pipe" on his painting of a pipe. Since *Dasein* is not intended to be a noun (although it can be taken as one grammatically), it is actually meant to describe man as a being in process in a way that transcends the ordinary use of descriptions of subjectivity or objectivity. Existing below the subject/object split, it is neither subject or object but actually a process (the alive being who is there); there is an indivisible divide between the individual, the process of living, and the object of relation (being-in-the-world). Attempts to scientize or objectify *Dasein* are bound to fail.

Perhaps psychoanalysts can come closer to understanding this by considering the difference between actually experiencing the therapeutic process ("being there") and the attempt to conceptualize it, especially in objective terms. No matter how astute the conception, every psychoanalyst knows in his heart that the full understanding of the therapeutic process remains ineffable—the "being" aspect is nearly impossible to capture. For the purpose of explanation, the process can be viewed as being tantamount to pure being. As soon as one begins to work with it, language, technology (in the form of technique), and prescribed meanings (in the form of interpretations) are brought to bear on it in an attempt to single out some aspect the analyst deems important. It is extremely difficult to accomplish this singling out without imposing some degree of objectification, which begins to dissect and objectify *Dasein*. Clinically speaking, the great potential of existential thinking is found in the fact that it can serve as a watchman whose sole purpose is to ensure that the true nature of *Dasein* is taken into consideration. As will be seen shortly, the clinical preservation of the integrity of experience is precisely the main intent of the phenomenological approach.

It just may be that only a "language" such as music can truly convey the sense of the motion involved in "being"—there is no content that can be grasped, yet it is there. As it changes from moment to moment before it concludes, it conveys an integrity and a meaning that cannot be definitively deciphered. In short, the nature of *Dasein* is such that it cannot be objectified without doing some injustice to its true nature. Consistent with the idea that God is dead, the concept of *Dasein* or being can be viewed as a replacement for God, in that it is a vitalizing presence that is intimately involved in all aspects of living.

BEING AND NONBEING

This brings us to a consideration of the basic existential choice between being and nonbeing, the ultimate frame and grounding of psychic experience. According to existential thought, man's basic awareness of his being always includes an awareness of the possibility of nonbeing, or death. As much as man's subjectivity and sense of self is rooted in his knowledge of both his separateness from nature and the concomitant awareness that he exists, it is also intimately related to the awareness of nonbeing. Life and death, being and nonbeing, everything and nothing are inextricably woven into the very fabric of existence—one implies the other. Within the tragic limits of life demarcated by birth at one end and death at the other, man lives out his existence while wrestling with a profound sense of aloneness that is intimately connected to the sense of finitude. Heidegger's insight was that, more than any other factor, it is the inevitability of death that actually constitutes man's separateness or aloneness. Heidegger felt that man had a strong tendency to forfeit much of his potential authenticity and individuality by conforming to others ("the they"). Death was considered the only experience that could not be given away in this fashion. He writes:

> When, by anticipation, one becomes free *for* one's own death, one is liberated from lostness in those possibilities which may accidentally thrust themselves upon one; and one is liberated in such a way that for the first time one can authentically understand and choose among the factical possibilities lying ahead of that possibility which is not to be outstripped. (1927/1962, p. 308)

In toto, existential man is driven by the need to reckon with the tragic dimension of life by attempting to find meaningful ways of relating to the world that diminish both the sense of aloneness as well as the terror of the nothingness that ultimately awaits him.

Although the terror of the nothingness that accompanies the awareness of nonbeing haunts existence, paradoxically, it is actually responsible for establishing the conditions that potentiate meaning itself.

Without the dark shadow cast by death, life has no meaning. This idea is fundamental to existential thought, as it reflects the basic paradoxical nature of being. Rollo May et al. (1959) succinctly sum up this existential paradox by stating, "Death in any of its aspects is the fact which makes of the present hour something of absolute value" (p. 90).

Even more important than the actuality of physical demise is the fact that death has its representative in all of the ways that man refuses or resists the use of the resources available to him to actualize his potential, that is, live fully. Given the freedom to choose, to carve out his existence, man is confronted with the tremendous burden of answering Kierkegaard's question ("How can I become an individual?") by finding meaningful ways to bring himself into full relation to the world. Existential guilt arises whenever there is a sense that one is failing at this task. Becker (1973) labels this quest the finding of "individuality within finitude" (p. 26).

In describing this paradoxical plight and its relation to meaning, Basescu (1961a) writes,

> Awareness of one's being in the natural world demands an immediate awareness of possible and eventual nonbeing. What lives is born, grows and dies, often unexpectedly, tragically and arbitrarily. Physical death is the most obvious instance of non-being. . . . But there is nonbeing in life as well as in death, *the non-being of meaninglessness.* With neither a fixed nature to unfold instinctually, nor a clear cut transcendentally imposed destiny, man becomes what he makes of himself continually confronted with the absolute necessity of making choices based on the fundamental option of affirming his being or denying it. (pp. 150–151, italics added)

The major role that the awareness of finitude plays in the existential view of man cannot be overstated. As is clear from the above, all meaning is ultimately grounded in the context established by the limits imposed by death and the way in which an individual's choices are either an expression of alive being or stagnant nonbeing—"to be or not to be" is always the question that pervades all choice. In fact, from an existential perspective, the possibility of the choice of suicide constitutes an important fact of existence. In effect, it means that since man could choose to die, he is actually choosing life instead.

Given the gravity and power that surround death in both its actual and symbolic forms, it is striking that most psychoanalytic theory is blatantly lacking in any conception that adequately matches the immensity of death's psychological significance. It seems to lie outside the purview of technique. Hence, the issue of death is rarely brought more directly into the corpus of clinical work. In this sense, it appears that the psycho-analytic conception seems to mirror the cultural denial of death, especially in America. It is not an accident that existentialism originated in Europe and behaviorism was developed in America. Not only does this fact reflect the difference in sensitivity to the awareness of death between the two cultures, but it also clearly reveals how the scientific-technological orientation toward life that is more characteristic of America always gravitates toward the elimination or blunting of the ontological categories of experience, that is, the categories of experience intimately related to being. Mostly it accomplishes this loss of the sense of being via the compartmentalization and high degree of objectification that lie at the core of this approach. In contrast, following Heidegger's direction, the more that death is in awareness, the more that the individual experiences himself as alone and the more this sense of aloneness becomes the casing for a deeper relationship to one's own subjectivity. In sum, there exists an intimate and direct correlation between the repression of the awareness of death and the objectification of being, with the loss of the importance of subjectivity as the final result.

A poignant example of this can be found in Freud's attempts to include the issue of mortality in his theorizing. It demonstrates the havoc that the scientific model wreaks on the ontological realm. In essence, Freud lost the deeper existential feel or ontological sense of death by converting it to a biological drive (death instinct) and reducing the enormity of its psychological significance to a mere derivative of castration anxiety. In other words, in this instance the all-pervasive, foundational sense of being is converted into a language and format that ultimately depend on the scientific model for their form. The incompatibility between the concept of being and its ontological concomitants such as love, courage, will, and authenticity, on one hand, and the scientific model, on the other, seems evident. The basic objective format of the scientific model is simply the wrong container for the highly subjective orientation of being.

In contrast, in more recent times Irwin Hoffman (1998) is one of the few psychoanalysts who has attempted to make the issue of mortality a main consideration in everyday clinical work while maintaining the true ontological flavor of the concept of being. Consistent with the dialectical-constructivist view that he developed, Hoffman sees the relationship between being and nonbeing in dialectical terms. He writes:

> The relationship between our sense of being and our anticipation of nonbeing is an example of a dialectic. There is a tension between the two experiences and yet neither could exist without

the other. When one is figure, the other is ground, but together they comprise a whole that is incorporated into our sense of self. . . . But the dialectic of our sense of being and our sense of our mortality is superordinate to all the others because it is the paradoxical foundation for our sense of meaning. (p. 19)

Throughout his book, Hoffman demonstrates a profound existential understanding of the relationship between mortality and many facets of the psychoanalytic endeavor. For instance, in describing the relationship between narcissistic injury and the more overriding tragic dimension of life that he refers to as "the darker side," Hoffman cogently describes the way in which blows to self-esteem in both the developing child and the analytic patient are infused with and directly related to the awareness of mortality. His existential sensibility is further demonstrated by his drawing attention to the fact that aspects of the analytic frame are the equivalent of or a representative of the darker side of the human condition. His view is presented here as an example of the way in which the sense of being and nonbeing can be maintained and brought directly into a psychoanalytic context. In describing the way in which the analyst's affirmation can serve to aid the patient in the struggle against damaged esteem within the larger context of the loss of life itself, Hoffman (1998) sensitively writes

Life itself can be viewed as a seduction that is followed by disillusionment, abandonment, and death—in other words, as a cruel deception. The love of parental figures in critical periods of childhood helps to buffer the impact of reflective human consciousness, particularly as it comes up against the terror of mortality. When the injuries of childhood are sufficiently traumatizing, the added insults of the human condition can be unbearable. The analyst is in a position to counter these assaults on the patient's sense of worth through a powerful kind of affirmation, one that is born out of the dialectic of psychoanalytic ritual and personal spontaneity. The interplay of the two can triumph over cynicism and despair and cultivate the patient's capacity for expansive and committed living. (p. xxvii)

Of course, one can always raise the question of precisely what it is that is considered to be affirming. Given the plurality of perspectives that now exist in contemporary psychoanalysis, there would inevitably be a wide range of opinions on this matter. Obviously, Hoffman is suggesting that the element of spontaneity is useful in this regard. Contained within the analyst's spontaneity is a freer, less restrained, more personal version of the analyst's self that transcends the usual bounds of psychoanalytic restraint. This more personal and alive form of participation signals that the analyst cares; his willingness to bring more of himself into the process deepens his involvement and demonstrates his vulnerability. In other terms, the analyst's spontaneity is a way of humanizing the process by transcending the normal bounds (the ritualized technical aspect) by bringing more of his subjectivity into view. Naturally, this would serve to make the patient feel less alone in his personal struggle with his aloneness and attempts to achieve his individuality within finitude. The sharing of the analyst's vitality becomes a source of affirmation and helps in the never-ending struggle against the despair and cynicism that can easily follow in the footsteps of the awareness of death and the fragile nature of existence. The sense of being is affirmed by the infusion of the analyst's subjectivity via the expression of spontaneity.

In contrast, Paul Tillich (1952), in a very interesting statement, reminds us that the individual's ability to look death straight in the eyes seems to be affirming in and of itself. Tillich defined courage as being the ability to self-affirm in the face of death. He stated, "The self-affirmation of a being is stronger the more nonbeing it can take into itself" (p. 87). This can be interpreted as meaning that one strengthens oneself by developing "the courage to be," which is accomplished by accepting the nothingness that exists in both the actual inevitability of physical demise and all of the forms of nonbeing that one has to contend with in both oneself and others. Although a more thorough expansion of this area of experience goes beyond the scope of this introduction, it is worth noting that quite often the destructiveness of the patient is missed because the analyst is unwilling to experience the extent to which the patient has no use for the analyst's being. As the anxiety associated with nonbeing approaches, the analyst is very likely to try to do something to avoid a deeper experience of this symbolic death. The analyst tends to draw on technical considerations, thereby bringing into the process a degree of objectivity, which could serve to further diminish the sense of being. Hence an inauthentic encounter would ensue, based in part on the analyst's inability to cope with his own death anxiety.

At the end of the day, existentialism, like psychoanalysis, can be interpreted as being a plea for man to live a more passionate and fuller existence. In analysis, man faces his castration anxiety and thereby becomes less afraid of being more alive and productive. By resolving his Oedipal issues, man becomes free to be more potent (that is, to actualize his potential), and he separates from the illusion of security provided by remaining in the tight harbor associated with maternal ministrations. This enhances his capacity to both deal with and perceive reality and, according to Freud, transforms his neurotic suffering into the misery of everyday life that normally plagues all humans. Obviously, the Oedipal scenario can easily be viewed as being a derivative of death anxiety, especially if it avoids the pitfall of being taken too literally. However, the difference lies in the fact that the power and gravity of what it means to face death are hidden in the use of metaphors that serve to mask the raw sense of passion derived from more directly encountering the terror of the nothingness associated with nonbeing. In existential terminology, this would be a firsthand example of avoiding the more basic ontological realm of experience by remaining within a system of thinking that is fashioned after the model of the hard-core sciences. Ultimately, this way of thinking returns conception to a place where the subject/object split is reinstated and the true nature of being is both missed and truncated.

In sum, it appears that both psychoanalysis and existentialism call for man to live more meaningfully by passionately bringing his subjectivity into a fuller relation to his world. This seems to be the only constructive palliative that can be used to treat the angst associated with nonbeing. Basically, both systems of thought interpret any type of holding back as a form of defense. Laing (1960) quotes Kafka's very compelling summary of the paradoxical nature of the issues just described: "You can hold yourself back from the sufferings of the world, this is something you are free to do and is in accord with your nature, but perhaps precisely this holding back is the only suffering that you might be able to avoid" (p. 82).

PHENOMENOLOGY

In founding his method of transcendental phenomenology, Edmund Husserl (1859–1938) was contending with developments in the field of philosophy and psychology that he felt were serious impediments to man's search for pure knowledge or universal truth. Husserl feared that philosophy was losing ground to the sciences, which were in ascendance; more particularly, he feared that psychology was poised to replace philosophy by becoming the source of absolute knowledge. Believing that philosophy should possess the status it formerly had, Husserl took as his mission to turn philosophy into a rigorous science in the pursuit of absolute knowledge. In an attempt to detract from the validity of the findings of both the philosophy and psychology of his day, Husserl pointed out the flaws in their foundational beliefs. *Transcendental phenomenology* was formulated as a methodology that was supposed to correct for the shortcomings that prevented these disciplines from making a claim to the attainment of universal knowledge.

In particular, Husserl strongly disagreed with *Weltanschauung* (worldview) philosophy (Jennings, 1986). It was the belief of this philosophy that all knowledge is relative to its historical age. This notion was particularly distasteful to Husserl because it implicitly negated the possibility of achieving the kind of universal knowledge that he was after. Obviously, in order for knowledge to be universal, it would have to be able to transcend time and place. The other major premise that Husserl was in strong disagreement with is what he termed *naturalism*. Husserl coined this term to refer to the implicit assumption found in philosophy, the social sciences, and psychology that ultimately all of reality consists of physical being (the natural). According to Husserl, the most dangerous implication of reducing all phenomena to "physical stuff" is that all of natural being, including consciousness, can be reduced to the properties of physical material, and thus can be manipulated and measured using the experimental method. Husserl strongly felt that phenomena such as consciousness and other forms of essence do not have the same kind of being that natural or physical things possess. Husserl provides the example of attempting to study the experience of sound by experimentally viewing it as a function of "air vibration" and the "stimulation of the auditory sense." Husserl understood that this theory could explain sound but that it could not claim to explain the *experience* of sound.

The distinction that Husserl draws between the experimental definition of a phenomenon and the actual experience is an essential aspect of phenomenological thinking. Here one can begin to detect the shades of the clinical implications of the all-important difference between experience and conception. Most of the relevance of phenomenology to psychoanalysis comes from the far-reaching implications of this distinction. From a historical vantage point, it was the acceptance of a plurality of metapsychologies that resulted in the understanding that different psychoanalytic theories simply reflected the unique perspective of a particular theorist rather than being an accurate scientific description of actual experience. In essence, this restored the metaphoric meaning of *meta-* (above) in the term *metapsychology*. Although from a contemporary standpoint the idea that psychoanalytic theories are just different perspectives that do not accurately reflect the unique experience of any particular individual seems mundane, it was this development that opened up the field to other conceptual possibilities, thereby facilitating the major paradigmatic shift in the field. In turn, the change-over to a two-person approach brought with it a greater appreciation of the uniqueness and integrity of individual experience. As will be seen momentarily, adhering to the basic premises of a two-person model actually requires that a phenomenological approach be used.

Phenomenology's emphasis on the uniqueness of experience arose because Husserl wanted to understand the source of knowledge that he believed was to be found in consciousness. He located this source in the knowing subject, the "I–myself" or the ego, which exists relative to a world of which it is conscious. Atwood and Stolorow (1984) succinctly describe Husserl's aim and methodological principle:

> Whereas traditional science takes the existence of the world for granted as a "pregiven" reality, transcendental phenomenology suspends or "brackets" assumptions regarding the nature of objective reality and studies instead the world's manifestation to consciousness as pure phenomenon. The procedure by which this suspension or belief occurs is known as the phenomenological reduction or *epoche*. (p. 9)

The *epoche* involves the creation of a new mind-set that begins with the bracketing of the *natural attitude*—the everyday assumption that the world exists "out there" and that there is a shared reality that is the same for others. Husserl was never totally clear about the exact procedures involved in accomplishing the phenomenological reduction. However, the main intent was to purify consciousness in order to eliminate the contaminating effects of presupposition. In actuality, nothing is changed by the reduction except that the natural attitude is put aside and the act of consciousness itself comes into focus as the essential factor in the way the world is perceived.

Husserl believed that by studying the act of consciousness itself, the hidden presuppositions that normally control perception and understanding would become apparent. Therefore, consciousness would be purified and his goal of achieving absolute knowledge could be achieved. Note that while Husserl performed the *epoche* in a state of solitude, for obvious reasons analysts do not have this luxury.

Whether or not it is possible to develop a transcendental ego or purified state of consciousness is open to question. However, what is most important to the study of psychoanalysis is the basic spirit and intent of phenomenological methodology. To a large extent, all psychoanalytic theorizing involves the creation of sets of presuppositions that arm the analyst with ways to organize clinical material on an a priori basis. These presuppositions are very powerful and contain many layers of assumptions that are not entirely explicit. From a phenomenological perspective, this would mean that the patient is potentially in danger of having his experience understood in terms of the analyst's theoretical bias. Although it sounds like a rather strong critique, in actuality this means that most psychoanalytic theorizing could benefit from being more open to the highly individualized or idiosyncratic ways that each individual chooses to construct his world. By using a phenomenological approach, theories or aspects of them could be evaluated as to the extent to which they are open to accommodating the unique vicissitudes of subjective experience or, conversely, the extent to which they call for experience to be assimilated into the categories of understanding that they deem essential.

In other words, psychoanalytic theories and specific constructs within a theory vary qualitatively according to how many degrees of phenomenological freedom they possess. For example, the Kleinian notion that the infant's experience is primarily determined by the aggressive drive or Freud's notion that the infant exists in a state of unrelated primary narcissism are concepts that clearly define experience on an a priori basis. Hence they would be considered to have very little phenomenological freedom, and this could potentially constrain the practitioner in capturing the essence of the patient's unique experience. In contrast, Sullivan's (1940) conception that any facet of psychic experience can fall under the deleterious influence of anxiety depending on the actual history of interpersonal events clearly has a greater degree of phenomenological freedom. Here the analyst has no specific map as to exactly which experiences contributed to the construction of the patient's difficulties other than the central theoretical notion that the most formative events were interpersonal.

Although Sullivan's position may come closer to being "experience-near" in that it makes a conceptual demand that the clinician look more closely at the actual behavior that constituted historical events in order to understand the pathogenic effects of anxiety, the structure of the theory, being purely interpersonal, precluded other domains of experience that can be considered important. It is a well-known fact that Sullivan (1950) had little use for the idea of unique subjective experience or the concomitant concept of a self—his interpersonal bias precluded it. Sullivan's position was more open in some respects, but like most psychoanalytic theories, it clearly delimited the scope of psychoanalytic inquiry on an a priori basis.

The extent to which psychoanalytic theories define and structure clinical inquiry on an a priori basis becomes readily apparent from examining the three *modes of world*, or domains of experience, that describe the scope of clinical inquiry by existential analysts. Each of these modes characterizes our existence as beings-in-the-world. The first realm is the *Umwelt*. This is the world of objects outside us—the natural world, including the biological instincts. The second mode is the *Mitwelt*, or the world of interpersonal relations. Finally, the third mode is the *Eigenwelt*, or self-world. The *Eigenwelt* circumscribes the experience of the self's relationship to itself and it is considered to be the center of self-awareness and experience that determines the way in which the world is related to. Whereas Freud focused on the *Umwelt* and Sullivanian and relational theories work within the *Mitwelt*, only an existential-phenomenological approach includes all three and makes the *Eigenwelt* central. Although there are many implications that directly flow from this analysis, it is easy to see that an exclusive emphasis on any one realm implicitly precludes significant aspects of experience and therefore could be considered to be reductive to some degree.

Although a fuller discussion of this issue goes beyond the scope of this introduction, it is worth noting that the basic premises of the two-person model, if taken to their ultimate conclusion, call for a phenomenological reading of the clinical material. Briefly, the foundational belief of the two-person model is that the interaction between patient and analyst consists of the way the unique subjectivity of each participant interacts with the other's. Hence, there is no theoretical map that can account for the idiosyncratic nature of the relationship that develops. From the analyst's position, the interaction must be understood on its own terms; it is a "thing to itself" and therefore calls out to be understood on a phenomenological basis. However, it should be noted that a more purely existentially oriented phenomenological model would focus primarily on the patient's experience of the interaction rather than on the meaning of the interaction itself, as would be the case if an interpersonal or relational approach were being utilized. In fact, all psychoanalytic applications of phenomenology would be considered to be bastardized versions if the original intent and methodology of Husserl's transcendental phenomenology is used as a baseline. Technically speaking, in regard to the two-person paradigm, using a phenomenological approach has come to refer to the attempt to capture the uniqueness of the nature of the therapeutic interaction by describing it without reference to any theoretical presuppositions. In other words, the uniqueness of the interaction would be the unit of analysis and would be looked at with the intent of preserving all the uniqueness implied by the phenomenological expression "a thing to itself."

The description of the application of the phenomenological approach to the two-person paradigm serves as an example of the attempt to remain true to Husserl's original intent of removing all sources of preconception by purifying consciousness. Hence, it can readily be seen that the primary clinical usefulness of the phenomenological method has been to avoid the narrowing of conceptual focus that is inherent in most psychoanalytic theories. Mostly this is accomplished by describing what is seen rather than prescribing meanings according to the dictates of preordained, metapsychological constructs. In this way, the phenomenological method avoids the objectification of experience by incorporating as much of the patient's unique subjectivity as is possible into any interpretative formulation. Protecting and respecting the sanctity of unique, individualized experience enhances and preserves the integrity of the self, and thereby both validates and vitalizes the sense of being.

It seems reasonable to assume that no analyst would want to objectify a patient's experience or deprive him of an enhanced sense of self. Yet psychoanalysis generally has not entirely embraced phenomenology's sensitivity to the integrity of subjective experience. Interpretations based more on theoretical considerations than on a closer reading of the patient's experience are still plentiful. It seems reasonable to assume that no theory or technique, including phenomenology, can guarantee that the patient's subjectivity will be fully respected. In the end, it is the actual way in which an analyst chooses to participate that will determine this. Of course, this is precisely the point: Conception *does not* determine experience. Experience is a "thing to itself."

CONCLUSION

For the most part, existentialism and phenomenology have never been fully or directly incorporated into the corpus of mainstream psychoanalytic theorizing. However, like the experience of being itself, existential thinking—or, more accurately, an existential sensibility—seems to be like an aura that surrounds and frames each analytic session. Grains of sand flowing through the hourglass create a familiar tune that is so deafening that frequently it cannot be heard. This song of being has its own rhythm that will either lull one into a numbing somnambulistic state or will get one to wake up to aliveness and dance. Being fully familiar with this music, every analyst knows that the present hour will never be recaptured or lived again. Without a sense of urgency based on the awareness of the finitude of one's being there would be no meaning to the choices one makes. Resistances and defenses would merely be idle indulgences, experiments in freezing life and thawing it out according to one's will. Finding their expression in a lack of passion, if the existential melody becomes blunted, constrictions in living would simply not reverberate in the same way—their deadening pulse could not be detected.

It is hard to imagine an analyst who lacks an awareness of this basic existential sensibility; after all, in his own way Freud, like Nietzsche, declared that God was dead. Clearly, analysts differ in the degree to which this awareness is in focus, and they certainly differ in regard to how much of this sensibility is directly incorporated into their clinical work. However, at the foundation of psychoanalysis is an awareness that the person is at the center of his own being and that ultimately it is he alone who must willfully carve out an existence. It would be interesting to see what would happen if difficulties in living were more directly interpreted as an avoidance of being in all its forms—being more "out there," being more related, being more alive, being more loving, being more aware of being itself.

In helping patients answer the age-old question of whether they will choose "to be" or "not to be," both analysts and patients would greatly benefit from a greater attunement to the general existential sentiment of using passionate relation to combat the meaninglessness and despair that result when man stops listening to the existential melody and lives life aimlessly, as if time and life itself were unreal. In a culture that is increasingly becoming less real and more virtual, keeping an eye on the nature of being and the sensitivity that this brings may be the necessary remedy for the dehumanizing effects of the cybernetic age. Hence, the existential sensibility seems more relevant than ever before.

POSTSCRIPT: SABE AND I

I first met Sabert Basescu in 1973, when I began my psychoanalytic training at age 27 in the New York University Postdoctoral Program. At that time, Sabe was the head of the interpersonal track, which in those days was called the "humanistic-existential-interpersonal track." Eventually, the "humanistic-existential" designation was dropped because of the awkwardness it presented. However, the original name reflected the kinship that existed between the existential-phenomenological and interpersonal approaches. In addition to the phenomenological attitude that characterized Sullivan's work (as described above), the interpersonalists and existentialists of that era shared a deep conviction about the importance of freedom and individuality. In this regard, they were influenced by Fromm and their firsthand experience of the devastation wrought by authoritarian regimes in World War II Europe and McCarthyism in America. All of this culminated in the antiauthoritarianism of the 1960s, which further fueled the spirit of freedom.

As I observed the interpersonal group at that time, with Sabe at the helm, it seemed to me that the drive to achieve both personal and clinical freedom was almost characterological. Unfortunately, this resulted in many bitter disputes between people within the track as well as with individuals who subscribed to other theoretical orientations. (Of course, the history of psychoanalysis is replete with battles that were both personal and theoretical.) In the early to mid-1970s, the classical position was dominant and the interpersonal or two-person paradigm was not accepted as a legitimate brand of analysis. Primarily, it was the struggle for acceptance of the importance of interpersonal experience that fueled the ongoing debate in both the field at large and the NYU program in particular.

From the time I met Sabe, I was struck by his capacity to stay out of this fray. I believe that he was able to do this because, true to his theoretical position, he had a great deal of respect for all of the individuals involved. Also, as George Goldstein mentioned in the preface, Sabe came from a phenomenological point of view and fully understood that the actual experience of therapy was determined more by the relationship than by the theory to which any particular analyst subscribes. To remain separate in this way not only is testimony to Sabe's high degree of respect for all but also reflects a kind of wisdom that he possesses. Again, this characteristic is consistent with Sabe's phenomenological approach in that it allows for the cutting away of all the distractions and external noise so that the issue itself can be more directly seen. In dealing with any problem, whether it be clinical or otherwise, I was always impressed by Sabe's capacity to do this. He had a way of untangling the most complicated knots with a simplicity that led to a clearer understanding that provided relief. This quality of Sabe's thinking can be described as producing a kind of profound simplicity. In the clinical situation, this way of being and conceptualizing was both freeing and enlightening.

As time passed, I had the good fortune to get to know Sabe both personally and professionally. In my third year of training, I entered supervision with him. I found the supervision to be so productive that I continued for another year. Although I am not as purely phenomenological as he is, what he taught me about his approach has become an integral part of my everyday work. I have come to believe that there is no substitute for staying deeply attuned to the patient's experience in the way that the phenomenological attitude suggests. I would like to take this opportunity to express my deep appreciation for the enduring contribution that he made to my training.

On a more personal note, I had the chance to get to know Sabe in a variety of settings. Eventually, we became colleagues at both NYU and the Westchester Center, of which he is a founding member. We were roommates at many NYU and Westchester Center weekend retreats. Unfortunately for my ego, we were pitted against each other on the tennis courts of Martha's Vineyard. In all these instances, I found Sabe to be a delightful, charming gentleman who was full of a quiet kind of certitude and respect. Also, I would be greatly remiss if I failed to mention how much fun we had given the quickness of Sabe's wit and his wry sense of humor.

Sabe has made an enduring contribution to the field of psychoanalysis. Whereas Rollo May humbly considered himself to simply be the "importer" of existentialism, it can be said that Sabe was the main "retailer." His career as a lecturer, teacher, author, supervisor, and analyst lasted for over 50 years. Sabe was the main spokesman for the existential position within the New York psychoanalytic community. Although he had to confront the tragedy of an accident that greatly diminished his capacity, his passionate commitment to imparting his knowledge of existentialism continues on in the lives of all of those he touched with his gracious hand.

A recent visit to his apartment in Manhattan served to demonstrate that even a brain injury could not squelch his generous spirit. When I arrived, he was eating dinner; he immediately and somewhat insistently asked if I wanted to eat something. As I continued to say no, he queried, "Where did you learn to be so definitive?" I spontaneously replied, "You taught me that!"

REFERENCES

Atwood, G., & Stolorow, R. (1984). *Structures of subjectivity: Explorations in psychoanalytic phenomenology*. Hillsdale, NJ: Analytic Press.

Basescu, S. (1961a). Human nature and psychotherapy: An existential review. *Review of Existential Psychology and Psychiatry*, *2*(2), 149–157.

Basescu, S. (1961b). Phenomenology and existential analysis. In E. Lawrence (Ed.), *Progress in Clinical Psychology: Vol. 6*. (pp. 67–78). New York: Grune & Stratton.

Becker, E. (1973). *The denial of death*. New York: Free Press.

Heidegger, M. (1962). *Being and time* (J. Macquarrie & E. Robinson, Trans.). New York: Harper & Row. (Original work published 1927)

Hoffman, I. (1998). *Ritual and spontaneity in the psychoanalytic process: A dialectical-constructivist view*. Hillsdale, NJ: Analytic Press.

Husserl, E. (1965). *Phenomenology and the crisis of philosophy*. Trans. Q. Lauer. New York: Harper & Row.

Jennings, J. (1986). The forgotten distinction between psychology and phenomenology. *American Psychologist*, *41*(11), 1231–1241.

Laing, R. D. (1960). *The divided self*. New York: Random House.

May, R. (1960). *Existential psychology*. New York: Random House.

May, R., Angel, E., & Ellenberger, H. (1959). *Existence: A new dimension in psychiatry and psychology*. New York: Basic Books.

Sartre, J.-P. (1970). *Existentialism and human emotions*. Secaucus, NJ: Castle Books.

Seigel, J. (2005). *The idea of the self: Thought and experience in Western Europe since the seventeenth century*. Cambridge, UK: Cambridge University Press.

Sullivan, H. S. (1940). *Conceptions of modern psychiatry*. New York: W. W. Norton & Co.

Sullivan, H. S. (1950). The illusion of personal individuality. *Psychiatry*, *13*(1), 317–332.

Tillich, P. (1952). *The courage to be*. New Haven, CT: Yale University Press.

1

ANXIETIES IN THE ANALYST

An Autobiographical Account (1977)

COMMENTARY BY IRWIN Z. HOFFMAN

Finding oneself reflected in the sensibility and writings of another is an unusual, validating, and sometimes even uncanny experience. It's more than just finding certain points of agreement. Sometimes the wording, the flow of ideas, or the combination of thoughts and feelings yields something more than that, something hard to describe. There is a sense of a whole that is more than the sum of its parts and of a match between that whole and oneself. In fact, that sense of connection is not overridden by certain points of disagreement because the overall spirit of the other's perspective seems so like one's own.

Such was my experience in reading Sabert Basescu's "Anxieties in the Analyst: An Autobiographical Account" in February 2002. He had sent it to me along with one other article after reading my book, *Ritual and Spontaneity in the Psychoanalytic Process* (Hoffman, 1998). In his handwritten cover letter he said: "Since I so much sense a kindred spirit in you, I've taken the liberty of enclosing two articles I wrote some 15–25 years ago, which gave me a good time in the writing." And indeed so much in this very rich, personal, informal, self-revealing essay seemed to correspond with what I had written about somewhat more formally over a 20-year period. Sabe's essay antedates the book, in which much of my work was collected, by 21 years. I regret that I didn't discover it, or Sabe's contributions generally, which were so ahead of their time, until that moment.

I will have to be very selective in the points I take up because I found myself resonating continually with Sabe's account of his experience, and reporting on all of it would be impossible. So here are some of the ideas that stood out for me.

A central conviction that can be viewed as a kind of wellspring for everything Sabe is teaching us through his account of his experience as a therapist is simply that the therapist or analyst is a person, a human being, and that the analytic role, however it affects the nature of the analyst's involvement, does not negate that simple reality. I've become accustomed to the realization that in psychoanalysis sometimes the assertion of the most seemingly obvious truths can amount to revolutionary developments. So Sabe, with his characteristic self-effacing, wry humor, states the following:

> I know that the conception of the role of the therapist has evolved from that of the anonymous reflector, through that of the participant observer, to the current standard of the therapist as human being. It is not so easy for me to be a human being. I think it would be easier for me to be a mirror. The rules for being a mirror are more clear-cut than the rules for being human. (p. 159)

Well, I would say that the standard of being human within the role of therapist is one that 30 years later is still not fully accepted, much less met, in theory or practice, even though anything to the contrary would be disclaimed. But wouldn't the same thing have been the case in 1977? I mean, would anyone holding to the model of therapist as mirror (he means in the classical sense, not the self-psychological sense) or the model of therapist as participant observer have thought that he or she was advocating or being anything other than a human analyst? Surely not. And yet it is so interesting to me that Basescu in 1977 had the idea that being a human being is a late development in conceptions of what it means to be a therapist. Beyond that, he has the sense that what seems like a virtual truism does not go without saying. The genius is in the recognition that it is necessary to say it and to spell out its implications, and in the awareness that saying it captures something that might well be missed if it were left unspoken. What is the context, by implication, of that realization? I believe that it is the appetite for dehumanizing, "clear-cut" rules (like, as Sabe says, "the rules for being a mirror") that create grounds for knowing how one should work analytically from moment to moment, an appetite that was active in 1977 and is active even now. Sabe was at war with that mechanistic, standardizing tendency back then. I would submit, however, that that war is going on to this day. Indeed, by its nature, it may be a perpetual struggle to which

Sabe Basescu's quietly passionate, humanistic convictions will always be relevant.

It's noteworthy, however, that the standard of humanness that Sabe adopts in his role as therapist does not imply that he intends to participate in the therapeutic relationship as he would in social life outside that role. Sabe spells out various attitudes that the role of therapist precludes in their full form.

> A therapy relationship is not a mutual relationship for me, although there are certainly aspects of mutuality in it. It is not a friendship, although there are certain qualities of friendship about it. It's not love, marriage, or parenthood either, although there are analogies to those relationships. As a therapist, my awareness of purpose is very different for me from other truly interpersonal relationships. That is, the purpose of being there, the purpose for the relationship existing is always an overriding presence which exerts a pressure on me that I am more or less aware of all the time. (p. 159)

I am reminded of a related statement of my own:

> Every interaction . . . is experienced by the analyst as a psychoanalytic interaction. There are no exceptions. Whether the analyst is reacting emotionally, talking about the weather, or talking about the patient's childhood, the stamp of the analytic situation should never be lost on the participants. (1998, p. 177)

Sabe continues:

> That awareness does not exist in the same way for me in other kinds of relationships, even those that can be described as purposeful. The combination of my awareness of purpose and the feeling I have that being open and "human" is desirable is, I think, what gives rise to my moments of doubt about what is going on when I talk about myself or expose my feelings (or avoid talking about myself). (p. 159)

What Sabe encourages here, in line with my own viewpoint, is the interplay, the dialectic, of the analyst's personal, spontaneous responsiveness and certain constants that are inherent in the unique role of analyst. Aware of the importance of this combination, Sabe is determined not to let go of either aspect. He doesn't use the term dialectical, but in my view it is clear that he is talking about that kind of relationship. And when one thinks in terms of dialectical relationships, language fails. On one hand, we are talking about two factors that seem to be opposites in some sense, or at least distinct and contrasting. On the other hand, we want to show that each factor includes the other as part of it, even as integral to it, which shatters the nondialectical and, perhaps, conventional meanings of the terms. So, for example, the kind of analytic "presence" that Sabe feels is always inherent in his sense of his role as analyst sets this relationship apart from "other truly interpersonal relationships." However, the experience of presence is itself an interpersonal one, just as overtly mutual interpersonal moments—moments of disclosure, for example—are not devoid of consciousness of the importance of sustaining and protecting a special kind of presence in the patient's life. Each pole—the relatively constant sense of a unique kind of presence and the openness to immediate, personal, fluctuating qualities of engagement—is embedded in the other. The sense of contrast, even tension, coexists with a sense of synthesis.

I would say the poles in a dialectical relationship are complementary in that each has the opposite figure-ground relationship embodied within it. Consider the dialectic of ritual and spontaneity. When we are acting in accord with the standard ritual requirements of the analytic role, we may also be expressing something personally meaningful, but the relatively standard behavior (for example, starting and ending at certain regular times, or listening to what the patient has on his or her mind) is in the foreground. When we deviate and express ourselves more personally in the moment, we may have in mind the importance of judiciousness relative to the protection of that special kind of presence that we want to construct, but now the spontaneous self-expression is in the foreground (Hoffman, 1998).

What pulls it all together experientially is the sense of uncertainty that Sabe speaks of. That uncertainty, and the anxiety that goes with it, is highly personal but at the same time is absolutely integral to an optimal kind of analytic presence and analytic attitude. Again, Sabe says (like many of his comments, it bears repeating):

> The combination of my awareness of purpose and the feeling I have that being open and "human" is desirable is, I think, what gives rise to my moments of doubt about what is going on when I talk about myself or expose my feelings (or avoid talking about myself). (p. 159)

It is so important, I think, that Sabe's sense of doubt accompanies not only the more controversial talking about himself but also (parentheses notwithstanding) the more standard avoidance of such talk. For Sabe, to have the patient's long-term interests in mind, via the special kind of presence that his responsibility entails, does not mean yielding to a comforting belief that it is possible to know the "right" thing to do in order to optimize the quality of that presence. Sabe recognizes, first, that each moment with each patient is unique so that mechanical generalizations are not possible, and second, that it is inescapable that his own behavior will be shot through with his personal, subjective involvement from moment to moment. Therefore, uncertainty about the meaning and merit of what he is doing is inevitable. Paradoxically, I think it's that uncertainty itself that might be embraced as integral to the new experience that an analyst might strive to provide. The sense of uncertainty, and with it a sense of openness to criticism and to possibilities other than those one has pursued, becomes integral to an optimal analytic attitude.

The following is a sample of my own musings on the interplay among the analyst's personal participation in the process, the special kind of presence that the analyst has in the patient's life, and the analyst's struggle with uncertainty with respect to the balance between the two. I believe that the analyst's presence entails a degree of authority that is fostered by the ritualized asymmetry of the analytic situation:

> Corresponding, again, with what several authors have discussed in terms of an interplay between the "principle of mutuality" and the "principle of asymmetry" . . . there is an ongoing dialectic between the patient's perception of the analyst as a person like himself or herself and the patient's perception of the analyst as a person with superior knowledge, wisdom, judgment, and power. Each way of viewing the analyst is very much colored by the other. Whichever is in the foreground, the other is always in the background. What the balance should be for any particular analytic dyad, at any particular moment or over time, is very difficult to determine or control. Also, it must emerge from an authentic kind of participation by the analyst rather than from adherence to some technical formula. The patient may benefit, however, simply from his or her recognition of the sincerity of the analyst's struggle with the issue. . . .
>
> The very fact that we usually maintain the analytic frame even after termination to the extent that, for example, we do not become friends with or socialize with our patients in the usual sense, indicates that we want to preserve rather than undo the special kind of presence in our patients' lives that the analytic situation fosters. So those of us who are interested in developing more mutual and egalitarian relationships with our patients should not deny the extent to which we are drawing upon the ritualized asymmetry of

the analytic situation to give that mutuality its power. The asymmetry makes our participation in the spirit of mutuality matter to our patients in an intensified way, one that helps to build or construct our patients' views of themselves as creative agents and as persons ultimately deserving of love. (1998, pp. 83–85)

Sabe tells us that there are a number of feelings stirred up in his analytic work with which he is uncomfortable. One of them is the feeling of being admired by a patient, especially when he has the sense that he "needs" the admiration. He writes in that regard:

Why shouldn't somebody have good feelings about me, especially if I'm tuned in and the work is going well? I can experience that without too many twinges of anxiety as long as it doesn't happen too often. But if I start to feel that I need the admiration, the love, the affection, the praise, I get very anxious and guilty. There are so many opportunities and temptations for self-aggrandizement and self-gratification in this kind of work, and since I'm no more calloused to admiration than I am to criticism, it's very easy for me to feel suspicious, and then anxious, and then guilty in the face of praise from my patients. Many times I'm right! (p. 155)

On one hand, there is so much in this that I think is warranted. At the heart of the attitude Sabe conveys is a kind of "worrying" about his motivation. Without such worry, he could drift toward complacent self-satisfaction, toward being uncritically enamored of his way of doing things, and that just wouldn't be Sabe, nor in fact would it be good. On the other hand, I think there might be an excessive concern here, possibly proportional to insufficient theorizing about the dialectic of the analyst's and the patient's needs. Yes, it is certainly important to worry about the exploitative potentials of the analytic situation, what I've called "the dark side of the analytic frame." The potential for abuse of power, moreover, does not reside only on the side of deviations from the ritualized asymmetry of expression of need. Rigid adherence to the frame can also reflect a "power play" in which the analyst is always in control, always above feeling vulnerable, always beyond needing something from the patient.

Wisely, Sabe acknowledges, again in parentheses, a truth that is the opposite of the one he seems most worried about. He says, "I realize, incidentally, that serving my needs has its place and therapeutic value in my work, but that doesn't simplify the problem of my doubts. It complicates it" (p. 159). One way to formulate that complication with respect to therapeutic action is to say that the patient needs, in some measure, to be needed, even by his or her analyst. There is a certain kind of respect and recognition that the patient cannot get unless there are interludes in which he or she can be appreciated for being a source of positive, caring influence on the analyst. Perhaps there is an ongoing unspoken current in every successful analysis in which the analyst is the beneficiary of the patient's therapeutic impact (cf. Searles, 1975). But that factor cannot be overdone either. The analytic relationship, overall, should be asymmetrical in the other direction. So in the end, the analyst is always thinking on the spot, always thinking and struggling and, as Sabe says, doubting whether his or her actions have been optimal for the patient's long-term well-being.

It gets really complicated when you consider that analytic ritual—the fundamental structure of the frame that presumably privileges the patient's needs over the analyst's—is the very framework that may encourage the admiration, even the idealization, with which Sabe is uncomfortable to the extent that he feels he needs it. Given that context, the analyst revealing some need overtly can, paradoxically, mean sacrificing something for the patient's sake, whereas adhering to the rule of abstinence can mean stubbornly holding on to one's power and all the rewards that go with it.

One of Sabe's many departures from convention in his way of working is his eschewing of exploration of the patient's history as a priority. He writes, "I think that what is significant about the past is active in the present in such a way that a full understanding of what is going on now is sufficient without necessitating an understanding of how and why it got to be that way" (p. 161). To my mind, Sabe underestimates the importance of the history in two ways. First, understanding the origins of a person's repetitive patterns and symptoms can help free him or her of their grip. Exposing the possible origins of certain problematic ways of being means showing their relativity to particular childhood experiences, thereby helping to free the patient of the sense that they are essential components of his or her "nature." Second, the history colors the patient's experiences in the present insofar as they seem familiar or unfamiliar, resonating with or contrasting with experiences in the past. In that sense the history emerges not just as explanatory but as integral to the quality of immediate experience. I believe Sabe's thinking about the past and the present is too dichotomous in that the past is not sufficiently recognized as a live dimension of the phenomenology of the present.

Perhaps one factor that contributes to Sabe's disinterest in the history is its traditional association with psychoanalytic zeal about determinism. Traditionally, the drives determine childhood experience, and childhood experience, in turn, determines experience in adult life. But the paradigm of determinism is anathema to Sabe, although it makes him anxious to turn away from something so entrenched and widely accepted. Instead his focus is on the individual as a free agent who is responsible for his or her choices, however influenced they may be by internal pressures and surrounding conditions. I could not agree more with Sabe's simple, brave assertion that "unconscious processes and their influence on behavior . . . are often dealt with in psychoanalytic work in a way that induces passivity, and a discounting of the effectiveness of a person's will" (p. 162; cf. Hoffman, 2006). Among psychoanalytic theorists, it is perhaps only Otto Rank who gives human willing the kind of status that Sabe feels it deserves.

It is Sabe's radical existential sensibility that brings us full circle, back to his anxieties as an analyst. Sabe recognizes that at the heart of what it means to be human within his analytic role, he is, at every moment, a choosing subject, aware of his inevitable uncertainty and yet fully responsible for his actions as they bear on his own and another person's life. Theories of technique, traditional rules, the pressures of the transference and of the countertransference, the opinions of others, and untold other considerations are powerful sources of influence, but they do not eliminate, for Sabe, his obligation to participate courageously in the process in a personal, self-expressive, responsible way, exercising his judgment as best he can as a free agent. In the end, it is Sabe's extraordinary, profound integrity as a person that his patients and students could count on, and by which all of us stand to be inspired.

References

Hoffman, I. Z. (1998). *Ritual and spontaneity in the psychoanalytic process: A dialectical-constructivist view*. Hillsdale, NJ: Analytic Press.

Hoffman, I. Z. (2006). The myths of free association and the potentials of the analytic relationship. *International Journal of Psychoanalysis, 87*, 43–61.

Searles, H. F. (1975). The patient as therapist to his analyst. In P. L. Giovacchini (Ed.), *Tactics and techniques in psychoanalytic therapy: Vol. 2. Countertransferences* (pp. 95–151). New York: Jason Aronson.

ANXIETIES IN THE ANALYST: AN AUTOBIOGRAPHICAL ACCOUNT*

In the family in which I live there are four people of whom I am afraid. Three of these four people are afraid of me, and each of

---

* This chapter originally appeared in K. A. Frank (Ed.), *The Human Dimension in Psychoanalytic Practice* (pp. 154–164), New York: Grune & Stratton, 1977. Reprinted with permission.

these three is afraid of the other two. Only one member of the family is not afraid of any of the others, and that one is an idiot.

—Joseph Heller, *Something Happened* (1974)

I am used to being told by people I see in psychotherapy that I seem so calm and unruffled. I know I appear that way and it really does reflect an aspect of my being as a therapist. It's not that I make any effort to appear that way. It's just the way I am. But it's not the whole story, not by any means. When I make a point of noting the stream of thoughts and fleeting feelings that flow through me during my work, I am amazed at how many things I am uneasy about and afraid of.

For example, whenever someone I'm seeing (I don't really think of the people I see as patients, or clients, or analysands, and I usually feel a twinge of uneasiness—see what I mean?—when I refer to them that way, so I mostly refer to them as people I see or work with. But that can get to be semantically awkward at times, so I sometimes refer to them as patients and put up with the twinges). Well, when someone I'm seeing begins to describe himself (there's another one of those problematic designations that gives me a twinge because I can anticipate the reactions of the liberated women in my life to it. I am going to resolve that one in this essay by using "him" when the person I'm thinking of is male, and "her" when she's female) as despairing or discouraged or hopeless (and in this line of work that is a fairly frequent occurrence), I immediately expect it to be the beginning of a criticism of me. Since I've never become completely calloused to criticisms—even criticism I can successfully pass off to myself as transference—I start to feel some sense of unease. The discomfort can disappear pretty quickly (especially if it's clear that I'm not being criticized, or even if I am), but it can also linger on and become more intense.

Criticism of me has taken many forms—that I don't say enough, do enough, explain enough, react enough, care enough, give enough (once even that I don't charge enough). Also, that my clothes are too square or too informal, that my office is too quiet, or too noisy, or too small, or too uncomfortable, or too cozy. That I go too fast or too slow, that I understand too little or too much, that I'm too healthy, too well-adjusted, and too secure (this paper should set that straight!) to empathize with what life is like for somebody with problems. The list goes on. That I don't go deep enough, that I don't sleep enough, that I move around too much in my chair, that there's not enough fresh air, that I'm not a Jungian, that I sound just like a Freudian, and why don't I do hypnosis. It may sound funny, but if you don't believe that a continuous daily barrage like that takes its toll, you ought to see a therapist . . . or be one.

Since very few people are crazy enough to miss the mark completely, most such comments have their kernel of truth. I find myself having two kinds of anxious reactions to these kernels of truth. When they link up with things I've been told by others, especially my family, I worry about what's the matter with me and about the difficulties others have living or being with me. And I worry about how my work as a therapist would be different, that is, better, if I were different.

Sometimes—not too often—the barrage gets to be too much for me. I've reacted by thinking that the person was about to quit therapy. I was flooded by feelings of failure and worries about lost income. I thought of who it was that referred him to me and who would know about his quitting and what they would think about me—and felt intensely uncomfortable. Just then I felt a wave of relief at the thought of his quitting. I wouldn't have to be exposed to this buffeting about anymore. I wouldn't have to struggle against feeling demoralized. And besides, I could really use the free time. I did such a good job on myself that I was almost disappointed when he didn't quit. In fact, quitting wasn't even on his mind.

It is much easier to contend with such worries when I'm feeling generally good than when I feel low or self-doubting. But even feeling good doesn't prevent the worries from registering.

You would think that, given my sensitivity to criticism from the people I work with, I would rejoice in expressions of praise or gratitude from them. No such luck. That's not to say that I don't like the fondness and respect for me that this kind of work often generated, but it brings with it a fair share of anxious concerns and uneasiness—some of it even more problematic for me than that caused by criticism. We therapists have all learned that the admiration, attraction, idealization, and so forth coming our way has mostly to do with somebody else, is probably masking some pretty angry feelings, and is elicited by the structure of the therapeutic situation (see, I know the rules). But there are times when I think maybe it really does have to do with me. After all, I'm a pretty good guy in many ways. (My mother thinks I'm great.) Why shouldn't somebody have good feelings about me, especially if I'm tuned in and the work is going well? I can experience that without too many twinges of anxiety as long as it doesn't happen too often. But if I start to feel that I *need* the admiration, the love, the affection, the praise, I get very anxious and guilty. There are so many opportunities and temptations for self-aggrandizement and self-gratification in this kind of work, and since I'm no more calloused to admiration than I am to criticism, it's very easy for me to feel suspicious, and then anxious, and then guilty in the face of praise from my patients. Many times I'm right!

I once had a dream that a woman I was working with was like a rag doll—my rag doll—the floppy kind whose limbs and torso I could put in any position I wanted—and I did! I put her arms around me and her legs around me, and it was sexy and great. And I woke up with a start! The whole thing suddenly got too obvious. Of course, it made what was going on in the session painfully obvious, too. She and I were accomplices in setting me up as the powerful manipulator and her as the obedient puppet. We were both getting our respective neurotic kicks from that combination. I can't say I felt too good about myself with the realization. Then I started to wonder why I had the dream about her that night. I couldn't recall anything striking about that day's session with her, but I did remember a fight I had had with my wife that night, after which I felt self-righteously angry and unappreciated. It seemed pretty clear then; if I couldn't get the treatment I deserved at home, I surely knew where I could get it and apparently had been getting it. The next thing that hit me was the realization of what I was really angry at my wife about. She wasn't willing to be my rag doll. Then I felt terrible all over again (about me, but really good about her). Ah, well, all in a day's work—and a night's dream. That's the trouble with this profession. It keeps you working day and night. The person who told me I didn't sleep enough was right.

Praise is more problematic for me than criticism when the praise makes me feel caught in a cover-up, my cover-up. As I think about it, it's not surprising that the self-doubting feelings I'm willing to acknowledge in the face of criticism must be less of a threat to my self-esteem than those I keep under the wraps of admiration from others. The moral of the story is that it is better to look a gift horse in the mouth—as self-depriving as that feels—than to turn your back and risk getting kicked in the head.

There is another kind of "spoiler" that I feel required to be at times that makes me uneasy—the spoiler of the other person's good feelings. It is not unusual for troubled people to endow external objects of their environment with the power to make them happy. A new possession, a promotion, a trip, a new relationship, a new twist of any kind may be the occasion for a surge of good feeling and the announcement that "all my problems are solved." When somebody who has been suffering latches on to the illusion of joy, I don't feel especially good about being the one who says, in effect, "you are kidding yourself." This leads to people saying things like, "I felt pretty good when I came in but now I feel lousy, thanks to you." I don't feel anxiety about this, since I know that the new experience is more likely to be a positive one if it is not expected to provide something it cannot provide. But the immediate experience for me may be of the other person's disappointment and anger, and I don't find that especially pleasant.

Perhaps the most unpleasant experience that I confront in my work as a psychotherapist is the experience of feeling intimidated. By intimidated I mean scared and paralyzed, knowing full well that something is wrong but feeling helpless to do anything about it, although knowing I should be able to do something about it. I'll give you an example of what I mean.

The very first time I ever saw Mary, a bright and energetic five and a half year old who had just been banished forever from kindergarten because of disruptive behavior, she entered the playroom and began to destroy it. Without even a "Hello," she managed to dump three shelves of toys on to the floor and was stomping on them by the time I overcame my surprise and got out of my chair to stop her. Subsequent sessions continued to be messy (in more ways than one), and I established the procedure of announcing, ten minutes before each session was scheduled to end, "We have to clean up now." "We" turned out to be a euphemism for "I," since Mary didn't see much need for any cleaning up, that is, until one session in which she used, or rather, abused finger paints. She placed a large sheet of paper on the floor and began with the paints innocently enough. Then she discovered the creative possibilities inherent in elbow painting, wrist painting, chin painting, and knee painting. I made my clean-up announcement fifteen minutes before the session's end that day. But Mary was full of surprises. She decided the room needed cleaning, and she was determined to see the job done properly. She ran around the room wiping spots on the walls, windows, shelves, floor, and furniture. Covered in finger paint as she was, each wipe smeared a rainbow of color on whatever she touched, and she became ever more enthusiastic in "helping" me clean up. And I became ever more tense and helpless to end the session (which was by then overdue) and get her out of there. Some time later, when a colleague asked why I didn't just take her firmly by the shoulders and walk her out of the room, I realized that I was in such an impotent rage that touching her would have been like hitting her, and that was what I was afraid I would do.

I think my fear of being destructive or attacking is always at the root of my feeling of being intimidated by the people I see. I'm really intimidated by the possibilities of my own anger when I can't allow myself to be angry because I feel I shouldn't be. I shouldn't be angry just because someone is self-righteous, or self-justifying, or presumptuous, or overbearing, or skeptical, or rigid. I wouldn't be angry unless I felt that this was going on at my expense, that my needs were being thwarted, especially the need to experience myself as effective. Come to think of it, my feeling intimidated arises only when I feel ineffectual with people I see as effective—when I see myself as a competitive loser. It takes two to make for competition. When I'm one of the two and a patient of mine is the other, I feel guilty about being competitive and angry about being a loser. Until all of that comes to light, I am intimidated and to some extent paralyzed.

A woman telephoned for an appointment. When she arrived, she introduced herself quite pointedly as "Dr. R." She was a forceful, attractive, articulate, impressive-looking career woman about twenty years older than I, on a university faculty, nationally known as a leading authority in her special field, a field somewhat related to my own. She was also referred to me by my psychoanalyst, who was a friend of hers. (I assume I don't have to spell out the loaded impact on me of that array of presenting facts.) In our work together, she often said things like, "I've been using such and such a teaching method with my students and it works marvelously. You really ought to try it." Or she would tell me, in the course of discussing a problem of hers, what a favorable reaction an audience had to one of the many speeches she gave. In addition, she was an avid reader of the literature of the social sciences and always assumed I read everything she did and more. She would say something like, "I've been reading Blabberman's books, which I'm sure you're quite familiar with. . . ." More often than not, I was not only unfamiliar with it but hadn't even heard of it. I rarely acknowledged that.

The combination of her style, my problems, and the special needs I had in this situation to prove myself left me feeling increasingly tongue-tied and impotent. In session after session, I felt like a child disguised as a psychoanalyst, about to be found out. I was a loser. Finally, out of desperation, I told her I felt intimidated by her. She bolted upright, thoroughly surprised, and said, "How could you be frightened of me? I'm so frightened of you." That surprised me as much as what I said surprised her, and it was the beginning of the end of that anxiety-laden impasse. In fact, the whole interchange had an unexpected payoff in that she realized part of her difficulty with her faculty colleagues followed exactly the same pattern. She was frightened of them without realizing that their behavior toward her was indicative of their feeling intimidated by her.

Although this very troublesome situation had something of a "happy ending" attributable (maybe) in part to my saying what I felt, don't think that I am advocating that therapists should lay out their anxieties for their patients to react to as a general policy. In view of what I have already described about my own reactions to people telling me about their bad feelings, I could hardly think it desirable to dump an added load onto people who are seeing me because the loads they're carrying are already too much for them. I felt driven by my feelings rather than in touch with them, and I was not really clear about what was going on with me until after the experience passed its peak. I think my anxieties can be generally useful to me in my work when they are not getting the better of me. Then they can serve as clues to understanding what is going on in the relationship. It would be easy to assume that because I felt intimidated by Dr. R., she was trying to intimidate me, especially since her colleagues also felt intimidated by her. Some therapists would immediately confront her with trying to intimidate others and in that sense hold her responsible for their feeling intimidated. I would prefer to examine her behavior in relation to her feelings rather than mine, namely her need to bolster her self-esteem by impressing others. My reaction is helpful in understanding something about the impact of her behavior on others, an impact that she did not intend and was puzzled by but frequently, although not always, encountered. Even if, at some less focal level of consciousness, she did intend to frighten others, I think that could best be brought to awareness by first focusing on what she did in relation to what she was aware of feeling.

However, the whole issue of disclosing myself in my work as a therapist is one that is shot through with nagging anxieties for me because I wonder what my real intentions are when I answer personal questions or deliberately describe something about myself—an experience, event or feeling—and I wonder about the kind of impact it has on the other person. I know that the conception of the role of the therapist has evolved from that of the anonymous reflector, through that of the participant observer, to the current standard of the therapist as a human being. It is not so easy for me to be a human being. I think it would be easier for me to be a mirror. The rules for being a mirror are more clear-cut than the rules for being human. I think the people who say you should "just let it all hang out" are trying to make being a therapist, which I think is a hard job, into something easy or at least something that sounds easy. (Even "letting it all hang out," which I am trying to do here, is not easy. When I first started to study psychology, my grandfather, who was in the insurance business, would say to me that he was a psychologist, too. He said he had to be in his work. That made me furious.)

A therapy relationship is not a mutual relationship for me, although there are certainly aspects of mutuality in it. It is not a friendship, although there are qualities of friendship about it. It's not love, marriage, or parenthood either, although there are analogies to those relationships. As a therapist, my awareness of purpose is very different for me from other truly interpersonal relationships. That is, the purpose for being there, the purpose for the relationship existing is always an overriding presence which exerts a pressure on mc that I am more or less aware of all the time. That awareness does not exist in the same way for me in the other kinds of relationships, even those that can be described as purposeful. The combination of my awareness of purpose and the feeling I have that being open and "human" is desirable is, I think, what gives rise to my moments of doubt about what is going on when I talk about myself or expose my feelings (or avoid talking about myself).

Am I looking for attention or creating an impression? Am I playing a role? Am I giving in to pressure? Am I cooperating with avoiding something? Am I serving my needs or the other person's? (I realize, incidentally, that serving my needs has its place and therapeutic value in my work, but that doesn't simplify the problem of my doubts. It complicates it.) Am I conveying understanding by describing a similar experience of my own? Am I being reassuring by saying I have experiences like yours? Am I just being me as a way of saying, "it's all right for you to just be yourself"?

I saw a young man of twenty, only a child, whose father had been killed a month before he was born and whose mother had committed suicide when he was fourteen. He had spent some time in a reformatory and in a military academy before his mother died. After, he was adopted by a gang of thieves as their mascot, and he lived in a house with them and their "molls." Then he lived alone and was essentially an isolate. The point of these facts is that, in the lexicon of our profession, he had never had an adequate male identification model. Nor had he ever had a suit of clothes.

In one of our meetings, he talked about his clothes, or rather the lack of them, and then asked me where I bought my clothes. The context led me to feel the question had to do with both clothes and father figures. I answered that question as well as a few others having to do with the cost of my suits and men's clothing stores in New York City. (He had been in this city only a few months.) Then he asked whether I shaved with a blade or an electric razor. That question puzzled me, and I asked why he wanted to know, since he had been shaving for a number of years. I supposed he could have still been trying to find out what kind of a man or father I was, or what kind of questions I would answer. He said he was just curious, and then he quickly and sarcastically asked me how often I had intercourse with my wife and if I had extramarital affairs. I didn't answer those questions but rather commented on his sarcasm and suggested that something about my answering his earlier questions made him anxious.

I felt clear during the session itself about what I was doing, but I was beset with doubts after it. Should I have answered the first questions in the fatherly way that I did? And if the first, why not the others? Was I made uneasy by the sexual questions, and was he reacting to my uneasiness? Or was he made anxious by the exposure of his own need for a father and the responsiveness it evoked in me? There were other questions then and even more now in retrospect. My point is that as the value of self-disclosure by the therapist has become recognized, it has provided me with, among other things, additional opportunities to worry and wonder. It is much easier to avoid all self-disclosure than to have to decide what is or is not desirable to express. But is it more therapeutic?

Money makes me anxious, too. Getting it or having it doesn't, but dealing with it does. I am referring mainly to the problems created by fees for missed appointments—when to charge for a missed appointment and when not to. I know of procedures that avoid such dilemmas, like charging for all appointments whether kept or not, for whatever reason, or charging a regular monthly fee. These procedures keep the therapist from having a financial stake in any judgments made. They also facilitate a guaranteed annual income. I also know of therapists who do not charge for *any* appointments cancelled in advance (the meaning of "in advance" varies from hours to days), but these therapists tend to have other sources of financial support.

I don't feel comfortable (as yet, although I could imagine it happening) in either always charging or never charging for cancelled appointments. (Of course, I always charge for an appointment missed without any notice given, or do I? What about the person trapped in a stalled subway train for two hours on the way to the appointment? Arranging a make-up appointment spares me from such dilemmas.) So I end up with a set of rules of thumb that work well (that is, keep me and the people I see agreeable) most of the time but which confront me with disquieting decisions and conflicts some of the time.

In discussing my anxieties as a psychotherapist, I have, up to this point, focused on the interpersonal occasions for my uneasiness. There are other sources of anxiety for me that have to do with theoretical views I have that I experience as differing from traditional or predominant views. My attitude toward personal history is such an issue. I think that what is significant about the past is active in the present in such a way that a full understanding of what is going on now is sufficient without necessitating an understanding of how and why it got to be that way. I realize that, oftentimes a person's history can be helpful to the therapist in clarifying the structure of present behavior, especially if the analyst is interested in how things got to be the way they are. But that just isn't a major interest of mine in psychotherapy and, therefore, not one I frequently resort to in my attempts to understand the nature of the other person's world. I think a knowledge of history is necessary for a theory of development but not for expanding one's awareness. I don't feel uneasy in stating that, but I sometimes do feel anxious in operating on that basis. I believe that I am not as attentive to or familiar with the personal life histories of the people I see as most therapists are. And that can make me anxious. Am I lazy? Am I missing something I shouldn't be? When I read about or hear elaborate case histories tracing the development of pathological patterns from the potty to the present, I think to myself, I can't do that with the people I see. Maybe I should be able to. Everybody else seems able to.

However, I believe there are a number of routes to the same goal—the increased awareness of self and experience. Dreams, fantasies, personal history, current experiences, and the patient–therapist relationship are all relevant areas deserving of attention. Different therapists use them differently because of varying interests, sensitivities, and skills. My own interests are less in the area of personal history than in other areas. Therefore, I don't as often rely on a person's history to shed light on what's going on with that person as other therapists might. That's not to say I never do.

I have a similar ambivalent feeling about the emphasis I place on the related issues of choice and responsibility for oneself. Although I adhere to the concept of unconscious processes and their influence on behavior, I think they are often dealt with in psychoanalytic work in a way that induces passivity, and a discounting of the effectiveness of a person's will. (I think this is what underlies the meaning of the statement that psychoanalysis is the disease for which it purports to be the cure.) Someone I see, a psychologist, said to me, "I haven't done a lot of things I know I ought to do because it would take a conscious decision and a struggle to do them. That seems unnatural. I've been waiting for them to happen spontaneously." On the one hand, it is striking that consciously deciding something and struggling to implement it gets equated with unnaturalness. On the other hand, it is exactly what could be expected from the omission of will.

Most often, unconscious content is seen to be the consequence of childhood repressions. I think it is also the consequence of conscious choices. That is, the ways in which one chooses to structure his or her world influences the nature of one's unconscious experience. What is unconscious is a function of the self and its projects and is determined by them. Unconsciously determined behavior is a result of prior choice and commitment. In that sense, the unconscious influences consciousness and consciousness influences the unconscious. Psychoanalysis has traditionally concerned itself with the former, not the latter. I think I try to emphasize the latter (without neglecting the former), but I do it with recurring twinges of trepidation.

I feel anxious because I experience myself in a minority and that minority does not have a long-standing or extensive theoretical tradition. Volition is a topic that is notably absent in personality theory and psychoanalytic literature. Psychoanalytic work is so filled with intangibles. Consequently, so much depends on personal judgments, and it is easy for me to raise doubts about mine. I wonder if I overemphasize responsibility for one's behavior and oneself. I can substantiate my views theoretically, but I become uneasy when confronted with comments like, "I can't get myself to do it differently," or "I don't know why I do things like that. I certainly don't want to."

There are times when personal concerns, as opposed to professional ones, preoccupy me. Since I find it very difficult to listen to another person when that is the case, I try to lay aside my personal anxieties when I work. I have found the best way for me to do that is to concentrate on what is bothering me and to be as clear about it as I possibly can. I try to set aside some time before my sessions in which to do this. I don't orient myself to trying to resolve my personal anxieties but just to being clear about what bothers me. It is as if I am making a list of things to be attended to at the proper time. Having that list seems to leave me freer to stop worrying about those things than trying to ignore them does.

I have attempted to present a wide-ranging sample of the kinds of experience that make me anxious in my work as a psychotherapist. I have by no means exhausted the list of problematic issues and situations that make this work something other than the idyllic enterprise it is sometimes romantically portrayed to be. It has for me its fair share of rewards, joys, and deep satisfactions, but I think I am more aware of these feelings in between sessions than during the sessions themselves. When I think of the changes in my anxieties as a therapist over the twenty-five years I have been one, the single most important change is that I am continually less anxious about being anxious. I accept it and expect it as part of the work. The more I can do that, the better able I feel I am to use my anxieties as a resource for understanding and clarifying the structure of the interpersonal world in which I find myself

Postscript

My work as a therapist is not the only thing about which I sense anxieties. At this point I feel uneasy that I have created an image of myself as so beset with anxiety that my ability to function effectively is highly questionable. I fear that I might have presented myself as anticipating criticism at every turn, as thoroughly intimidated, as continually in need of reassurance, as indecisive, as unaware of the significant events in the lives of the people I work with, and as paying only lip service to my theoretical convictions. Do you think anyone without a great deal of self-assurance could risk all that?

2

BEHIND THE "SEENS"

The Inner Experience of at Least One Psychoanalyst (1987)

"CHOOSE LIFE": COMMENTARY BY LEWIS ARON

In his teaching, supervision, and writing, Sabert Basescu placed emphasis on the therapist's contribution to the therapeutic relationship. As Sabe points out early on in this rich and deeply personal paper, such a focus on the therapist's contribution has become a hallmark of contemporary psychoanalysis across the schools, although each theoretical orientation speaks of it in its own language. Sabe's focus on the therapist's contribution is at once a personal statement reflecting his character as well as a clear derivative of his chosen theoretical orientation. Drawing on the existential tradition, Sabe's theoretical emphasis places the immediacy of experience at the center of practice.

Merriam-Webster's Collegiate Dictionary defines experience as the "direct observation of or participation in events as a basis of knowledge," and as "the fact or state of having been affected by or gained knowledge through direct observation or participation." The word experience, like experiment, derives from the Latin meaning "to try" or "to test out." Because in testing things out one is affected by the trying, the word took on the meaning of "feeling," "suffering," or "undergoing." The dictionary definition repeatedly refers to the duality of direct observation and participation, and so is strikingly evocative of Sullivan's (1940) methodological emphasis on participant observation. Sabe, rooted in the interpersonal tradition with an existential accent, consistently puts his emphasis on sticking with immediate experience, the experience one gains by trying, struggling to engage the other, testing out that engagement, suffering with the other, and so proceeding not through the linear application of theory or metapsychology but through the trial and error of direct observation and participation. And here, speaking of suffering brings to mind the root meaning of the word patient. We might note that Sabe talks about working not with patients but with people, with others—this man, that woman. Referring to patients smacks of too much hierarchy for Sabe, and here one sees the greater symmetry in his existential approach where the analyst tries, suffers, elaborates, feels, plays, and free-associates.

Included in Sabe's methodology is an emphasis on what in recent psychoanalytic writing has been called reflective function and meta-cognitive awareness (Fonagy, Gergely, Jurist, & Target, 2002). Sabe calls it "listening to myself listening to the other." Reflection on one's own participation is an important aspect of participant observation, and it includes the recognition that such reflection is itself one aspect of the continual cycle of participation. Enactment does not end when one observes; even in observing oneself one is engaging in some ongoing participation with the patient. Observing experience is itself an experience; thinking may itself be experiential. The experiential does not imply a lack of observation, cognition, and metacognition.

Haydée Faimberg's (2005) important contribution about "listening to listening" (p. 76) refers to the analyst's listening to how the patient listens to the analyst's interpretations. Sabe was describing what we might think of as an important complement to Faimberg's notion, that is, he was describing the importance of listening to our own listening. It seems essential that we bring together these two descriptions of listening to listening.

It is for this reason that Sabe can say so simply, so forthrightly—and, once said, so obviously—that "free association seems more consistently to describe what I'm doing than what the other is doing. That doesn't surprise me, because I've often thought that free association, rather than being a technique of psychoanalysis, is its goal" (p. 257). Here Sabe describes a method akin to Tom Ogden's (1997) much celebrated description of reverie, what Sabe describes as "the continual stream of associations—thoughts, words, images, recollections, feelings" (p. 256). Sabe forthrightly owns up to the fact that sometimes such a focus on his own associations leads him away from the patient. He makes no excuses about this; it is, one might say, an occupational hazard. Sabe simply asserts that when this happens he tries once again to get back on track—that is, on the patient's track. But by associating in this way, by entering what Freud had called this evenly hovering state of consciousness, Sabe believes that one elaborates on and plays with what is activated in one's own mind in the service of connecting with what the other person is conveying. Repeatedly one sees in reading Sabe that this connecting is his goal. All of his associating, playing, elaborating, and trying ideas on for size is in the service of connecting to the other person and grasping what this other person is trying to convey to him.

Sabe begins this very personal article with a reference to his first analyst, Erwin Singer, and ends with a reference to Irvin Yalom, but he does not spell out the theoretical connection or system of influences, so let me insert some relevant background. Singer's most significant influence was Erich Fromm (on Fromm's existentialism, see Burston, 1991). He wrote and worked in the tradition of humanistic psychoanalysis. Yalom's textbook *Existential Psychotherapy* (1980), cited here by Sabe, explains that the major voices of humanistic psychoanalysis, including Fromm, were forerunners of contemporary existential psychotherapy. I believe that in bracketing his article with references to Singer and Yalom, Sabe was attempting to situate himself both personally and theoretically within the existential-interpersonal psychoanalytic tradition. The existential tradition represents one subspecies within the interpersonal-relational psychoanalytic family tree, albeit an often neglected breed. Frie (2002) has pointed out, "Curiously, contemporary interpersonal and relational psychoanalysts seldom cite existential-phenomenological clinicians or recognize them as forerunners of their work" (p. 636). Similarly, Fiscalini (2005) writes:

> Existential-phenomenological analysis, particularly in its focus on a personal self, and its corollary emphasis on personal agency, responsibility, and will forms a natural complement to interpersonal and relational foci. In fact, a number of interpersonal analysts of an earlier generation, such as May, Fromm, Farber, Singer, and Wolstein, show a definite existential-like sensibility. The existential influence in America, however, has declined considerably in the last thirty years, contributing to what may be called the forgotten experiential tradition in interpersonal theory. An integration of existential-phenomenological and interpersonal conceptions would make for a robust, comprehensive, and flexible interpersonal psychoanalysis. Such integration would, in fact, enrich both approaches. (p. 550)

The above quotations lead me to some comments about the place of these existential concerns within the contemporary psychoanalytic literature. In my view, relational theory has been unfairly criticized as neglecting existential concerns and the place of personal agency (Mills,

2005; Thompson, 2005). From our critics' point of view, relational psychoanalysis is overly identified with postmodernism and so abandons as essentialist such notions as the self; consequently, for these critics, relational psychoanalysis cannot adequately theorize the fear of loss of the self, the centrality of death anxiety, or the loss of agency. I would argue quite to the contrary, and I am in agreement with Reis (2005) that existentialist philosophy has in fact been a significant influence on relational psychoanalysis, perhaps having even a more fundamental impact than postmodernism. The relational vision of a healthy subjectivity, to paraphrase Reis, is one of "an inclusive abundance of experience" (p. 89), of a self that stands in the spaces (Bromberg, 1998) and builds bridges between isolated moments of experience (Pizer, 1998).

This may be a good place to remind ourselves that in his groundbreaking *Relational Concepts in Psychoanalysis* (1988), Stephen Mitchell included an important discussion of the existentialist critiques of psychoanalysis, the standard analytic responses, and the ways in which he felt he had been influenced by this debate. Drawing especially on such psychoanalytic theorists as Otto Rank and Fromm, he outlined a program for a relational psychoanalysis that, while taking into account the recognition that we are shaped by our prior experiences, nevertheless also highlighted the individual's creative will in shaping experience. In Mitchell's version of relational psychoanalysis, the self was not neglected or deconstructed out of existence; rather, self-organization remained one of the basic ingredients of mind, along with attachment to others and transactional patterns, which taken together constitute the relational matrix. For Mitchell, "the analysand is not just the fly caught in the web, but is the spider, the designer of the web, as well" (p. 257). Mitchell's metaphor of the fly and the spider also alludes to the life and death themes emphasized by existential philosophy. In Hoffman's *Ritual and Spontaneity in the Psychoanalytic Process* (1998), the first two chapters are titled "The Dialectic of Meaning and Mortality in the Psychoanalytic Process" and "Death Anxiety and Adaptation to Mortality in Psychoanalytic Theory." Hoffman initiated a sustained confrontation between psychoanalysis and existentialism and called on us to integrate the awareness of mortality into contemporary psychoanalytic theory.

In *A Meeting of Minds* (1996), I tried to trace some of the existential dimensions of relational theory back to the influence of Rank, which I believe well complements the more clearly relational influence of Sándor Ferenczi. I agree with Reis that "the self is alive and well and living in relational psychoanalysis" (2005, p. 86), but I would acknowledge that our critics have a legitimate point: These existential influences have not been given their due attention within much of the relational or interpersonal literature.

And so with this bit of background in regard to existential theory and contemporary psychoanalysis, I return to Sabe. Sabe writes not as a theoretician but as a clinician. He downplays theory, instead emphasizing phenomenological experience or suggesting that he listens to what dreams say, rather than trying to decipher what they mean. But of course Sabe knows quite a lot of theory, and he certainly knows that one cannot hear clinical material without having one's implicit theories and preconceptions at least affect what one hears. Whenever one is listening to oneself listening, one is listening with the benefits and detriments of theory. So how to resolve this seeming contradiction?

Here I believe that Rollo May's idea of "disciplined naiveté" (cited by Yalom, 1980, p. 25) best captures what Sabe was striving for in his teaching. It is not easy to "bracket" one's personal experience, one's preconceptions, one's theoretical points of departure. It takes a great deal of professional discipline and expertise not to let one's theory get in the way of clinical work. In his writing and teaching, Sabe struggled to teach his students and his readers to attempt just that. It's not a matter of neglecting theory or not learning it; rather, one needs to learn it well enough so that one can forget it and let it go. In the paper presented here, Sabe tells us the story of how and why he had to end his analysis with Erwin Singer, who was at that time not yet a training analyst. He does not mention here, though it is most relevant in understanding Sabe's influences, that he continued his formal training analysis with May.

I believe that one of May's most important contributions was his critique of technical rationality in psychotherapy. This critique is elaborated in two of his own essays in his classic text *Existence* (1958a, 1958b). He wrote (1958a), "We are now in a position to see the crucial significance of the existential psychotherapy movement. It is precisely the movement that protests against the tendency to identify psychotherapy with technical reason" (p. 35). May was attempting to determine how to study the person without fragmentation, without analyzing the person into dehumanized mechanistic parts. One cannot do this through disinterested rationality, indifference, or neutrality; rather, one can do it only through passionate involvement and active presence. In Buber's (1923/1970) related terms, it is through not "I-it" but "I-Thou," dialogic relations.

It is presence that Sabe illustrates and even enacts with us through his writing. I think that speaking of our presence is in many ways more useful than focusing only on self-disclosure. For one thing, self-disclosure can become yet another technique, another prescription for the therapist's behavior, and as such it suffers from all of the problems associated with technical rationality. Speaking of presence seems less a matter of technique than of analytic attitude and experiential state, a mind-body state of congruence and authenticity in which one expresses what one genuinely feels.

Sabe tells us, as he tells his patients, what seems relevant to further communication and engagement. He tells us, and his patients, very personal things. He tells us that he feels pressure to make himself felt or known and that he enjoys being clever or pithy; he even alludes to worries about his own sexual performance—what could be more personal? And yet one does not feel that he is exhibiting himself just for the sake of it or that it is a distraction from what he is teaching. Quite to the contrary, his revelations all seem in the service of engagement and the enrichment of experience. In this sense self-disclosure is used not as a technique but rather as an aspect of his presence and authenticity (Bromberg, 1994).

This article contains one of the funniest interpretations in the entire history of psychoanalysis. When Sabe's female patient, herself a therapist, in her idealization of Sabe, tells him what a great husband he'd make, he tells her, "You know, my wife says the same thing—about her therapist" (p. 258). Sabe clearly enjoyed that inspired interpretation, but one could certainly point to the limitations of this intervention. After all, Sabe might have said this to his patient because of his own discomfort with being so idealized, and it could have led to premature deidealization; its self-deprecating but clever humor and self-exposure might just as likely have contributed to even further idealization. Was Sabe bringing in his wife as a third so as to disrupt the intimacy of the erotic therapeutic dyad? I'm tempted to answer, as I suspect Sabe would, that of course he was. So it was an enactment as much as an interpretation, a defensive avoidance or coresistance as much as a progressive communication, perhaps even a self-indulgent exhibition as much as a therapeutic self-disclosure. And yet we judge it not by technical rules and principles but rather pragmatically, on the unfolding and deepening of the therapeutic process, relationship, and engagement. I happily admit to having told this story on numerous occasions to students and to patients. I will tell you that when I have so used it, it has had mixed results. But I attribute this not to technical principles but to the authenticity and timing with which I have delivered the punch line. And yes, even someone else's story or joke can be told authentically.

Sabe ended by referring to Irvin Yalom, and so will I. While there is a risk that what follows may seem like yet another technical principle, that is not the spirit in which Yalom offered this observation. He recently said, "Therapist disclosure begets patient disclosure" (2008, p.

262). Sabe is certainly not the only analyst whose spouse loves and idealizes her own therapist. But Sabe shows us how even such a personal aspect of the analyst's marital life can be employed constructively and therapeutically if the analyst uses it in the service of deepening the relational connection and intimate communication with the person with whom he or she is engaged.

Existential psychotherapy, as we have seen, places special emphasis on life and death—not only biological life and death but experiential life and death as well. Sabe is particularly good at evoking how enlivening and vitalizing psychotherapy can be in its good moments, but he can do this so well precisely because he is nondefensive, revealing, and self-reflective about his own anxieties and vulnerabilities. Sabe's existential philosophy may be summed up in the biblical directive to "choose life" (Deuteronomy 30:19).

References

Aron, L. (1996). *A meeting of minds: Mutuality in psychoanalysis*. Hillsdale, NJ: Analytic Press.

Bromberg, P. (1994). "Speak! That I may see you": Some reflections on dissociation, reality, and psychoanalytic listening. *Psychoanalytic Dialogues, 4*, 517–547.

Bromberg, P. (1998). *Standing in the spaces: Essays on clinical process, trauma, and dissociation*. Hillsdale, NJ: Analytic Press.

Buber, M. (1970). *I and thou* (W. Kaufman, Trans.). New York: Charles Scribner's Sons. (Original work published 1923)

Burston, D. (1991). *The legacy of Erich Fromm*. Cambridge, MA: Harvard University Press.

Faimberg, H. (2005). *The telescoping of generations*. London: Routledge.

Fiscalini, J. (2005). Of existence and experience. *Contemporary Psychoanalysis, 41*, 545–556.

Fonagy, P., Gergely, G., Jurist, E., & Target, M. (2002). *Affect regulation, mentalization, and the development of the self*. New York: Other Press.

Frie, R. (2002). Modernism or postmodernism? *Contemporary Psychoanalysis, 38*, 635–673.

Hoffman, I. Z. (1998). *Ritual and spontaneity in the psychoanalytic process: A dialectical-constructivist view*. Hillsdale, NJ: Analytic Press.

May, R. (1958a). The origins and significance of the existential movement in psychology. In R. May, E. Angel, and H. F. Ellenberger (Eds.), *Existence* (pp. 3–36). New York: Simon & Schuster.

May, R. (1958b). Contributions of existential psychotherapy. In R. May, E. Angel, and H. F. Ellenberger (Eds.), *Existence* (pp. 37–91). New York: Simon & Schuster.

Mills, J. (2005). Introduction. In J. Mills (Ed.), *Relational and intersubjective perspectives in psychoanalysis: A critique* (pp. ix–xix). Northvale, NJ: Jason Aronson.

Mitchell, S. (1988). *Relational concepts in psychoanalysis.* Cambridge, MA: Harvard University Press.

Ogden, T. (1997). Reverie and metaphor. *International Journal of Psychoanalysis, 78,* 719–732.

Pizer, S. A. (1998). *Building bridges: The negotiation of paradox in psychoanalysis.* Hillsdale, NJ: Analytic Press.

Reis, B. (2005). The self is alive and well and living in relational psychoanalysis. *Psychoanalytic Psychology, 22,* 86–95.

Sullivan, H. S. (1940). *Conceptions of modern psychiatry.* New York: W. W. Norton.

Thompson, M. G. (2005). Phenomenology of intersubjectivity: An historical overview and its clinical implications. In J. Mills (Ed.), *Relational and intersubjective perspectives in psychoanalysis: A critique* (pp. 35–70). Northvale, NJ: Jason Aronson.

Yalom, I. (1980). *Existential psychotherapy.* New York: Basic Books.

Yalom, I. (2008). *Staring at the sun.* San Francisco: Jossey-Bass.

BEHIND THE "SEENS": THE INNER EXPERIENCE OF AT LEAST ONE PSYCHOANALYST[*]

Clinical psychoanalysis has increasingly concerned itself with the contributions made to the psychoanalytic relationship by the therapist's personality, transferences, and countertransferences. In keeping with that concern, this article focuses on my own thoughts and feelings as I've observed them in the course of my functioning as a psychoanalyst. Questions like: What's the ongoing nature of my experience in sessions? How come I say what I do say? What prompts the interventions I make? have guided my observations. My intention is to contribute to our understanding of what really goes on in analytic sessions, not simply what is formally portrayed.

About 35 years ago, fresh out of graduate school, I decided to go into personal analysis. I called the White Institute and asked for a low-cost referral. I was given the names of three senior candidates, a woman and two men, and had a consultation with each of them. I chose not to see the woman because I was afraid I'd spend the hours trying to seduce her. At least that's what I told myself. One of the men turned me off by making an elaborate psychodynamic interpretation of my squinting, at which point I told him that I usually wore glasses but had broken them and could see a little better by squinting. I liked the other man a lot and arranged to continue working with him. His name was Erwin Singer.

---

[*] This paper originally appeared in *Psychoanalytic Psychology, 4,* 1987, 255–265. Reprinted with permission. A version of this article was presented as the Fifth Annual Erwin Singer Memorial Lecture, New York University, November 1985.

What I liked about him was the way he listened to me. I don't remember anything he said in that first session, or if, in fact, he did say anything at all. But I do have a vivid image of him sprawled out in his sling chair listening intently to me. However, I will tell you something he said to me in one of our last sessions about 2 years later. I had applied to a psychoanalytic training institute and was told that I would have to change analysts because Erwin was still in training himself. I was furious and said to Erwin, "I'm going to tell them they can shove their training program up their asses." He calmly said to me, "You do that and you'll prove to them they're right in requiring you to change." Well, of course, I didn't tell them what to do with their training program, and I did change analysts. Erwin and I subsequently became colleagues and friends.

I am recounting this bit of personal history for two reasons: (a) it is important and meaningful for me to make a link, especially on this occasion, with Erwin; (b) given the nature of the material I am going to discuss, it is not amiss for me to begin with a reference to my own experience in analysis.

A major contemporary focus in clinical psychoanalysis is on the therapist's contribution to the nature of the therapeutic relationship. That contribution has been discussed under the headings of the therapist's personality structure, the therapist's transferences, and the therapist's countertransferences—induced or otherwise. I want to continue that discussion but reduce the level of abstraction somewhat. That is, I intend to talk about observations I've made of my own thoughts and feelings in the course of my functioning as a psychoanalyst. I've previously written on my anxieties as an analyst, but my focus in this presentation is not limited to anxiety. It's really more on the ongoing nature of my experience in sessions, what is said and when, and the interventions chosen.

Probably the most frequent intervention that any of us makes, except those with a theoretical position against it, is to ask questions. Although there may be many reasons, even defensive ones, for asking questions, it's generally not too hard to figure out what stimulates them, nor do they give the particular analytic relationship its unique cast. Questions are mainly in the service of gathering and clarifying information. How one listens to that information, as well as to all the other data available, and what the therapist does with it, seems more to the point in discussing the therapist's contribution.

For me, listening seems to be a dual process—listening to the other person and listening to myself, or listening to myself listening to the other. What I note is a continual stream of associations—thoughts, words, images, recollections, feelings—some distinctly related to the other person, some related to my own experiences, some seemingly unrelated to either one of us, like a joke, a line from a song, or a brief image. I feel like I continually free associate to what the other person is conveying. In fact, free associating seems more consistently to describe what I'm doing than what the other is doing. That doesn't surprise me, because I've often thought that free association, rather than being a technique of psychoanalysis, is its goal. Blocked associating is more accurately descriptive of what the patient is doing.

The risk in relying on my associations as much as I do is that they may have more to do with me than with the other person, and there are times when that clearly happens. I think I can tell when it's happening because I lose my sense of connectedness. I may even literally stop hearing what the other person is saying. It feels like I have to get back on the track and tune in again.

Most of the associations I have quickly fade, but some become compelling and stand out in different ways—by being repeated, by persisting, by being elaborated on, and by my, in a sense, playing with them and seeing how they connect with what the other person is conveying to me. At times I say something to myself first and then say it aloud, as if I'm trying it on for size. But it's generally the compelling associations that are expressed in interventions. For example, a woman was describing competitive feelings on her job. She felt overlooked and left out but was ashamed to bring them up because they seemed so trivial and uncalled for. I imaged an experience she previously described of her father playing ball with her brother and her feeling left out. So I said just that, "I have an image of your father and brother playing ball." I didn't elaborate on it at all, but she did.

A man said he feels like his life is a blank page and he can't think of anything to say. I was reminded of the blank card on the Thematic Apperception Test and I said, "If you keep looking at it long enough, perhaps you'll begin to see something." He subsequently used the image of the page to convey the status of his feelings, saying things like, "my page is glowing today." He apparently told a friend about our interchange. On his birthday the friend gave him an elaborately wrapped gift box inside of which was a blank sheet of paper. He really liked that gift.

There are a number of factors I'm aware of that may lead to my saying something I'm thinking. Relevance is one of them. My conscious intention is to make clear what's going on, and when what I'm thinking serves that purpose, I generally say it. I'm also aware of responding to messages from the other person. Those messages may take a variety of forms—such as direct questions, subtle beseeching glances, or angry, insistent commands. It isn't that I always comply, but I always react.

I'm not always happy about what my reactions lead to—especially if I respond out of a sense of intimidation rather than out of a sense of clarity of purpose.

Sometimes I experience an inner pressure to say something to make my presence known or felt. For example, with someone using the couch, I know I've deliberately cleared my throat or moved in my chair, not because I needed to, but because it was a way of saying I'm here. I've also said "I'm here." Perhaps there's some amorphous sense of timing for something to be said. I think there are inherent rhythms in all relationships that enter into determining how long people are comfortable being together, apart, silent, or talkative. The rhythms vary with the particular people and combinations, but I sense they play a part in determining the timing of things I say in therapy sessions.

The recollections of my personal analyses are sometimes powerfully operative. At times I recognize myself saying something just like my analyst would have said it, or wondering how my analyst would have responded under the circumstances, or recalling whole experiences that then impact on what, when, and how I communicate something.

Associations of mine become especially compelling when I think they are clever or pithy in their cogency, when a little says a lot about what's going on. I enjoy my own cleverness and I feel good about making clear what the other person's experience is, or what is transpiring between us. That, incidentally, is the focus I am most conscious of having throughout my analytic work trying to clarify what's going on.

A woman, also an experienced therapist (which is relevant in that it presumes a sophisticated understanding of transference), was talking about what a good husband she thought I would make. She used words like understanding, compassionate, kind, wise, and so on. Going through my mind, in addition, of course, to the more psychological appraisals of resistance, were thoughts like these: "Boy, don't I wish it"; "My family should hear this"; "What a joke." I certainly enjoyed hearing what she was saying about me but I couldn't let either of us get away with it. I said to her, "You know, my wife says the same thing—about her therapist." I thought that was one of the better transference interpretations I've made.

At a later time in our work she said to me, "Husbands are a dime a dozen, but a good therapist is hard to find. I'd rather keep you as a therapist." I suppose that could be seen as more of the same, but I didn't say anything about it.

I've been describing primarily what my inner experience is like when I'm relaxed, at ease, unpressured, not feeling anxiously compelled to do something or make something happen. That is the way I feel most of the time, at least in recent years, thanks in part to a lot of experience. However, I obviously don't always feel that way.

I think there is an inverse correlation between the degree of tension I feel and the extent to which I can let associations come to me: the less tension, the more I trust my associations and the more readily they flow; the more tension, the more I experience myself pushing to try to formulate something and that almost invariably turns out poorly.

I see a man who is in the real estate business. He's in therapy because he's not doing well and has never done well in prior, different businesses. He talks obsessively about the details of every deal he's trying to negotiate. I've heard so much about real estate that I'm ready for the broker's licensing examination.

In the sessions, I often feel jammed up, even physically awkward and uncoordinated, and I think, "This is going nowhere. I've got to get us off this subject." But he's more skilled at keeping us on it than I am at getting us off it. There is a frightened, pleading look on his face, and he expresses desperation about earning a living. He also reports leaving a previous therapist because he wasn't helped to increase his income. When the pressure from him works on me, I feel myself grasping, saying things that feel forced, intellectualized, cognitive, and explanatory, in spite of my awareness, even at the time, that my interventions are at best useless and at worst counterproductive. Telling myself what I should or should not be doing doesn't work any better with me than with him.

It's the forced quality of my response that is most disturbing. There's a distinct difference between my experience of letting meanings and understanding emerge and trying to figure things out. In this sense, psychoanalytic work at its best resembles a Zen activity, or perhaps an artistically creative one. It's at these times that I feel most tuned in to the experiential field, and get most joy and satisfaction from the work.

The contrast between the pressured attempt to puzzle something out and the relaxed but attentive listening to what is evoked in me is clearest when working with dreams. Dreams are more meaningful when I don't set myself the task of interpreting them. That is especially true with long, complex, multi-scened dreams. Attempts to decipher them often deteriorate into intellectual exercises for the dreamer and me. I find it more productive to ask myself what the dream says rather than what it means.

Here's an example of the kind of response to a dream I wish I could have more often. A young man dreamt that his parents, his sister, and he were watching an eclipse of the sun. I simply said, "How do you spell 'sun'?"

Dream interpretation, as it is traditionally meant, doesn't play a large role in my work, nor, I suspect, in the work of many interpersonal psychoanalysts. That is not to say I don't work with dreams; I do, a lot—but as communications, not as puzzles.

According to the books, at least some books, psychoanalysts are not supposed to answer questions. I answer some questions, especially those that are about what is going on with me at the time in the session. For example, a woman was describing lifelong feelings of depression and feeling unloved. Her feelings focused on me even though she feels cared for by me. She said, "It's strange to feel most disappointed in the one who I feel most cares. Why can't I enjoy what I've got?" Then, accurately perceiving something about me, she said, "You look like you were off someplace. Where were you?" I said, "Las Vegas," and then told her I had an image of a gambling casino where a woman won $10,000 from a slot machine but the jackpot was $50,000. She smiled, but then I felt uneasy and explained that I didn't mean she should settle for less. She said, "Are you afraid I'll misunderstand? I understand."

In the following session she said she felt good that I cared enough about her feelings to be concerned that she shouldn't misunderstand. She also felt good about my looking off somewhere. For her it made me more human. I often ask, what are you thinking? And I often answer it when it's asked of me.

My answering such questions and, in this case, explaining further what I didn't mean, were both prompted by a strong feeling I have in my work that I don't want to contribute to the clouding or mystification of people's experience. Obviously this is not an intention that's unique to me. However, I think that too often, with the intention of allowing the patient's fantasies and projections free rein, analysts avoid the kind of self-disclosure that can have far greater therapeutic value. Getting direct, open, forthright feedback about the impact one has on others may be one of the most important aspects of the therapeutic experience—for both participants. Of course, one has to be ready to hear it.

The whole issue of the analyst's self disclosure has become a focal point in recent years. Judgments about its appropriateness and therapeutic consequences must take into account the context in which it occurs, and the conscious and unconscious intentions motivating its use. Although it can be helpful in clarifying what is going on in the therapeutic relationship, it may also serve controlling, self-aggrandizing, and competitive needs of the analyst, and end up constricting, intimidating, or burdening the patient.

I find that I react quickly to what I perceive to be discrepancies between the way people describe themselves or their experiences and the way I perceive them to be. I don't always immediately say something about these discrepancies, but I often do.

A young married man I see has anxiety about his sexual performance because he loses his erection every so often. On one occasion he said, "I have a sexual problem," and I said, "Sometimes." He found that helpful and told his wife what I said. She said it was helpful to her as well.

On another occasion, after a weekend, he was upset because he lost his erection. In spelling out the details, he indicated that he had successful intercourse three or four times and failed once. I said, "That reminds me of a joke," and then told him about the man who went to the druggist on Friday night and bought a gross of condoms. On Monday morning he informed the druggist that there were only 143 condoms in the package. The druggist said, "Gee, I'm sorry. I hope that didn't ruin your weekend."

Another joke I've told more than a few times is about the man who gets a flat tire on a country road and doesn't have a jack. As he walks to a nearby farmhouse, he starts to imagine a conversation that involves some pretty unsympathetic responses on the farmer's part. He gets to the house, rings the bell, the farmer opens the door, and the man shouts, "You can keep your damn jack," and stalks away. It's an old joke but makes a useful point.

One might get the impression from what I've described thus far that I'm a bundle of spontaneity easily letting it all hang out. Here are some of the reactions of the people with whom I work: One said, "I need you to be more involved"; another stated, "I need something from you"; and another mentioned, "You do 'the right thing.' You're too careful about that"; a fourth said, "I want your reactions as a person, not as an analyst." These people are all therapists themselves.

Another person, also an analyst, said to me, "You're too pure, too analytical. I want you to be spontaneous, responsive. It would make it easier for me to talk. Sometimes you are, sometimes not." I responded to this comment by expressing some of my own doubts and questions about the meaning and usefulness of a lot of spontaneous responsiveness. She then expressed uneasiness about my possible reaction to her pressuring me. In the following session she began by saying, "I thought of a number of theoretical justifications for being more responsive." And I said, "So I shouldn't have doubts about it?"

But, of course, I do have doubts—doubts about what I do and say and think, and about what I don't do or say or think. The one thing I don't have any doubt at all about is that psychoanalytic work is beset with uncertainty and doubt—but so is living. It has been said that the quest for certainty impedes the search for meaning. Once accepting uncertainty as characterizing the work, its presence is not debilitating, just anxiety-provoking. I do have serious doubts about psychoanalysts who have no doubts about what they're doing.

Although some form of the accusation, "You're acting like an analyst, not like a person," comes up often enough, I don't experience myself as forfeiting my personhood when I work. That is not to say that my behavior in an analytic session doesn't differ from my behavior in a social situation, on a tennis court, in bed, with my family, or teaching a class. It does differ, and it differs in each context compared to each other. The differences are a function of varying meanings, purposes, and intentions, not of being more or less of a person. I don't feel inhibited, constrained, or constricted because I'm working as an analyst, although anxieties arising in the course of the work may result in that. Nor do I feel less human because I react one way to something occurring in a therapeutic relationship and another way to the same thing happening in a friendship. The context is different, and therefore, the impact and meaning are different. In other words, the same thing isn't really the same thing in different situations.

In fact, at times, analytic work feels expansive and exhilarating. The intensity of the feeling of connectedness with another person, the multiple levels of understanding, the experience of mutual trust, the openness to profound emotionality are all liberating aspects of the therapeutic relationship for both participants. They have been for me; at such moments I've felt alive, excited, and even high.

I have a sense that the authority conferred on me by virtue of being the analyst in this essentially asymmetrical relationship is an important factor in its liberating consequences for me. Similarly, the defined role as patient has liberating consequences for the other. By accepting the respective designations, each of us has a structured place from which to experience and explore the relationship. We don't have to jockey for position, establish a pecking order, compete for attention, maintain a social facade, save face, or involve ourselves in the myriad political maneuvers to set up interpersonal relationships. They are set up by definition, so to speak. I think that accounts for the rather remarkable fact that people can, and do, begin to reveal the most intimate details of their personal lives to total strangers (psychoanalysts) within minutes of first meeting them. And we analysts experience a confidence in our emotional reactions and intellectual understanding that allows us to use them as the basis for laying bare meanings and clarifying interactions. This is not to say that every kind of interpersonal maneuvering doesn't go on in the therapeutic relationship, but rather that it goes on within an agreed on framework. Of course, the contract can be broken by either the analyst relinquishing or the patient withdrawing the authority, in which case therapy is over— although it may take some time for either or both participants to realize or acknowledge it.

There is another sense in which analytic work is therapeutic for me. As I listen to myself listening to the other, I sometimes become aware of a change in perspective about myself or the possibility of a change. I see myself in relief.

A woman was speaking about her mother's recent death and her reactions to it. In such situations it's not unusual for me to associate to my own encounters with death—most often my father's death. But this time I suddenly realized, with a jolt, that I wasn't thinking of my father's death but of my own, and imagining my children's reactions to it. This happened around the time I became older than my father was when he died. The timing was clearly not a matter of coincidence.

Aside from the strictly personal significance of this reaction, it has left me with a profound realization of how I really am old enough to be the father of some of the people I see in analysis, although that has been factually true for a long time. On the one hand, that puts me more in touch with a feeling of vulnerability. On the other hand, it contributes to my sense of personal and professional authority— without which, incidentally, I doubt very much if I would be telling you all of this.

A funny thing happened one day on the way to this presentation (see Acknowledgment). Once I decided, quite a few months ago, that I would try to talk about my inner experience as a psychoanalyst, I started a new level of listening to what went on with me in analytic sessions and to make some notes on my observations. From time to time I would look over the notes to get an idea where I was going. On this particular day, it suddenly struck me that I had noted nothing about sexual reactions. That kicked off a whole chain of questions, doubts, and anxieties. How could I talk about inner experience and not talk about sex? What did I have to say about sexual reactions anyway? Furthermore, what did I have to say about inner experience that was worth saying? That night I had the following dream.

I'm in a big auditorium with a lot of people. A tall basketball player comes in. Apparently, I'm expected to be afraid. I say, "What makes you think I'd be afraid?" People react angrily as if I'm hiding my feelings. I try to say that I saw him play last night and that's why I'm not afraid of him, but nobody listens. A young woman speaks to the people. She says, "This guy acts like nothing bothers him." I begin to get very frightened that they'll gang up on me, physically, to break down my composure, to show how upset I can get.

Among the many things the dream brought to mind was the previous article I'd written, about my anxieties as an analyst. It began with the following:

> I am used to being told by people I see in psychotherapy that I seem so calm and unruffled. I know I appear that way, and it really does reflect an aspect of my being as a therapist. It's not that I make any effort to appear that way. It's just the way I am. But it's not the whole story, not by any means. When I make a point of noting the stream of thoughts and fleeting feelings that flow through me during my work, I am amazed at how many things I am uneasy about and afraid of. (1977, p. 153)

Okay, so now I've told you how anxious this whole enterprise can make me feel—although anxiety is by no means the only reaction I have to it. I guess I've also made a plea for you not to gang up on me. With that hope in mind, I'll discuss sex.

In one sense, my reactions to sexual material are no different from my reactions to any other kind of material. That is, I'm aware of a range of associations that may include recollections of sexual experiences of my own that are similar or contrastingly different. I may imagine myself in the situation being described and sensing my own feelings about it. It puzzles me, for example, that a woman whom I see as sexually attractive keeps being treated by the men in her life as if she weren't. I express that puzzlement to her and it helps gets us further into relevant details that make clear she presents herself as a sexual doormat. Doormats don't get loved, they get stepped on. Then I wonder about the ways she's a doormat with me and how that affects my view of her as attractive. So, hopefully, we both understand something about her and I learn something about me.

In the case of the young man I referred to previously with the sometimes problem of impotence, my thought was that he has the problem partly because he worries about having the problem. If he didn't worry about it, it wouldn't happen. Or if it did happen, so what—no big deal. If it happened to me I sure wouldn't worry about it. Then it happened to me and I worried about it. It markedly changed my understanding of what he goes through. It was as if I had to give myself a lesson in humility and I did it through identifying with him. Again, I understand something about him and about myself.

At one time or another, I have some kind of sexual reaction to almost everybody I see, most generally to the women as partners and to the men (as you might have picked up from my dream) as competitors, but sometimes as partners too. These reactions tend to be more reflective than genital. That is, I get a feeling about the person's sexual impact on me, which I find helpful to be aware of, but I deliberately don't elaborate that impact in a sexual fantasy about me and the other person.

The fact that therapists are often the focus of their patients' sexual fantasies provides fertile ground for narcissistic ego trips of one form or another. My own experience in both taking those trips and avoiding them has led me to conclude it's better to avoid them. Not fantasizing myself, leaves me freer to inquire about the other's sexual experience and fantasies without feeling uneasy that I'm indulging myself or "getting kicks"—especially when the topic is feelings and fantasies about me.

In the introduction to his book *Existential Psychotherapy* (1980), Yalom described a cooking class he attended, taught by a woman who spoke no English. She taught by demonstration, but the students were never able to duplicate the special taste of her dishes. Then one day Yalom noticed that after she prepared a dish she gave it to her servant to take to the kitchen and put in the oven. On the way to the oven the servant threw in a few handfuls of assorted spices and condiments.

Similarly, he wrote:

> Formal texts, journal articles, and lectures portray therapy as precise and systematic, with carefully delineated stages, strategic technical interventions, the methodical development and resolution of transference, analysis of object relations, and a careful, rational program of insight-offering interpretations. Yet I believe deeply that when no one is looking the therapist throws in the "real thing." (p. 3)

My intention here has been to describe at least some of what Yalom would call the "real thing" in my own psychoanalytic work. I don't think it has any greater claim on realness than everything else that goes on in the therapeutic encounter, but it surely is part of the recipe. I also don't think that therapists throw in the "real thing" surreptitiously most of the time. Rather, our clinical theory has not developed sufficiently to treat it as relevant data. Therefore, we don't have an appropriate scientific or professional language in which to talk about it, nor to evaluate its impact. So we can only talk about it anecdotally, and that's frowned upon. When it is done surreptitiously, it's probably because, as Yalom indicates, it isn't in the books. In that case, too bad for the books—we'll have to write new ones.

References

Basescu, S. (1977). Anxieties in the analyst: An autobiographical account. In K. A. Frank (Ed.), *The human dimension in psychoanalytic practice* (pp. 153–163). New York: Grune & Stratton.
Yalom, I. (1980). *Existential psychotherapy*. New York: Basic Books.

3

THE THERAPEUTIC PROCESS (1988)

COMMENTARY BY IRWIN HIRSCH

I had the good fortune to begin psychoanalytic training at a time when both the theoretical and clinical winds were shifting—as Bob Dylan sang, "the times they are a-changin'"—and a 40-something Sabe Basescu was my first teacher. It was 1970, and the United States and much of the Western world was in revolution, with challenges to tradition and to hierarchical structure at a level not evident for long years before and not since. Authorities in all realms of life were being questioned, from government to family structure, the military, the corporate world, academia, and the previously cherished value of age as reflecting wisdom. This country was involved in a war that led to unprecedented mass protest, a movement that, amazingly, led eventually to the government's recognition that the war could not be sustained. In tandem with this there existed an equally unprecedented mass movement to alter a horrendous tradition of white racism in America. More individuals than ever before began to link the authoritarian elements of government and big business that brought the country into an unwarranted war with the same power structure that perpetuated a racist underclass. In parallel with these social forces flourished what came to be known as the women's movement. I am not at all equipped to be a chronicler or a historian of these times, though I can say that it was an electric time to be in sympathy with these developments and to witness the erosion (to a degree) of authoritarian leadership, racism, and sexism. Of course, in subsequent years other social forces brought our culture back to old and familiar structures of power and hierarchy—the so-called revolution was only a small part of an evolution, particularly with respect to racism and sexism. Unfortunately, the will of the people over time preferred a return to a more authoritarian government and to military and civil liberties policies that have gone even further toward the abuse of power than before what at the time felt like a true social revolution.

Fortunately, the profession of psychoanalysis has never regressed back to the mean of strong power and authority, and the forces operative during the period just prior to and during my analytic training have had a profound and lasting impact on the direction of psychoanalytic theory and practice. During this era we began to see the waning of the influence of the medical profession on psychoanalysis, the proliferation of analytic training institutes that admitted psychologists and social workers, and the enormous influx of women into psychoanalysis. In the psychoanalytic profession in this country today, psychologists and social workers outnumber psychiatrists and women outnumber men. Though it is foolish to stereotype psychiatrists and men as keepers of the authoritarian flame, it is difficult not to find some meaning in a correlation between a breakdown in absolute standards of knowledge and authority (Hirsch, 1980; Mitchell, 1988; Aron, 1996; Hoffman, 1998) and the changing demographics of the psychoanalytic profession. Sullivan's (1953) view of the psychoanalyst as a subjective observer (participant observer), in contrast to the previous model of the analyst as an allegedly objective observer, did not gain currency in the broader field until the social forces of the late 1960s began to challenge some hierarchical psychoanalytic traditions. Up until this point a relatively small group of analysts, almost exclusively in New York City (primarily at the William Alanson White Institute and the New York University Postdoctoral Program in Psychotherapy and Psychoanalysis) and identified as interpersonalists, were the only analytic subculture to appreciate the degree of the analyst's subjective and unwitting participation in the analytic couple. The view of the analyst as a subjective coparticipant in a decreasingly asymmetrical analytic dyad belatedly opened up the whole examination of countertransference in all forms (e.g., Thompson, 1952; Wolstein, 1954; Searles, 1965; Racker, 1968; Singer, 1965; Epstein & Feiner, 1979; Gill, 1982; Jacobs, 1986; Gabbard, 1995; Hirsch, 1995). The conception of analytic process as a two-person psychology and as a largely unwitting and lived experience between two subjectivities originally had relatively few adherents, but it eventually heralded the relational turn and the decline in interest in metapsychologies, and it has now taken psychoanalysis into the postmodern era (Wolstein, 1954; Levenson, 1972; Greenberg & Mitchell, 1983; Aron, 1996; Stern, 1997;

Hoffman, 1998), currently associated more with the designation relational than with the term interpersonal.

With teachers very early in my analytic training at NYU such as Sabe Basescu and Erwin Singer, I have always felt that I was in on the ground floor of psychoanalysis' relational turn. This is so despite my own and my teachers' identification with the interpersonal subgroup at NYU, even after the relational group broke away from their interpersonal colleagues and initiated their own track in the middle 1980s.* Sabe was always one of the most popular teachers and supervisors at NYU. He was handsome, sharp-witted, quick on his feet, and charismatic. The women often had crushes on him and the men identified with him. For at least one year beyond my full-year introductory course with Sabe, I identified myself theoretically as an existentialist, and I was not unique in this regard. We read very little—his focus was clinical, and in thirty weeks there was rarely a dull moment in his clinical seminar. He seemed to me extraordinarily attuned to his immediate experience in the context of any interaction—in the clinical material he reported, in his responses to students' clinical material, and in the immediacy of classroom interactions. For learning purposes more than anything else, he eschewed interest in psychoanalytic theory, patients' life-historical data, and interpretations that explained motivation and behavior. He pushed us to be skeptical about any conclusions that seemed like certain insights into the meaning of experience and about any notion that we knew for sure what another person was experiencing. He warned us that theory would always give us the answers we were looking for, give us closure, and make us comfortable in our quest for linearity. He pitched a focus on the "what" of experience in preference to the "why," because the latter is explanatory and inevitably theory-driven. He pushed us to bracket life-historical material, to try to know our patients by attuning to their immediate experience, and of course to pay careful attention to our own subjective experience when with patients. He cautioned us that none of these pieces of awareness gives us any objective information, though anyone becomes a stronger person to the extent that he or she is attuned to his or her immediate experience. It was very important for him to convey to us that we are totally responsible for what we do, that we are always making choices, and that we are neither determined by our past nor victims of our past experiences, no matter how abominable these experiences were. We learned that people evolve when they are optimally aware of their immediate experience and take full responsibility for their actions. The notion of

* For a discussion of the interpersonal-relational distinctions at NYU, see Hirsch (2006).

people as agentic meant everything to Sabe. This concept of agency represented hope for change. That is, if we can choose to perpetuate our unhappiness, we also have the power to choose to do things differently, whereas if we are victims of our troubled pasts and determined by them, we can only hope for others to provide us with compensatory experience—"the kindness of strangers." Sabe hated the passivity and the victim attitude that are implicit in the latter. He believed that people, no matter how troubled, had the power and potential initiative, when aware of their experience, to choose to engage the world in unfamiliar ways. He imbued us with an optimism about the mutative potential of our psychoanalytic work, and about the power of people to control their own destinies. He excited us by dispensing with boring and overly intellectualized theoretical constructs, and by encouraging us to be present as fully as possible in the here and now of each lived moment with ourselves and with our patients. In class with Sabe, I was always very present, and his lessons about the significance of attention to the here-and-now transference-countertransference interaction has remained with me as a central underpinning of my clinical work. As well, I have never forgotten his cautions about excessive focus on theoretical explanation, the need to be aware of the absolute subjectivity of all theoretical and historical formulations, and the need to focus on the patient as the active shaper of his or her life. This last point has been extraordinarily meaningful to me because it helps me see patients as having the capacity to make choices different from those that have led to a rigid, albeit perhaps comfortable, stagnation. All of Sabe's teaching that I have just summarized was compatible with what I subsequently learned from my teachers identified as interpersonal, and it seems to me that it was also a precursor to many of the essences of what later became known as relational thought or the relational turn in psychoanalysis.

Sabe's lessons to us captured the revolutionary spirit of the time, and this is effectively illustrated and summarized in the paper presented here. His primary influences came from his interest in existential philosophy and the work of psychoanalysts identified as "existential analysts" (e.g., Farber, 1966; Becker, 1973), and from his interpersonal friends and colleagues in New York City, particularly Singer (e.g., 1965) and Levenson (c.g., 1972). Both of these analytic perspectives, and these voices in particular, were considered quite radical at this time in history. As Sabe articulates, their emphasis was on creating an optimal awareness of the experience of the moment, both within each analytic participant and in the transference-countertransference exchange. The coparticipating analyst is perceived as every bit as subjective as the patient, echoing the trailblazing ideas of interpersonal thinkers such as Sullivan (1953) and Wolstein (1954) and dramatically veering away from the Freudian psychoanalytic hegemony of this era. Sabe embodies this revolutionary psychoanalysis. He writes about not retreating to potentially intellectualized explanations about patients' lives, but being satisfied with efforts to be attuned to our own experience, to encourage patients to do the same, and to create an atmosphere where this can be openly described (in contrast to being explained). He is highly critical of facile efforts to explain patients' ways of being, for these interpretations were often stock and were frequently a retreat from affect toward the intellectualized. Sabe argues that attunement to immediate experience may very well reflect parallel past experience, but he cautions us to be careful about cause-and-effect thinking. He predates the important writing of Spence (1982) and Schafer (1983) in conveying to his readers that one can never truly know about the facts of the past, and that speculations about past experience are subjective narratives at best and never facts. At this time in history interpretation was largely considered the key mutative analytic activity, and alleged knowledge of past events and their current ramifications reflected the primary psychoanalytic striving. This was so despite Freud's caution (1912/1958) that psychoanalysis is not an explanatory art. When Sabe was writing, the majority of practicing analysts paid lip service to Freud's warning and tended to view interpretations as accurate reconstructions of the past; thus they did not recognize the extent to which one's theory will inform one's interpretation. As he notes, the striving for closure and for coherent narrative often took priority over facing the affective immediacy of experience. For these reasons, and in some contrast to what is visible in his written work, Sabe taught us to ignore history and any effort to understand the present through the lens of past narrative. He pushed us to be ahistorical. In retrospect I believe he did this to wean his students from what had become a reflex of cause-and-effect interpretive explanations that were either shared with a patient or held privately until the patient was deemed ready to hear these "objective truths." As one can see from his writing, Sabe did not really believe that analysts should ignore curiosity about historical reporting; instead, he wished for his students to develop the skills to be with patients without leaning on historical explanations. This radical exercise immeasurably helped me and so many other young students become more sensitive and less intellectualized clinicians.

Sabe's writing touches all of the significant keys of the existential and interpersonal theorizing that became the building blocks of the current relational perspective. As I see it, these essentials include the analyst as a thoroughly subjective coparticipant; historical understanding as narrative rather than fact; primary attention to understanding patients (and one's own) experience in preference to interpreting this experience; the here-and-now mutual interaction between analyst and patient as primary data in efforts to explicate essential aspects of patients; and the analytic relationship as curative more because it provides opportunity for new experience and the assumption of responsibility for having shaped one's life to repeat the troubles of the past than either because of insight per se or because the nurturing analyst replaces the hurtful caretakers of one's early years. Though small in quantity as well as wonderfully pithy in style (all of his papers are mercifully brief and easy to read), his theses are thoroughly contemporary; indeed, they foreshadow what is now a dominant and widely embraced mode of psychoanalytic thought.

Perhaps this last point is nowhere more clear than in Sabe's portrayal in this paper of what he views as mutative in analytic work. In this regard he was strongly influenced by Levenson (1972), whom he found both instructive and profoundly compatible with his own existential background. Sabe, as Thompson (1952), Fromm (1964), Searles (1965), and Singer (1965) before him, views the purview of psychoanalysis as centering not on how individuals were damaged by early relationships but instead on how people re-create and rigidly perpetuate these hurtful experiences to conform to the troubled, albeit comfortable and familiar, past. Though not specifically articulated in this paper, he sees personality as shaped by the internalization of self-other interpersonal experiences, and any individual's sense of his or her current world as viewed through the lens of (in current parlance) implicit relational knowing. People adapt to the hand they were dealt, and for most of us these adaptations, no matter how miserable, are usually the most comfortable and equilibrium-producing ways of being. This is the world that is most known, and new experience and alternative ways of being in the world are unpredictable, risky, and often frightening. When one enters into analysis, before long the analytic relationship begins to resemble a patient's early interactions as well as current ones. As Sabe notes, leaning on Levenson, the analyst becomes drawn into a mutual relationship that we may assume bears some resemblance to patients' standard operating forms of being in the world. That is, the patient is viewed as an agent in creating a troubled world and is most decidedly not a passive victim of a world not of their choosing. Sabe sees the tendency that many analysts have to portray people as victimized to be a fundamental castration of free will and freedom. Sabe assumes that all people choose to re-create their familiar and troubled past (albeit not with total consciousness), and nowhere is there better opportunity to explore this essential matter than in the cocreated psychoanalytic relationship. As Gill (1982) emphasizes in his effort to interpersonalize the concept of transference, the clearest and most immediate data for exploring how life history is likely re-created and sustained are within the transference-countertransference matrix (Mitchell, 1988). The element of what people do with what has happened to them is what Sabe refers to as "the area of freedom." This area provides the sense of free will and choice, which in turn makes psychoanalysis an optimistic enterprise. If people are simply passive victims, all they are able to do is to suffer bitterly and/or hope for relief from outside themselves. On the other hand, if within the analytic dyad patients are encouraged to explore what has transpired between analyst and patient, they are able to see more clearly the interpersonal configurations that they have chosen and constructed, as well as what new choices might be available as a way of breaking entrenched patterns of being in the world of others.

Sabe's views about the ideal nature of analytic relationship and how this might afford the opportunity to disconfirm what is expected, what is most comfortable and familiar, are prescient. What is so effectively captured in this pithy paper is a combination of his profound interest in existentialism, the influence of his exposure to the interpersonal analytic tradition, and his foreshadowing of what has emerged as central tenets of the most contemporary psychoanalytic thinking. During the exciting period in our culture and in psychoanalysis when Sabe was my teacher, his ideas were radical. Though our broader culture has maintained only some of the productive upheaval of the early 1970s, psychoanalysis has been forever changed by yielding to the influence of psychoanalysts of the caliber of Sabert Basescu.

References

Aron, L. (1996). *A meeting of minds: Mutuality in psychoanalysis.* Hillsdale, NJ: Analytic Press.

Becker, E. (1973). *The denial of death.* New York: Free Press.

Epstein, L., & Feiner, A., Eds. (1979). *Countertransference.* New York: Jason Aronson.

Farber, L. (1966). *The ways of the will: Essays toward a psychology and psychopathology of will.* New York: Basic Books.

Freud, S. (1958). Papers on technique: The dynamics of transference. In J. Strachey (Ed. & Trans.), *The standard edition of the complete psychological works of Sigmund Freud* (Vol. 12, pp. 97–108). London: Hogarth Press. (Original work published 1912)

Fromm, E. (1964). *The heart of man.* New York: Harper & Row.

Gabbard, G. (1995). Countertransference: The emerging common ground. *International Journal of Psychoanalysis, 76,* 475–485.

Gill, M. (1982). *The analysis of transference: Vol. 1.* New York: International Universities Press.

Greenberg, J., & Mitchell, S. (1983). *Object relations in psychoanalytic theory.* Cambridge, MA: Harvard University Press.

Hirsch, I. (1980). Authoritarian aspects of the psychoanalytic relationship. *Review of Existential Psychology & Psychiatry, 17,* 105–133.

Hirsch, I. (1995). Therapeutic uses of countertransference. In M. Lionells et al. (Eds.), *Handbook of interpersonal psychoanalysis* (pp. 643–660). Hillsdale, NJ: Analytic Press.

Hirsch, I. (2006). The interpersonal roots of relational thinking. *Contemporary Psychoanalysis, 42,* 551–556.

Hoffman, I. (1998). *Ritual and spontaneity in the psychoanalytic process: A dialectical-constructivist view.* Hillsdale, NJ: Analytic Press.

Jacobs, T. (1986). On countertransference enactments. *Journal of the American Psychoanalytic Association, 34,* 289–307.

Levenson, E. (1972). *The fallacy of understanding.* New York: Basic Books.

Mitchell, S. (1988). *Relational concepts in psychoanalysis.* Cambridge, MA: Harvard University Press.

Racker, H. (1968). *Transference and countertransference.* New York: International Universities Press.

Schafer, R. (1983). *The analytic attitude.* New York: Basic Books.

Searles, H. (1965). *Collected papers on schizophrenia and related subjects.* New York: International Universities Press.

Singer, E. (1965). *Key concepts in psychotherapy.* New York: Basic Books.

Spence, D. (1982). *Narrative truth and historical truth.* New York: Norton.

Stern, D. B. (1997). *Unformulated experience: From dissociation to imagination in psychoanalysis.* Hillsdale, NJ: Analytic Press.

Sullivan, H. S. (1953). *The interpersonal theory of psychiatry.* New York: Norton.

Thompson, C. (1952). Countertransference. *Samiksa, 6,* 205–211.

Wolstein, B. (1954). *Transference.* New York: Grune & Stratton.

THE THERAPEUTIC PROCESS*

I frequently have the impression in reading the relevant literature that we are often involved in conceptualizing our concepts rather than conceptualizing the therapeutic process. That is, the abstract nature of the conceptualizations seems remote from my experience of the therapeutic work.

Another related observation has to do with hearing of people's experiences in analysis with other analysts whom I know personally, or whom I've heard speak, or whose writings I've read. I am so often

* This paper originally appeared in *Contemporary Psychoanalysis, 24,* 1988, 121–125. Reprinted with permission.

surprised by a discrepancy between what I hear from the patients or ex-patients and what I would have expected on the basis of the analysts' formal or informal presentations. I now feel it's a very risky business to try to predict how analysts actually work. Incidentally, I assume the same is true of me.

All of this tends to confirm Clara Thompson's observation that the therapeutic relationship is like a marriage in that it's very difficult to convey to someone outside the relationship what the experience of being in it is really like. And yet, to advance our understanding of the process, we have to keep trying. Here's the way I think about the therapeutic process—most of the time, but not all of it. My orientation is, as with good therapy, to present my thinking concretely—that is, to reduce the level of abstraction as much as possible.

Psychoanalytic work takes place essentially between two poles—that of victimization and responsibility. That is, people become patients because they experience themselves as victimized. They feel victimized by other people, by their families past and present, by the circumstances of their lives, by their jobs, by the world and by themselves. They feel victimized by their emotions, their thoughts, their desires and their actions. They experience themselves existing in a world that's not of their own making, or if of their own making, then not of their own choosing.

And to a substantial extent they are right. We are all, to some degree, created by our world, shaped by our societal and personal histories and limited in our freedom to be otherwise. In psychoanalytic work we are presented with the accounts of victimization. We attempt to understand what it's like to be in the world of the other. Too often our anxieties push us to explanations rather than understanding, and instead of paying attention to the person, our theoretical models get in the way.

We often talk about the importance of building a relationship but rarely detail how to do it. I think what I have just described is the essential first step. That is, the analyst comes to understand the subjective, phenomenological, experiential world of the other and communicates that understanding to the person.

But in so doing, an unexpected thing happens. We find ourselves part of the very patterns being described. We realize that, in fact, we are not simply listeners, but also co-participants in creating the patient's world with ourselves in it. The analyst invariably comes to be experienced as one of the victimizers, and may actually act in ways that confirm it. Similarly, the analyst is likely to experience him or herself as victimized by the patient. Levenson (1972) has cogently described this process of transformation. How we deal with this phenomenon, or fail to, is at the root of the major pitfalls, as well as the unique opportunities of the psychoanalytic work.

A woman I saw, in describing her previous therapy, said, "We had a rough time with each other. She [the analyst] seemed to get defensive and was always trying to convince me that what I felt was going on wasn't true." This woman attributed her good feeling about our work to my giving her "space" to explore her experience—especially her experience of our relationship.

Another woman I worked with some time ago told me in one session that she felt I was angry at her in the previous session. I spent most of that session and the next two in effect trying to show her I hadn't been angry. The standoff continued until I finally wised up and got down to exploring her experience of my being angry. Then she said to me, "It's about time you realized I have a right to feel you were angry at me whether or not you really were."

While I wouldn't dispute the validity of her statement that she has a right to her own experience, no matter what it is, it does get us to the other pole of the therapeutic process—the ontological responsibility for creating the world in which we experience ourselves as victimized.

No matter what the degree of being determined, acted upon or limited, there is always an area of freedom—even if, as Bettelheim (1960) describes with regard to the concentration camp experience, it is restricted to deciding how you feel about what's happening to you. I recall saying in my first public professional presentation about 30 years ago, "The fact that your mother didn't love you is only part of the story. What you did about it and continue to do about it must be the primary focus of any therapy worth its salt, and the only area you can do anything about. Otherwise, like Miniver Cheevy, you are left to curse your fate and keep on drinking."

So the therapeutic process continually moves between the poles of the person as victim and the person as responsible, between being determined by others and self-determining, chosen and choosing, finite and free. I think this is descriptive of the process as a whole with the earlier phases more focused on the victimized aspects of experience and the later phases more on the person's participation in creating his or her world. But I think it is also descriptive of the way any experience focused upon in the therapeutic process is likely to be explored. Even in a first session one may deal with both these dimensions of experience, and we tend to feel it's a good first session when they are dealt with. I think many of the subjective evaluations that analysts make about the progress of the work, the suitability or "goodness" of the patient, and the quality of sessions are, more than anything else, a function of how far along the continuum to the pole of responsibility they experience the patient to be.

The analytic work proceeds by laying bare the patterns of interpersonal relatedness and the role that each person plays in actively creating and maintaining these patterns. What is unique about psychoanalysis, as opposed to other psychotherapies, is the focus on the patient–therapist relationship as the most immediate and experientially cogent arena in which to explore these patterns. And in exploring them it becomes clear that both participate, both are victims and victimizers.

Furthermore, it is essential to be as clear as possible about the nature and structure of the therapeutic relationship since it colors the way in which all other experiences are dealt with. That is, it acts like a filter system through which other experiences are seen and processed. In fact, it is the exploration of this filter system itself which is the primary work of psychoanalysis.

A man had the following dream the night of his first session in therapy. "I was looking at myself in a mirror. I had a camera and was also taking pictures of myself in the mirror." After reporting the dream, he immediately said that looking at himself in the mirror was like therapy. When I asked about taking pictures he said, "The camera doesn't lie." He apparently felt we needed an independent, objective observer to counteract the effects of the filter system.

Does the relationship cure? Certainly not in the simplistic sense that having a good mother now will make up for the victimizations of the past. Rather the relationship enables. It develops through the medium of exploring the patient's life experience. But increasingly the focus shifts to exploring the experience of the therapeutic relationship itself, where one is exquisitely enabled to become aware of self-fulfilling expectations and self-perpetuated patterns.

What then of the relative roles of historical and narrative truth? To my mind the distinction, as far as psychoanalysis is concerned, is a bogus one. As Hermann Hesse wrote in *Magister Ludi* (1969) ". . . the writing of history—however dryly it is done and however sincere the desire for objectivity—remains literature. History's third dimension is always fiction" (p. 37). Or as the historian Bernard Berenson put it, "A history of an era tells as much about the period in which it was written as it does about the period about which it was written."

In other words, our focus as clinical psychoanalysts is always phenomenological, is always on the nature of the person's experience. Accurate reconstruction of the past is not our concern. Knowing how people got to be the way they are may be necessary for a theory of psychopathology, but it is not necessary for a theory of psychotherapy. That

is not to say it might or might not be useful. Nor is our concern the creation of coherent narratives. I find that inconsistencies abound in my
understanding of what's happening, and in my articulation of it. The
inconsistencies don't seem to impede the work but attempts to overcome them, motivated by the need to have things fit together, generate
an atmosphere of artificiality and intellectualization.

What makes the psychoanalytic relationship an enabling one, that
is, what empowers it to be an agent for change, is the truthfulness with
which the participants can explore and acknowledge what it is that's
going on between them. It is this more than anything else which pro-
motes the shift from the limited mode of being as victim to the expansive mode of being as responsible.

References

Bettelheim, B. (1960). *The informed heart*. New York: Free Press.
Hesse, H. (1969). *Magister Ludi*. New York: Bantam Books.
Levenson, E. (1972). *The fallacy of understanding*. New York: Basic Books.

4

BATTERED, BOTHERED, AND BEWILDERED
The Daily Life of an Analyst (1995)

COMMENTARY BY ELSA MENAKER

This paper by Sabe conveys, implicitly and explicitly, what has been most characteristic of his way of being as an analyst, and some of the attitudes and points of view that underlie that being.

He speaks about the ubiquitous "battering" of the analyst, not from an abstract perspective on theoretical or technical issues, but from a subjective one, staying with the phenomenon—the direct experience of both parties. No matter what might be the focus of a particular interaction, Sabe's way of being present in the work has been unique and, it seems to me, deserves a further emphasis, one that he himself perhaps would not make—because it is, as he has said, "just the way that I am" (Basescu, 1977, p. 153).

My thoughts about this derive from my own experience of him as my analyst. When I met Sabe I had had a few prior experiences, of varying length, with therapists, none of which I had allowed to really shake me up (it takes a lot to shake me up). Ready to begin my analytic training, I had scheduled consults with Sabe and two other analysts and conscientiously completed them, meanwhile becoming clear beyond a doubt that something exceptional was already happening in my relationship with Sabe. I believe that I share this experience with many of his analysands, and while no two therapies are the same, it may be possible to identify some aspects of his way of being as a therapist that made him uniquely helpful.

When I was thinking back to that time, 30 years ago, an image came to mind. I saw a wild horse, contained in a wide, green corral. Sabe keeps the corral big enough to give space to the frightened, angry, bewildered, and sad casting about of the horse. Sabe stays still, steady; I sense his whole being focused on what is going on. Just to be clear, it's his corral, but he is not interested in owning it for its own sake. He is comfortable in his own presence there, in his authority over himself, but he is not invested in holding authority over the other. In fact, once the horse has become a (skittish) partner, he can say: "Why do I have to do all the work?" (of maintaining the corral or boundary).

In some of his writing Sabe has described the goal of therapy (or analysis) as expansion of awareness. Perhaps, in an ultimate sense, that would cover what he did as an analyst, but it does not describe the particulars of the business in the corral: finding a way of being together.

For starters, I cannot recall a single conventional "explanatory" interpretation made by Sabe, only even, usually one-line, usually right-on statements about what might be going on, such as "You sound angry" or, when I was being plain mean, "Did I do something to deserve that?" He knew the difference between use, in Winnicott's sense, and ill use. Letting yourself be pushed around by the person you are working with is not helpful; in fact, as he points out, it represents a failure of presence in the relationship.

He rarely described me, categorized me, or talked about me. He waited until something was happening between us. Once when I commented, jealously, on someone else's importance to him, he said: "How come you are so good at seeing her impact and so lousy at seeing your own?" When I talked about something outside the work, he could say: "It's tempting to talk with you." That felt important; the outside thing no longer did.

I used to feel like a newly dug up field, exposed, uncertain of what could grow there, and full of possibility. I remember saying, "It feels good that you don't come to conclusions. It's never finished, it stays open forever."

True to his stated point of view, he really did not believe that reference to the past was particularly useful, in comparison with the intensity of the present relationship. The only reference vaguely related to my life history that I recall him making occurred a few years into the therapy, when he said casually, "How old are you, anyway?" If I couched an observation about us in terms of the past, he cut me off at the pass (for good reason): "Why do you call it transference?" Well, because it keeps the terror of real relationship at arm's length. During our work, I once had a powerful, unbidden image of being held firmly by Sabe, who was standing behind me (where he in fact sat, behind the couch), unseen but intensely present. I turned around in his arms and beat his chest with all the power I could muster.

It might be superfluous by now, but I should mention that my own lifelong attachment pattern, until I began work with Sabe, fell squarely into the "insecure avoidant" category—a "when upset, paddle your own canoe" strategy. What I felt was: "You matter too much. This hurts too much. I want to remove you from my internal space: 'destroy the object.'" It occurs to me that the degree of difficulty in permitting the reality of the other to matter, the need to destroy his importance, may vary with the attachment history of the partners involved.

For Winnicott (1971) the resolution resides in the survival of the object. He does not retaliate; he remains both real and close. And there is vitality and joy in finding reality out there. That feels true, but to more fully understand Sabe's part in this process, I turn to the findings of mother-infant research and the Boston Change Process Study Group, particularly the thinking of Sander and Lyons-Ruth. They make use of a concept from evolutionary biology, the "device of specificity": "achieving the possibility of specifically fitted activity with another." "Specifically fitted activity" refers to finely coordinated or mutually attuned interactions (beginning at birth), whether in the mode of procedural, implicit, relational knowing, or conscious reflection (Lyons-Ruth, 2000, p. 90).

Thinking of such specifically fitted activity, it is interesting to note a relevant finding from attachment research: The caregivers of insecure avoidant children tend to pick up their children just as often as caregivers of securely attached children do, but not when the child asks for it. The insecure avoidant child, in consequence, may turn to the caregiver, but not when it is in emotional distress (Main, Kaplan, & Cassidy, 1985). Thus affect regulation has, by adaptation to the caregiving environment, become a solitary task, setting the stage for particular challenges in the therapeutic relationship. Sabe's ability and willingness to "pick up" the other in response to a gesture of approach, no matter how awkward, was no small part of his gift as an analyst. Even when he feels "battered," as in the present paper, by the patient who tells him: "I want to kill you and that should make you happy and you should love me for it" (Basescu, 1995), Sabe does not focus on the hostility per se; he responds to the bid for connection and the fragile promise involved.

Perhaps most such coordinations take place so fast and so out of our awareness that they are never articulated. (Once when I was laboring to articulate, to talk about our interaction, Sabe said: "You could talk it to death.") What is important, however, is that they can make you feel profoundly good: known. They have the potential to "knit up the raveled sleeve of care." In the language of Sander, increased coherence of adaptation and inclusiveness of fit between the organism and its environment is experienced as vitalizing, as a sense of wholeness or coherence in the person—as the expansion of awareness that Sabe speaks of. Lyons-Ruth, speaking of the importance of the "process of becoming known" for our "sense of integration and well being" says,

> The moment of exposing to another one's own delicate source of self-organizing intention or initiative remains a life or death precipice at the heart of self-organization. (Lyons-Ruth, 2000, p. 89)

Sabe was a master at the "device of specificity," at making you feel known at the wellspring of your being. The lasting reverberation is a profound sense of gratitude.

References

Basescu, S. (1977). Anxieties of the analyst: An autobiographical account. In K. A. Frank (Ed.), *The human dimension in psychoanalytic practice* (pp. 154–164). New York: Grune & Stratton.

Basescu, S. (1990). Show and tell: Reflections on the analyst's self-disclosure. In G. Stricker & M. Fisher (Eds.), *Self-disclosure in the therapeutic relationship* (pp. TK–TK). New York: Plenum.

Lyons-Ruth, K. (2000). "I sense that you sense that I sense . . .": Sander's recognition process and the specificity of relational moves in the psychotherapy setting. *Infant Mental Health Journal, 21*(1–2), 85–98.

Main, M., Kaplan, N., & Cassidy, J. (1985). Security in infancy, childhood and adulthood: A move to the level of representation. In I. Bretherton & E. Waters (Eds.), *Growing points in attachment theory and research: Monographs of the society for research in child development* (pp. 41–65). Chicago: University of Chicago Press.

Winnicott, D. W. (1971). The use of an object and relating through identifications. In *Playing and reality*. New York: Basic Books.

BATTERED, BOTHERED, AND BEWILDERED: THE DAILY LIFE OF AN ANALYST*

The psychoanalytic process encourages and facilitates the patient's open expression of all thoughts and feelings. Consequently, the analyst frequently becomes the focus of the patient's accumulated frustrations, conflicts, anger and rage. This continual experience

---

* Versions of this paper were presented at colloquia at the Manhattan Institute for Psychoanalysis on February 3, 1995, and at the New York University Postdoctoral Program for Psychotherapy and Psychoanalysis on March 24, 1995.

as the target of hostility is likely to tap into the full range of the analyst's vulnerabilities. The course and outcome of therapy is largely determined by the manner in which the therapist approaches and deals with these recurrent challenges.

—Strupp (1989)

Any psychoanalytically oriented psychotherapy, in its broadest sense, is essentially a phenomenological discipline. That is, its focus is on subjective experience or subjective reality. Consequently, therapists encourage the people they work with to express whatever is on their minds, whatever thoughts and feelings occur, without regard to their validity, appropriateness, social acceptability, significance, relevance or rationality. In other words, we say, "Don't worry about being crazy, hurtful or right, just be."

At the same time, we therapists are well aware of the power of transference, again in its broadest sense. We know that the therapeutic relationship is conducive to stimulating and eliciting the other's deepest wishes, desires, needs, disappointments, frustrations, criticisms, fears, anger and rage.

Our conception of our involvement or participation in what the other person experiences has undergone a number of evolutionary changes or paradigm shifts, since the origin of psychoanalytic thinking. Specifically, there have been three major conceptions of the therapist's role (Levenson, 1972). The classical Freudian model is of the anonymous, *tabula rasa* or blank screen therapist—the one who stays out of it, offering no self-defining information or input. This is the model that represents a one-person psychology—so called because the patient's experience of the therapist is seen as totally a function of the patient's intrapsychic structure and dynamics, and not influenced by the therapist, since, by definition, the therapist offers no input. I say, by definition, to allow for questioning what some have called the myth of therapist anonymity.

The second model is the Sullivanian or interpersonal model, also known as the participant–observer role for the therapist. One might say, although I don't think it ever has been said, that this represents a one-and-a-half-person psychology. The therapist is both in and out of it at the same time—participant in the communication dynamics and processes that unfold in the therapeutic relationship, and observer of what the patient does with them.

The third model is harder to name but I like to call it the therapist-as-a-human-being—which is not meant to imply that therapists functioning in other roles are less than human, but rather this role conceptualizes a fuller participation by the therapist in the therapeutic relationship and a greater recognition of the impact of the therapist's personality, character and behavior. In this sense it epitomizes a two-person psychology, which views the transference-countertransference matrix as a function of the interaction of both participants. A further corollary is that neither participant has an exclusive claim on defining the other's reality.

It is probably rare that any contemporary analytic therapist functions consistently in one mode. It is likely that theoretical allegiance influences the adoption of a primary mode but variations take place with different patients and even different times with the same patient.

In any case, it is the recognition that the therapeutic relationship is in fact a relationship, with all that implies, that lays the ground for the experience of therapist vulnerability. We can no longer simply dismiss the other's experience of us that we don't like, or even that we do, as "transference distortion." We have to wonder what we've contributed, what aspects of our own personalities have played a part in others' experience of us. In other words, when we get battered we also get bothered and bewildered.

While it's true that "battering the analyst" is not the only game in town, it is a frequent one and probably the one that elicits the analyst's discomfort more than any other, in part because the patient's hostility "will, to some degree, be shaped to conform to the analyst's unconscious vulnerabilities" (Fiscalini, 1994, p. 122). Why then is hostility ubiquitous in therapeutic work? Here is what some people have said about reasons for their anger.

"I'll probably hate you, too. Can you stand it? I'm really mad at the world. In here I feel I can express my anger. Outside I feel like some cosmic force will strike me down, so I'm submissive. I feel like I'm going to get cut down."

"I'll never get what I want. Nothing can change. Nothing you tell me makes me feel it can be any different. Don't turn away from me. I'll reject everything you say and fight you and attack you and be angry. I could never be just what I feel. There was always some reason for not being allowed to, growing up. You'll reject me. You'll have to because I'm impossible."

"It's so important to me that you could take my anger. It's a way of connecting with you. I need to be able to get angry and not be afraid I'll lose you, that you won't like me or let me have my feelings. I can only be that way with you. Too scared with others. Couldn't with mother. I fought because I was able to. It was never allowed in my family. I needed you to be able to take it."

"I have to deal with my disappointments in you. If I don't, I lose the situation with you . . . if I don't express my disappointments I lose my connection with you or my experience. If I do express them, I upset you, make you feel unappreciated. I have to protect you so I don't lose you. I'm afraid when I complain about you, you'll give it too much reality. You'll jump up and down with 'why are you always so dissatisfied with me' instead of going on the adventure with me. I don't know where the dissatisfaction comes from. I wish I could feel free to go the limit—to call you a no-good bastard. I don't think you can handle my ambivalence. You won't feel appreciated. You really like my idolizing you."

There are a number of themes in what these people are saying. Expressing anger is dangerous because it can get you ostracized and leave you abandoned. But not expressing what you feel alienates you from yourself and disconnects you with others. So the therapeutic task for these people is engaged—how to be their rageful, contradictory, obnoxious selves and not be condemned or rejected for it. As one person said, "any disagreement is like killing or being killed." Another said, "I want to kill you and that should make you happy and you should love me for it." In a profound way, that is very true.

When people do "let loose," so to speak, the therapist is caught in what R. D. Laing would describe as knots. For example, one man describes himself as on the verge of a schizophrenic breakdown. He says his brain hurts. He is so oversensitive to stimuli that sounds are painful. He is always exhausted and he is fearful that others will see how disturbed he is. If I don't act alarmed or don't seem to be concerned about the possibility of his needing hospitalization, he furiously says I don't understand him, don't take him seriously and am afraid to confront the depth of his pathology. If I do seem to take it seriously, he accuses me of having no confidence in him and wanting to get rid of him. He says, "you're angry at me. You have me. You want me out of here. You're inaccessible/you're angry at my criticisms of you."

Someone else talks of cutting down our sessions or taking a break for a while. If I offer any objection I'm accused of trying to control him. If I don't object it's because I'm relieved to be rid of him.

One person saw everything about me and my life as perfect and felt disparaged because we live in such different worlds. When she overheard some others make critical comments about me, she was furious with me for behaving in a way that left her feeling defensive about my being her analyst.

One person informed her therapist that she would be away for three months and then attacked the therapist because she would not be having her sessions. I heard of a therapist who told a woman he was seeing that he'd be away for some weeks. When she reacted with panicky feelings he made himself available by phone and even offered a session in that period. She responded with dismay and anger. She felt she was being told she shouldn't feel what she felt about the therapist's absence. She didn't need to have him available then, but available now to hear how frightening the prospect of his absence was. A therapist's attempts at reassurance are often met with patient's anger—and for good reason. I recall my analyst saying to me once that in this business nice guys often finish last.

A man I see said to me in a tone and with an expression that was dripping with sarcasm, "I know it goes against your grain and you have to distort your natural way of being, but in your genius as a therapist you recreate exactly the environment I grew up in and the mother I hated, so I can live it all over again. That's the beauty of transference. It makes you feel so much at home."

One of the attributes ascribed to creative people is the ability to work with mutually contradictory ideas. The same is true of therapists but we work with mutually contradictory feelings and we call it ambivalence. Or as psychological reinforcement theorists would say, both we and the people with whom we work are continually caught up in approach-avoidance relationships. We can't help wondering to what extent our own ambivalent feelings, our own needs for confirmation, respect, appreciation, love and their frustration contribute to the ambivalence of the others who have their own independent and deeply ambivalent feelings toward us.

A therapist told me that a woman she sees said to her as part of a stream of criticisms, "you do all the analytic things but you don't care about me. My friend got a postcard from her therapist who was on a trip. It made her feel so good. You would never do that." The therapist said to me that aside from questioning it clinically, she felt she wouldn't be inclined to do that, but it made her wonder about her own shortcomings—to what extent she is emotionally withholding.

Oftentimes a patient's attack on a therapist is precipitated by the patient's own anxiety—anxiety that may be brought about by an interpretation, by feelings of dependence, by an experience of intimacy or gratification or some other sense of imbalance in power of neediness. The attack is in the service of shifting the focus from the patient's anxiety to the therapist's, thus providing a means for the patient to maintain his or her equilibrium. Furthermore, the patient may project the most hated parts of him- or herself onto the therapist, especially when there is an iota of fittingness, and then vilify the therapist as bad, worthless and incompetent (Sherby, 1989). As Boris (1994) points out, "The nature of disjunctures . . . can only be discerned in the transference by an analyst who is not easily driven to being resentful of being thrown about all the time."

An instance of my resentment at being thrown about occurred in connection with preparing this presentation. The man who described transference as wonderful because it makes him feel so much at home, constantly berated me for everything. He was extraordinarily percep- tive and almost always latched on to some grain of critical truth when he then expanded into the whole of the experience, blotting out every- thing else that was going on. I felt uncomfortably like I was on a glass slide under a microscope being observed by a Dr. Cyclops. One of his major criticisms of me was that he had no impact on me, just like with his mother, and that I would never acknowledge the rightness of any criticism he made. I knew I wanted to refer to my work with him in this paper and so I asked for his consent. However, instead of simply say- ing that I wanted to use some clinical material from our work—which he rightly told me I should have said—I tried to reassure him about having an impact and I told him that I wanted to use some of what I learned from working with him. He reacted with a fury that shook and confused me. "What did you learn from me? What do you think you learned? I don't want any half-assed answer." He fairly screamed at me, and I kept my mouth shut not knowing what to say. "That's not what I wanted to talk about today. Now I have to be concerned with what's on your mind, not mine." Incidentally, when I began working with him, he said he didn't want me to say a word for two years, or five or ten years— not even hello at the beginning of the session—because anything I said would be coercive, requiring him to deal with it, rather than leave him free to follow his own inclination. Although I didn't say very much in our sessions, I was not totally silent but I didn't greet him. I did end the sessions by saying, "we have to stop." Once I said "okay, we have to stop," and he was furious about that. "What do you mean okay? What's okay about it? Why is it okay today? I don't think it's okay at all." He, by the way, is also the man who said he wants to kill me and I should love him for it.

But back to my resentment. In the following session he continued to attack around the issue of how I asked for his consent and his lack of impact on me. I think I was trying to avoid my anxiety by pointing out that what I said must have made him anxious. It came out, "so I gave you what you wanted and you couldn't take it." I was shocked by what I said because it sounded so retaliatory, and not what I thought I wanted to convey. Of course, he immediately pounced on it, sneeringly imitat- ing me and picking up every nuance of aggressive superiority one could imagine. Surprisingly perhaps, my work with him became a source of continued stimulation for me and I looked forward to our meetings, generally without trepidation. It took a fair amount of time for me to arrive at that degree of comfort. When he often criticized me for not getting supervision for the ten million mistakes in technique I'd made with him, I would tell him I was getting all the supervision I needed from him. He, incidentally, had been a therapist himself. More about my work with him later.

A woman I worked with had told me repeatedly of the discomfort she felt in coming to our sessions. She felt that things were happening and her feelings in the sessions themselves were not bad, but the anticipation was always unpleasant. Then she told me the following two dreams: "You told me I had cancer and it was incurable," and "I moved out from my house, sold it. It was a mistaken decision and I couldn't move back." She immediately followed the dreams by saying, "I'll open the door here and find things so wrong. It will be like a psychic death," I said, "and I'll have caused it."

A few weeks after starting therapy with me a man came home from his office and found that his wife had moved out with almost all the furniture and the balance in the bank account. He came to his appointment with me in a rage, told me we weren't compatible and he couldn't work with me, stalked out and slammed the door so hard it literally shook loose from its hinges, something I had only seen in comic strips. I was thoroughly bewildered and I never saw him again. It was clear he was blaming me for his wife's departure.

Therapists are often seen as the coercive agents of disturbing self-reflection and self-awareness, and of unanticipated changes that at least initially can result in a great deal of uneasiness. People don't generally come to therapists because they really want to change. They come because they want to feel happy but not alter the familiar structures of their lives. That can be very scary. The reward for the therapist's working effectively can be getting kicked in the head. As my supervisor-patient says, "When I begin to trust you I'll show you how angry I really am." I sometimes wonder what that will be like.

So we see that people's fears, anxieties, disappointments, frustrations, and the anger and rage they generate, invariably become focused on the therapist—at times because in truth, the therapist fails to understand, empathize, confirm, gratify, support, listen, attend, care, respond or because that is the way the patient more or less experiences everything, or most because of some combination of the two. Fears of rejection, abandonment and retaliation have kept the true nature of these feelings knotted in their emotional insides. They need to experience them live and learn that they won't destroy the other or the relationship with the other. They need to reintegrate repressed, disowned aspects of their being and in doing so, take responsibility for them and have the options of choice and control. The analyst becomes the necessary partner in this crucial venture, playing the paradoxical role of guarantor of safety and target of hostility. How well the analyst fulfills this complex task often determines its outcome.

Transference is one of those central concepts whose meaning is continually being modified and expanded. One way of thinking about it that I find helpful in the context of working with these issues, is to see it as the process by which the patient makes the analyst into the person he or she needs in order to re-confront unresolved interpersonal interactions that have fostered pathological reactions. The patient has the hope that this time around the traumas can be resolved and the pathological reactions relinquished. This process inevitably involves both the unconscious and the conscious participation of the analyst. It incorporates what Levenson (1972) has describes as the transformation of the analyst, what Winnicott (1971) describes as the use of the object, and what Sampson (1994) calls transference testing.

Levenson sees the analyst as inevitably drawn into the structure of the patient's world and behaving in a way that more or less fits into the pattern of the patient's transferential expectations. The task for the analyst is to resist this transformation and continually work his or her way out of what is inevitably and continually taking place without, of course, alienating or rejecting the patient. It is in the working through of this that the therapy proceeds. This echoes what has always been for me a very cogent statement of Medard Boss (1963): "Countertransference can never be avoided. It can only be denied." Formerly, anything that looked like countertransference was seen as a failure on the part of the analyst and an impediment to the therapeutic process. Now it is more realistically seen, not only as an inevitable part of the process, but as the most "experience-near" source of information available to the analyst about what it's like to be in the world of the other. As such it is not without its risks and serious pitfalls.

Sampson describes the therapeutic process as one in which "the patient repeats, by carrying out a trial action involving the expression of an attitude, affective state, or behavior, what (the patient believes) led in childhood to a traumatic experience" (p. 358). Or the patient may behave like the traumatizing parent and actively inflict the trauma on the therapist. In both cases the patient tests and hopes for a reaction that disconfirms the patient's pathological belief. Whether the patient plays the role of a child or parent in these tests, the therapist is going to get battered.

Winnicott's concept of the use of the object has perhaps been most influential in understanding the hostile and otherwise distressing environment in which analysts so frequently find themselves. He distinguishes between object relating and object usage. Object relating, as distinct from interpersonal relating, involves a construction of the other that is based on projections, identification and fantasized elaboration. Object usage deals with the other as "real in the sense of being part of shared reality" (p. 88) and as having in independent existence, as a thing in itself. Then comes this enigmatic statement: "This change (from relating to usage) means that the subject destroys the object" (p. 89). Substitute patient for subject and analyst for object and you have the situation of the battered analyst. But what does destroying the object mean in this context? Certainly it means in part destroying the projected, fantasized construction of the analyst. More importantly it means that the patient has the live and lived experience of his or her anger, rage and destructiveness in the world of a real, separate person, and not simply an "as if" fantasy experience that leaves the patient as mixed in anxiety and uncertainty as before.

> This destructive activity is the patient's attempt to place the analyst outside the area of omnipotent control, that is, out in the world. Without the experience of maximum destructiveness . . . the subject never placed the analyst outside and therefore can never do more than experience a kind of self-analysis using the analyst as a projection of a part of the self. . . . The patient may even enjoy the analytic experience but will not fundamentally change. (p. 91)

So, for example, the man I've referred to, continually and relentlessly berates me for everything from the condition of my office to the errors of my interventions, from my failures in understanding him to my refusal to re-enter personal analysis and supervision, and from my unfamiliarity with all the relevant personal literature to my refusal to spend sufficient time, both before and after his appointments, pondering his dynamics and the significance of what transpires between us. It is important to realize that none of these charges is totally without merit. Each had at least its kernel of truth which often enough leaves me wondering and worrying why I can't get it right. However, he expands the kernel of truth into the whole of his perceptions thereby distorting the full picture of what is going on. As he says, he knows he is "certifiably insane" but he is absolutely committed, for the first time in his life, at all costs, to staying with and exploring his own experience. He frequently says he hates me and wants to kill me and that I should love him for it. He also says this is the most important experience in his life and I would only shut up, he could get on with it.

Which brings us to the remaining, equally crucial point in Winnicott's thesis, namely the importance of the analyst surviving destruction by the patient: "It is important that 'survive,' in this context, means 'not retaliate'" (p. 91). In other words, what needs to survive is the analytic relationship and the integrity of the therapeutic process. The analyst should not attack, or withdraw from, or collude with, or reject the patient, but should maintain what Schafer (1983) has described as the analytic attitude. Clearly this is descriptive of an ideal stance that is never fully achieved but only approached. However, just as Winnicott has spoken for the value of "good enough" mothering, so too there is good enough therapeutic relating. With repeated experiences of the patient's destructiveness and the analyst's survival, the relationship becomes more trustworthy, dependable and safe, and, as Epstein (1984) describes, "contributes to the development of a reality sense and to the capability of living in a world of shared reality" (p. 652). My patient says "when I attack you I feel scared and uneasy so I attack you some more. The more seriously I attack you, the safer I feel I learn the world doesn't fall apart if I express what I feel. Then I can relax."

Although there is no question about the analyst's survival being essential to any successful therapeutic outcome, what can be said that can contribute to enabling analysts to live through the storm of enactments and survive? Strupp (1989) has done extensive research on the process of psychotherapy. He writes,

> The great paradox of therapy is that by offering another person a benign and empathic relationship one simultaneously opens the door to becoming the target of his or her accumulated frustrations, wishes, conflicts, and fears. Thus, as a therapist, one cannot avoid becoming an unwilling co-actor in the patient's interpersonal drama. The course and outcome of therapy is largely determined by the manner in which the therapist approaches and deals with these recurrent challenges. (p. 719)

Among Strupp's findings are these:

1. Personal therapy for the analyst is important in dealing with one's own emotional reactions.
2. Interventions are best focused on the patient's anxieties and conflicts, not on performance.

3. It is important to avoid responding to provocations in a complementary manner. That is, the analyst should avoid assuming an assigned role.
4. Traditional interpretations often have a pejorative, blaming quality, especially when aimed at so-called resistances, and to that extent are contra-indicated.
5. Avoid power struggles.
6. Avoid confronting or challenging patients.
7. Attend mainly to conveying understanding of the patient's subjective world.

On the basis of my own experience I would add the following. However harsh the hostility or criticism directed at me, I try to hear the content as the other's analysis of me, telling me how I'm perceived, what impact I have, what my character or personality is like in the eyes of the other. In other words, I try to find what I can relate to as the kernel of truth about myself. I try not to be concerned, at the moment, with its exaggeration or distortion—or with any particular response to it, or changing it, but just with finding its place in my awareness of myself. I find that both interesting and challenging, and, at least at this point in my life, helpful in not becoming dismayed, disheartened and discourages. It also leads me back, most of the time, into thinking about our interaction—what it is about me that inflamed the other person, why it had the significance it did and so on. It also often results in an acknowledgment on my part of how I think I might fit the bill and how I think I might not (Basescu, 1990).

For example, I was angrily accused by a woman over a period of time of losing interest in her analysis and withdrawing from her. She was really quite incensed and critical and talked of quitting her work with me and looking for another analyst. I was troubled by the accusation and puzzled by it as well, since I was not aware of either losing interest in her or the analysis. But I did become aware of a change in the nature of my material, that is, until I became aware of it being too easy to stay with and then my involvement with her sexual fantasies cooled down. I told her this and then her anger gave way to some fruitful exploration of the pattern of sexuality in her life.

Paying attention to the content of an attack on me is easier when the emotional quality is something less than explosive. Of course, sometimes there is no real content, just fury. In the midst of any anxiety I might feel under these conditions, I try to keep in mind not to try to defend myself or explain anything at the moment, but just to hear it out, realizing that under the rage the other person is probably even more anxious than I am (Basescu, 1977). (Only once can I recall anger becoming physical. A rather large woman threw over a potted plant in her rage at me and then stalked out of the office. But she changed her mind, turned and headed back in. I grabbed a wooden pole and barred her way with it. I didn't want to touch her nor did I want her to come back in.)

Ehrenberg (1994) makes the point that the analyst's insistence on being treated respectfully is necessary to preserve the analytic frame. She further highlights the importance of addressing any abusive enactment, and of "establishing a context in which the patient feels the analyst can take care of himself or herself, even as he or she is vulnerable" (p. 309). I completely agree with these principles but I think what defines them in practice varies considerably among patients and analysts, and specific pairs of patient and analyst. When my patient-supervisor threatens to bring me up on ethics charges to the State Board of Examiners, he is not treating me disrespectfully. However, I can only imagine the same threat being made by someone as a form of blackmail that would effectively end the therapy. Similarly, I can imagine very different thresholds of safety for different analysts but the principle applies that both patient and analyst need to experience the relationship as essentially safe.

Another situation that may require the analyst's limit setting intervention was brought to my attention some years ago by Leslie Farber. If the other's abusiveness is such as to result in the patient's subsequently feeling humiliated by his or her behavior, it is antithetical to the therapeutic process to let it continue.

When all is said and done, the fact remains that analysts often feel abused, unappreciated, frustrated, disrespected, aggressed against and like failures. And they experience anxiety, impatience, hostility, hate, a wish to be rid of the other and even a wish to be rid of the job. Winnicott (1949) warns that the analyst

> must not deny hate that really exists in himself. Hate that is justified in the present setting has to be sorted out and kept in storage and available for eventual interpretation. . . . In certain analyses the analyst's hate is actually sought by the patient, and what is then needed is hate that is objective. If the patient seeks objective or justified hate he must be able to reach it, or else he cannot feel he can reach objective love. (pp. 70, 72)

I saw a woman for whom I was the 27th therapist in her life. Although she ended her contact with some of them herself, most terminated the work with her. They gave her all kinds of reasons for ending—moving out of town, changes in schedule, retiring, specializing in research, raising fees beyond what she could afford and her owing them money.

To put it most benignly, she had a very alienating personal style. She told me that the therapist she respected most was the one who ended because, as he told her, he had a headache after every session with her and it was too uncomfortable for him. She said she knew what she was like and she appreciated his leveling with her.

The denial of the other's hatefulness or alienating qualities may leave him or her feeling not understood, unknown to the therapist or without impact. If the therapist's reactions are falsified, they may generate a mistrust of any of the therapist's reactions and responses, including the therapist's love. However, there is a difference between the therapist's enactment of "hate in the countertransference" and the acknowledgment of the range of negative reactions on the therapist's part.

Poetry has been described as "the recollection of emotion in tranquility." In making known their emotions to their patients, therapists should be as poets. That is, the description of the therapist's feelings may be inappropriate and useful, but the heat rarely is. It is more likely to be anxiety-provoking and disruptive.

The title of this paper (as I'm sure many of you recognize) is a parody of a love song form the musical *Pal Joey*, and that is not an accident. No discussion of hostile attacks on the analyst, and the analyst's vulnerability and survival would be complete without a mention of the part that love plays in these interactions. Nobody has a greater desire for the analyst to survive than the patient does. The patient's psychic existence depends on it, and he or she may make both subtle and obvious efforts to protect the analyst and contribute to the survival of the analyst. For example, one person, in the midst of a critical attack, acknowledged giving me a hard time. Another interspersed the hostility with talk of how valued our relationship was. One person brought me a copy of Winnicott's paper on object usage to make sure I had the right take on what was going on. And the man I've mentioned before has said the following kinds of things to me at different times, often in the midst of a hostile attack: "I've relaxed enough so that I can move my arms and legs freely. . . . For the first time I'm beginning to be a recognizable person in my dreams. . . . I can hear the birds chirp. I never heard them before." I often feel that part of his reason for saying these things to me is to reassure me that good things are going on, and I shouldn't get discouraged by his attacks. Sometimes, he will very deliberately call me "mother," I think to make sure I know he's got some perspective on his hostility towards me.

Slochower (1994) comments on the "oddly satisfying" feeling of the intense contacts following the patient's accusations, and her own freedom to feel more fully with her patient. She further writes "that the analyst also may derive real pleasure from living through object usage with the patient. This pleasure is analogous to the mother's reaction to her infant's all-out use of her, which confirms her own aliveness and her internal richness" (p. 148). However, Bromberg (1994) warns that "if the analyst is feeling satisfaction for his willingness to be 'used as an object'—he is not really being used at all, at least not yet" (p. 525).

In my experience they are both correct. There is nothing pleasurable in being battered or used, but it is deeply satisfying to come out on the other side and achieve a new level of intimacy and openness. I don't think therapists are masochistic in choosing to go into a profession in which they know they will be exposed to the kind of hostility, probing and criticism I've discussed. I think it is the price they are willing to pay to participate in an extraordinarily interesting, and at times exciting adventure—the development of a person.

References

Basescu, S. (1977). Anxieties of the analyst: An autobiographical account. In K. A. Frank (Ed.), *The human dimension in psychoanalytic practice* (pp. 154–164). New York: Grune & Stratton.

Basescu, S. (1990). Show and tell: Reflections on the analyst's self-disclosure. In G. Stricker & M. Fisher (Eds.), *Self-disclosure in the therapeutic relationship* (pp. 47–59). New York: Plenum.

Boris, H. (1994). About time. *Contemporary Psychoanalysis, 30*(2), 301–322.

Boss, M. (1963). *Psychoanalysis and daseinanalysis.* New York: Basic Books.

Bromberg, P. (1994). "Speak! That I may see you": Some reflections on dissociation, reality, and psychoanalytic listening. *Psychoanalytic Dialogues, 4*(4), 514–547.

Ehrenberg, D. (1994). Reply to reviews. *Psychoanalytic Dialogues, 4*(2), 303–316.

Epstein, L. (1984). An interpersonal-object relations perspective on working with destructive aggression. *Contemporary Psychoanalysis, 20*(4), 651–662.

Fiscalini, J. (1994). The uniquely interpersonal and the interpersonally unique: On interpersonal psychoanalysis. *Contemporary Psychoanalysis, 30*(1), 114–134.

Levenson, E. (1972). *The fallacy of understanding.* New York: Basic Books.

Sampson, H. (1994). Repeating pathological relationships to disconfirm pathogenic beliefs. *Psychoanalytic Dialogues, 4*(3), 357–361.

Schafer, R. (1983). *The analytic attitude.* New York: Basic Books.

Sherby, L. (1989). Love and hate in the treatment of borderline patients. *Contemporary Psychoanalysis, 25*(4), 574–591.

Slochower, J. (1994). The evolution of object usage and the holding environment. *Contemporary Psychoanalysis, 30*(1), 135–151.

Strupp, H. (1989). Psychotherapy: Can the practitioner learn from the researcher? *American Psychologist, 44*(4), 717–724.

Winnicott, D. W. (1949). Hate in the counter-transference. *International Journal of Psycho-analysis*, *30*(2), 69–74.

5

CREATIVITY AND THE DIMENSIONS
OF CONSCIOUSNESS (1967)

"THE WOUND AND THE EMBRACE: CREATIVITY IN CONTEXT": COMMENTARY BY SPYROS D. ORFANOS

Creative expression, is above all, an act of freedom. I create means I am free—I become free. The message of art is a message of freedom.

—Mikis Theodorakis

Sabert Basescu's "Creativity and the Dimensions of Consciousness" is a splendid piece of work, particularly when we consider the time it was written and how different it is from Basescu's other, more clinical publications. He did not write much, but what he did publish tended to be clinical, brief, clear, and personal. In "Creativity and the Dimensions of Consciousness" he is erudite and makes use of systematic empirical research but is not personal. Clearly, there were many sides to Basescu's writing and thinking style. In this article, Basescu is reaching for something that was not done much in the 1950s and 1960s: to place the psychological study of creativity in context. This context involves both conscious and unconscious processes, all within a humanistic/existential view of the person.

A Time of Crisis

I believe that the importance of "Creativity and the Dimensions of Consciousness" lies in its challenge to convention. It indirectly identifies

99

a time of crisis in both psychoanalysis and academic psychology. This crisis was taking place in a particular cultural and political climate: the late 1960s, an era of both amazing creativity and destruction. Basescu did not label it as a time of crisis, but his worry about the prevailing deterministic views is present. I believe this worry was a partial motivation for this paper, so different from his others. In his teaching and supervision he seemed to always be interested in matters creative. Through in-depth discussions with a few of his former patients I can state with certainty that he was strongly interested in their creative endeavors, both those that were artistic and those that were personally expressive.

While Basescu begins at the beginning with biblical Adam and Eve, we can say the modern study of creativity has two historic beginnings: 1908 and 1950. Freud made only one cursory, albeit brilliant, attempt at a formulation on creativity, and that was his 1908 public lecture "Creative Writers and Daydreaming" (1908/1959). He spoke to 90 intellectuals at a Viennese booksellers. His talk was about the topic of play as common to both children and creative writers. In this talk, he speaks about how instead of "playing" the adult "now phantasies." This eventually leads Freud to the memories of creative writers and their wish to find some type of fulfillment in the creative work. Despite this tantalizing formulation, Freud never really probed further into the mysteries of creative phenomena. Unlike with dreams, for example, where he applied his Enlightenment-era attitudes of the power of science, he seemed to drop theorizing about creativity. He came to believe that "psychoanalysis must lay down its arms" in regard to creativity (1929/1961, p. 177). Perhaps this invaluable human ability was just too murky and challenging even for a man of Freud's intellectual courage.

The second historic moment of importance to the study of creativity was J. P. Guilford's 1950 presidential address to the American Psychological Association. Guilford spoke to hundreds of eager psychologists at Pennsylvania State College. The address was titled "Creativity," and his basic call, and subsequent empirical efforts, went a long way toward convincing psychologists about the possibility of being scientific about creativity. He argued that creativity was a "natural resource." This may be an example of zeitgeist, for Guilford's arguments were compatible with the assumptions and needs of the 1950s and the values of American capitalism and production (Runco, 2004).

Reductionism and the Third Force

What was the implicit crisis that Basescu was dealing with in this paper? Guilford's 1950 call to action led to a burst of study about creativity for about 15 years, till about the mid-1960s; after that the field saw a waning of innovative action during the next 20 years, up to the mid-1980s (Runco, 2004). The first 15-year period focused on (1) the psychometric measure of creativity, (2) the dominance of learning theory, (3) rigid methodology, and (4) the lack of agreement on criteria for researching creativity. It is my contention that in the 20 years that followed, creativity research stalled because its focus was on creativity in relation to intelligence and personality, both constructs that yielded little other than small correlations. From the mid-1980s to the present, advances in research methods and statistical analysis based on powerful technological innovations have allowed for a diverse and sometimes innovative application of creativity studies. Moreover, genius (creativity with a capital C) is now sharing publication space in psychology journals with everyday problem solving (creativity with a lowercase c).

Current empirical findings suggest different investigative domains such as person, product, press (the relationship of human beings and their environment), and process. Moreover, a myriad of studies have used disciplinary frameworks organized by behavioral, biological, clinical, cognitive, developmental, historiometric (quantitative analyses to date concerning historical individuals), organizational, psychometric, and social perspectives. Of particular note is the finding that while creativity may be a sort of deviance, it is not a kind of psychopathology. Overall, I am of the opinion that the systematic empirical approach to creativity, however, has not been as impressive as Guilford once hoped. While it has been beneficial, the costs in terms of research time, energy, and monies should be acknowledged (Runco, 2004).

When Basescu writes about the "so-called scientific attempts to understand" he is addressing psychoanalytic studies such as Ernest Kris' 1952 view that creativity is at the service of the ego, which controls defense mechanisms. Later in his article, Basescu relies on a widely referenced publication by Frank Barron in *Scientific American* (1958) titled "The Psychology of Imagination." Barron presents research on the aesthetic preferences of creative people. Interestingly, nearly five decades later Barron (1995) articulates an ecological orientation to the study of creativity, which represents a major opening to relational conceptualizations. Barron's relational conceptualization is reminiscent of the field and gestalt theories of the early interpersonalists (Sullivan, 1953; Schachtel, 1959) and the contributions of various postmodern therapists and analysts (Altman, 1995; Anderson, 1997; Benjamin, 1988; Hoffman, 1998; Stern, 1997).

In the decades of the 1950s and 1960s, reductionism was in full force in psychoanalytic treatments of creativity. This reductionism is criticized by Basescu in "Creativity and the Dimensions of Consciousness." The whole tendency of Freud's psychology was to establish the "naturalness" of artistic thought. But in his early work he made the error of treating the artist as a neurotic who escapes from reality by means of "substitute gratification." As Freud went forward he insisted less on this simple formulation, going so far at his seventieth-birthday celebration as to say that whatever he may have done for the systematic understanding of the unconscious, the credit for its discovery belonged to the literary masters (Trilling, 2000). The foundation, unfortunately, had been set for the unhappy-childhood theory of artists. This theory held that the normal pattern of artists is to endure a miserable childhood and then, in their adult work, to weave the straw into gold (Acocella, 2007). Basescu claims that art is about the "emergence of something new," not something determined. This leads him to the concept of freedom and vision. He writes,

> The significant unconscious material, significant from the point of view of the artistic product, that emerges in the creative process is not the repressed dynamics of the artist, but rather the latent potentiality for experiential transactions with the world. The repressed dynamics may be very significant in terms of the artist's motivation, work habits, choice of media and content, personal satisfaction and so on. But to the extent that the artist's unique dynamic limit the ambiguity or universality of his art by making it a reflection of his repressions, to that extent his work will be self-expressive and not art, a private representation, not a communicated one. Many of the same mechanisms are involved in the expression of idiosyncrasies and the pathological ideation as well as in artistic creativeness. The manner in which the private meanings are structurally integrated and articulated is of decisive importance. Although the criteria of art do not have the status of unanimously agreed upon and objectifiable propositions, it is clear that novelty and originality, while necessary are not sufficient. Art must also partake of vitality, communicability, general validity, aesthetic formal organization, and some would claim, vision. (p. 137)

Having laid the groundwork with a criticism of psychoanalytic reductionism, Basescu offers a gentle way out via the gathering momentum of the humanistic perspective—often called the "third force in psychology." This humanistic perspective was critical of both psychoanalytic and behavioral traditions and championed the transcendence of the subject-object dichotomy, the holistic approach, phenomenology, personal freedom, and a science of the person (Maslow, 1962).

In the marketplace of ideas, however, the humanistic approach also stalled after a promising start. It was replaced by the cognitive revolution of the 1970s and 1980s, which in turn seems to have been replaced by the explosion of neuroscience research. Basescu was fond of saying that the humanistic and existential views have not faded; they have just been subsumed into more contemporary interpersonal and relational ideas and practices. Perhaps with the increased awareness of a complex and uncertain world, the study of creativity will once again place high value on individuals and their relations to others as centers of experience and agency. Beyond the capital C and lowercase c ideas of creativity, we may return to a self-actualizing creativity, albeit one informed by our place, time, and culture. This third type of creativity was alluded to by Otto Rank when he wrote, "Creativity lies equally at the root of artistic production and of life experience" (1932, p. 38). Back in 1968, Basescu wrote,

> The parameters of will, decision making, choice behavior and responsibility are coming into their own in areas of respectable research interest. This has been made possible by the shifting zeitgeist, the shift from seeing man as natural-science determined organism to seeing him as a conscious being capable of bringing to bear his consciousness on his experience and behavior. This shift maintains itself in work of creativity. (p. 138)

It is not that he rejects inspiration and the unconscious processes involved in creativity. Basescu wants the conscious choice dimensions to be given their rightful status along with unconscious dimensions. His is not a dichotomous approach.

Psychoanalytic Amnesia

Understanding creativity in context necessitates one final comment on a broad vista. We suffer from an amnesia of sorts, or perhaps an intellectual dissociation, when it comes to history and culture (Gergen, 2000; Lippmann, 2003). For instance, contemporary concepts of creativity owe much to 19th-century romanticism in which we could imagine mysterious reservoirs of seething energy lurking within the depths of individual psyches. From these energetic reservoirs sprang the creative impulse. For example, the symbolic images of Beethoven range from brooding, haunting, and tormented—glaring eyes, hair almost blown back with creativity (as seen in the 1852 engraving by Carl Mayer)—to lovelorn, ranting, and tortured (as portrayed by the actor Gary Oldman in the film *Immortal Beloved*). Beethoven's life and work seem never to stop stirring pathos, curiosity, and wonder in scholars and amateurs alike (Morris, 2005). Lurking behind today's inquiries are the images of Van Gogh, Keats, Schiele, Coleridge, Nietzsche, and the "mad scientist." These images have led to a denial of the cultural and historical underpinnings of creative achievement. As implied earlier, when Freud laid "down his arms" in the face of creativity and did not use his strong beliefs in the scientific methods of his day, he may have inadvertently encouraged these romantic extravagances.

In the 1930s, the great Russian psychologist and humanist Lev Vygotsky (1997) argued that

> psychoanalysis displays not dynamic, but highly static, conservative, anti-dialectic and anti historical tendencies. It directly reduces the higher mental processes—both personal and collective ones to primitive, primordial, essentially prehistoric, prehuman roots, leaving no room for history. The key unlocks the creativity of a Dostoyevsky and the totem and taboo of primordial tribes, the Christian church, communism, the primitive horde—in psychoanalysis everything is reduced to the same source. (p. 263)

Thus, Freud's naturalistic view of the mind contradicts Vygotsky's sociohistorical view. I mention Vygotsky because he was one of the first to value individual subjectivity and agency in a manner akin to our current views. The thrust of his work leads to the conclusion that new meanings, constructions, conditions, and institutions are fashioned from existing social reality. His entire emphasis is on the socially mediated character of psychology. For Vygotsky, subjectivity is active. Even novel psychological phenomena that individuals construct are always motivated by our relation to others—to class, to gender, to groups.

A good example of our collective suppression of culture and history concerns Picasso and his treatment at the pen of psychoanalyst Mary Gedo. Gedo (1980) wrote a biography and did a compelling analysis of Picasso's intrapsychic issues when he painted *Guernica*, a monumental work about the murder of innocent civilians in a small village during the Spanish Civil War in 1937. Gedo does touch on the importance of the political situation. Still, her main focus is on Picasso's problems with womanizing, and she even probes into his early relationship with his sister. But according to the art historian and psychoanalyst Donald Kuspit, Gedo ignores everything that was happening in the art world at the time as well as the internal arc of Picasso's own work, specifically the decline of classical cubism (Whitebook, 1994). Psychology, politics, and developments in the art world intermingled to create one of the most important objects of the 20th century, and this was not captured in Gedo's biography. This kind of interplay and interaction points to the multiple levels of creativity in context. Culture and history do not merely act as influences and determinants but also are influenced by creativity (Runco, Richards, & Moger, 2009).

Relational Meaning

The postmodern theorist Kenneth J. Gergen (2000) convincingly argues that creativity is an outcome of coordinated activities—among human beings and between humans and the world. The action of any person is not a possession of the person alone, nor is it the outcome of forces acting upon the person from elsewhere. It is a manifestation of the coordination among people and their material surroundings. That we have artists who paint requires a tradition of culturally meaningful action, from actions constituting our institutions of training to highly precise movements of the hand and eyes as the brush is guided over the canvas. Of course, these actions cannot be separated from a range of coordinated artifacts (e.g., paint, canvas, previously existing paintings). Gergen holds that in addition to the coordination of action, there is also the closely linked relational generation of meaning.

> That we have institutions of art training, careers in art, genres of art, and the like requires a community of meanings—relations among persons in which the relevant discourses of the real and the good are given life. The very idea of "a creative work of art" requires a matrix of meaning in which there is recognition of a tradition, a value placed on deviation (e.g., "progress," an "avant garde"), and distinctions made as to what are proper and prized deviations as opposed to improper or banal. To treat the painter as a creative agent is to suppress the complex array of relationships of which the painterly act is but a single manifestation. . . . Like psychopathology, creativity lies neither within the actor nor the eye of the holder, but with the extended relational process. (p. 61)

Similarly to Gergen, I do not wish to abandon our appreciation for and celebration of unique, individual accomplishments. Our cultural life would be much poorer if we did that. But when creativity is conceptualized, as it is in much of the psychoanalytic literature, as a uniquely psychological phenomena (with or without biological substrates), we are being one-sided. Despite the work of the now mostly gone cultural school of psychoanalysis of the 1950s and the current relational views on gender, culture, class, history, and language, we have not really understood the social unconscious. In my view, by granting credibility to the most unique and independent within the individual, we favor these same tendencies within the culture and thus embark on a lonely and self-centered search for self.

Creativity is a topic that involves such an extensive journey that even a talent such as Sabert Basescu could not do it justice. But he had a felt sense of the crisis in academic psychology and psychoanalysis and the dangers of reductionism. He argued for a humanistic/existential perspective that emphasized both imagination and responsibility. In our post-Google era we often function as if we are suffering from amnesia when it comes to culture and history in relation to creativity. It may be a way to travel light, but it comes at a cost. The complexity of the relational generation of meaning is dangerous in that it necessitates a willingness to be naked with our limitations. But it may also help us get a better grip on our creative strengths.

Coda

Sabe Basescu was a master teacher and enjoyed speaking about the existential-phenomenological point of view. And I enjoyed listening to him speak and being taught by him. He liked making use of the essay "Art and Neurosis" by the literary critic Lionel Trilling (2000). Trilling resisted the idea of neurosis as a "wound." That is, he believed that the idea of the psychic damage suffered in childhood by artists was misleading. He also had little use for the causal connection between the fantasy of castration and artistic power. Trilling believed that weakness does not preclude strength nor strength weakness. It is from this standpoint that Sabe so frequently operated in his own professional and personal life. Further, Sabe taught that we must empathically enter into the other person's life and grasp the meanings of situations for him or her. Empathy, it seems to me, is an act that occurs in a context of the imaginative abilities of the initiator, who gives it his or her own expression and form and attains completion with the other. It is a full circle. Sabe was especially gifted at creating such circles.

In the spring of 2001, my daughter, Lina, gave a senior voice recital in Princeton, New Jersey. It was a college graduation requirement. Lina had a tragic health blow as a young adolescent, and Sabe knew about it intimately, for he was my wife's analyst. As a senior with a major in vocal studies, Lina was required to give a recital in various languages such as English, French, Italian, and German. In addition, she had the option to sing in another language of her choice. She decided on Greek. As a Greek, this pleased me to no end. Sabe attended the recital with his fiancée, Stefanie Glennon, a family friend of ours with her own sublime singing voice. Following Lina's last song, one of those life-affirming, heroic Greek songs by the composer and activist Mikis Theodorakis about olive trees blossoming, the audience gave Lina a standing ovation. People crowded around Lina, and I so deeply felt her triumph on so many levels. I noticed Sabe make his way though the horde and move straight toward me. He had tears in his eyes and gave me a big hug. I felt his tremendous empathy. I shall always cherish Sabe's embrace and the creative power behind it.

References

Acocella, J. (2007). *Twenty-eight artists and two saints: Essays.* New York: Pantheon Books.

Altman, N. (1995). *The analyst in the inner city: Race, class and culture through a psychoanalytic lens.* Hillsdale, NJ: Analytic Press.

Anderson, H. (1997). *Conversation, language, and possibilities.* New York: Basic Books.

Barron, F. (1958). The psychology of imagination. *Scientific American,* 151–165.

Barron, F. (1995). *No rootless flower: The ecology of creativity.* Berkeley: University of California Press.

Benjamin, J. (1988). *The bonds of love: Psychoanalysis, feminism, and the problem of domination.* New York: Pantheon Books.

Freud, S. (1959). Creative writers and daydreaming. In J. Strachey (Ed. & Trans.), *The standard edition of the complete psychological works of Sigmund Freud* (Vol. 9, pp. 141–153). London: Hogarth Press. (Original work published 1908)

Freud, S. (1961). Dostoyevsky and parricide. In J. Strachey (Ed. & Trans.), *The standard edition of the complete psychological works of Sigmund Freud* (Vol. 21, pp. 177–194). London: Hogarth Press. (Original work published 1929)

Gedo, M. (1980). *Picasso: Art as autobiography.* Chicago: University of Chicago Press.

Gergen, K. J. (2000). The collaborative achievement of creativity and psychopathology. *Bulletin of Psychology and the Arts, 1*(2), 61–62.

Guilford, J. P. (1950). Creativity. *American Psychologist, 4,* 444–445.

Hoffman, I. Z. (1998). *Ritual and spontaneity in the psychoanalytic process: A dialectical-constructivist view.* Hillsdale, NJ: Analytic Press.

Lippmann, P. (2003). Reflections on culture and psychoanalysis. In A. Roland, B. Ulanov, & C. Barbre (Eds.), *Creative dissent: Psychoanalysis in evolution* (pp. 197–216). Westport, CT: Praeger.

Maslow, A. (1962). *Toward a psychology of being.* Princeton, NJ: Van Nostrand.

Morris, E. (2005). *Beethoven: The universal composer.* New York: HarperCollins.

Rank, O. (1932). *Art and artists.* New York: Knopf.

Runco, M. A. (2004). Creativity. *Annual Review of Psychology, 44,* 657–687.

Runco, M. A., Richards, T., & Moger, A. (2009). Integration: Prospects for future journeys. In T. Richards, M. A. Runco, & S. Moger (Eds.), *The Routledge companion to creativity* (pp. 363–370). London & New York: Routledge.

Schachtel, E. (1959). *Metamorphosis*. New York: Basic Books.

Stern, D. B. (1997). *Unformulated experience: From dissociation to imagination in psychoanalysis*. Hillside, NJ: Analytic Press.

Sullivan, H. S. (1953). *The interpersonal theory of psychiatry*. New York: Basic Books.

Trilling, L. (2000). Artists and neurosis. In L. Wieseltier (Ed.), *The moral obligation to be intelligent: Selected essays* (pp. 87–104). New York: Farrar, Straus, & Giroux.

Vygotsky, L. S. (1997). *The collected works of L. S. Vygotsky: Vol. 3. The historical meaning of the crisis in psychology* (M. J. Hall., Trans.). New York: Plenum.

Whitebook, J. (1994). Sublimation: A frontier concept. In A. K. Richards & A. D. Richards (Eds.), *The spectrum of psychoanalysis: Essays in honor of Martin S. Bergmann* (pp. 321–336). Madison, CT: International University Press.

CREATIVITY AND THE DIMENSIONS OF CONSCIOUSNESS*

The biblical story of Adam and Eve in the Garden of Eden marks an event of major significance in the development of each individual as well as in the evolution of the species—the birth of consciousness. Adam and Eve were in the Garden, enjoying a life of total oneness with nature, when Eve violated the stricture of eating the fruit of the Tree of Knowledge, at which point, as the Bible says, "The eyes of them both were opened, and they knew that they were naked" (Genesis 3:7). That is, they saw themselves; they became aware of themselves and they experienced shame. A further consequence of their violation of the prohibition not to eat the forbidden fruit was that they were expelled from Eden, banished from unconscious communion or oneness with nature, and condemned to a life of toil.

This biblical story captures the essence of a process that marks the birth of man as a species and an event that occurs in the development of each individual human being. The birth of consciousness, of self-awareness, introduces a paradoxical relationship between man and nature—paradoxical in the sense that man is both immersed in and part of the natural world, but at the same time one who transcends it. He is able to look around at what is and evaluate it against what could be, even what ought to be. As we recall, the Tree of Knowledge in the Bible is the Tree of Knowledge of Good and Evil. In order to know and judge good and evil one must be aware of more than simply what exists. One must be

---

* Delivered at the Institute of Man Symposium on Personality and Aesthetics, November 18, 1967, this paper originally appeared in print in *Humanitas: Journal of the Institute of Man*, 4(2), 1968, pp. 133–144. Reprinted with permission.

aware of what might exist, what could exist. This awareness is based on consciousness, based on the capacity to be aware of oneself.

Man is determined by the physical, chemical, and biological laws of nature. He is subject to all of these natural laws. But as he is determined, so too is he self-determined. He is free and finite—not an unlimited, but a finite freedom, not a total finitude, but a degree of freedom within the limits of his finitude. Man is a *creature* of the world but also a *creator* of the world.

Consciousness is the fundamental attribute constituting the human condition, with, if you will, its good and its bad consequences. Because of consciousness we experience existential anxiety and its perversion in the form of pathological anxieties. Anxiety on the one hand and human culture on the other are in a sense the two ramifications of consciousness. It is in the development of human culture that man creates his world, and his unique medium is symbolic. Susanne Langer (1948) likens the mind to a powerful transformer by which raw sensory data are immediately sucked into the primary process of symbolization. Ernst Cassirer (1944) claims that this new acquisition transforms the whole of human life. As compared with other animals, man lives not merely in a broader reality; he lives so to speak in a new dimension of reality. Human development, both ontogenetically and phylogenetically, is characterized by the increasing interposition of symbol systems between the world of matter and man's dealing with this world. As Cassirer points out, we do not deal with the things themselves but only with our representations of them.

Creativity may be defined as the process by which the raw data, signals or sensations impinging on our receptor organs are transformed into the meaningful constituents, essentially symbolic in character, of the multiple realities in which we live and experience our being. All realms of culture reveal the creative process at work. Similarly, all forms of culture allow for some self-expression. In other words, some cultural forms are clearly more conducive to the expression of the individual than others. Ritualistic cultural forms allow less individual expression whereas the more artistic cultural forms allow greater self-expression. To the extent that individual needs, motives, style and subjectivity are reflected in behavior, to that extent it is self-expressive. Clearly, all art is both creative and self-expressive, but relatively little creativity and self-expression qualify as art. Dreams, for example, are certainly manifestations of self-expression and of creative activity. However, dreams are not art. The artist may use the symbols or images of his dreams as the basis of his artistic elaboration but it is the art work that creates art, not the dream work. The artist's dreams are not essentially different from the dreams of non-artists although it is probably possible to detect the dynamic life and personal style of the artist in both his work and his dreams.

Art concerns itself with the sensuous forms of being. If consciousness marked the end of man's unconscious communion or oneness with nature and consequent eviction from the Garden of Eden, artistic creativity marks the attempt to get back in. Art is man's way of bridging his existential alienation from nature by means of the reincorporation of sensuality into his experience of himself and his world.

It is interesting to note the artistic interest in both children's art and primitive art. I think part of the basis for this interest lies in the attempt to recapture the naïve, unsophisticated, open communion with the natural world. However, this reincorporation is not regressive, in the sense of involving a denial of the uniquely symbolic dimension of reality. The artist's interest in the artistic productions of children, for example, exists as an attempt to recapture the openness of the child— the child's direct perception of the world around him but within the enlarged capacities of the adult.

Art is the creation of sensual symbols by means of which the artist articulates, communicates, and assimilates some aspect of his perception of the world beyond the realm of the already familiar. Herbert Read, in a magnificent book entitled *Icon and Idea* (1955), maintains that artistic consciousness as represented in significant sensuous forms is the precondition for the development of all consciousness: "It follows that any extension of awareness of reality, any groping beyond the present threshold of knowledge, must first establish its sensuous imagery" (p. 53). Similarly, Ortega y Gasset has written: "In order that a man may stop believing in some things there must be germinating in him a confused faith in others. It is curious to note that almost always the dimension of life in which the new phase begins to establish itself is art." Whether or not one subscribes to this thesis, there is little or no disagreement about the importance of art in human functioning. Therefore, both the creative process and the creative person have held the interest of students of the human condition.

Some of the so-called scientific attempts to understand something about artists and the creative process may now be clarified. These attempts can be more or less seen as beginning with Freud's interest in the creative personality. Freud's study of Leonardo da Vinci would be a classical example of an early attempt to understand something about the creative person. Similarly, Ernst Kris' *Psychoanalytic Explorations in Art* (1952) is an extension and an application of Freud's psychodynamic approach to the artist and to the understanding of something about the nature of the artist's personality. These early attempts, which were extremely successful in exploring the relationship of the content of an artist's work to the major dynamic trends of his life, leave much to be desired when it comes to understanding the nature of creativity itself. Freud, for example, in his study of Dostoyevsky writes about Dostoyevsky's insanity, his wit, his personal needs, but Freud ends up by acknowledging that when it comes to understanding creativity itself, the psychoanalyst must lay down his arms.

I think that the psychoanalytic attempts to understand artists are intrinsically limited by the very nature of psychoanalytic theory. It is essentially a theory that deals with the ways in which man is determined by his past experience, his social, cultural, physiological and genetic background. But the essence of art, the essence of artistic creativity, is precisely that which is not determined, namely the emergence of something new. The essence of art is freedom. Because of the psychoanalytic commitment to the deterministic view of man, it is invariably unable to deal with the essence of freedom in artistic creativity. However, psychoanalytic theory is eminently successful in at least throwing light on those aspects of the artistic product that are determined by the artist's personality.

The psychodynamic, psychoanalytic approach to understanding art continues, certainly. As a matter of fact, in the *New York Times* of November 4, 1967, there was a report on the recently published study entitled "Clinical Aspects of Creativity." A summation of some of the terms the investigator uses to approach an understanding of the artist reveals the kind of finding and orientation that has been inherent in the psychoanalytic approach. For instance, the writer refers to "severe injury to infantile narcissism" among the artists he studied, "rich and florid fantasy lives," a "drive for restitution that is manifested in creativity." He continues, "The problem is not one of organ inferiority per se but rather one of body image formation, permanently distorted self-representation, cathectic imbalance, irreversible ego impairment and ego restitution." These descriptions highlight the emphasis and focus given to psychodynamic patterns, styles and trends in the artist's life that fall short of dealing with creativity as such.

The significant unconscious material, significant from the point of view of the artistic product, that emerges in the creative process is not the repressed dynamics of the artist, but rather the latent potentiality for experiential transactions with the world. The repressed dynamics may be very significant in terms of the artist's motivations, work habits, choice of media and content, personal satisfaction, and so on. But to the extent that the artist's unique dynamics limit the ambiguity or universality of his art by making it a reflection of his repressions, to that extent his work will be self-expressive and not art, a private representation, not a communicated one. Many of the same mechanisms are involved in the expression of idiosyncrasies and pathological ideation as well as in artistic creativeness. The manner in which the private meanings are structurally integrated and articulated is of decisive importance. Although the criteria of art do not have the status of unanimously agreed upon and objectifiable propositions, it is clear that novelty and originality, while necessary, are not sufficient. Art must also partake of vitality, communicability, general validity, aesthetic formal organization and, some would claim, vision.

More recently, the artistic research climate has shifted away from the study of unconscious dynamics and individual personality themes toward the area of cognitive processes and consciousness. In psychology, psychiatry and the study of human functioning in general, we have only recently passed through a period of overemphasis on the unconscious deterministic processes. This took place due to the prevailing natural-science view of man as a biological organism whose behavior is determined in the same way that the behavior of the rest of the animal kingdom is determined. More recently there has been an emergence of a humanistic view of man. This humanistic image provides a context for the developing interest in manifestations of consciousness. For example, in the psychoanalytic tradition itself, there has come about an emphasis on what is called ego psychology and conflict free spheres of the ego, that is, an emphasis on the conscious side of functioning as well as the unconscious side. Similarly in psychological work we find a great deal being done in the area of cognitive theory and research. The parameters of will, decision making, choice behavior and responsibility are coming into their own as areas of respectable research interest. This has been made possible by the shifting *zeitgeist*, the shift from seeing man as a natural-science determined organism to seeing him as a conscious being capable of bringing to bear his consciousness on his experience and behavior. This shift manifests itself in work in creativity. Researchers are investigating the conscious, cognitive behavior of gifted people.

One of the early transitional studies involved an attempt to learn something about personalities of highly creative artists through the administration of intelligence and personality tests (Roe, 1946). The results indicated that the artists revealed a variety of personality patterns and adjustment levels, but no reliable criteria of creativeness existed in their personality characteristics. In other words, as personalities, at least insofar as personality reflected itself in projective and personality tests, artists are not unique.

As far as intelligence is concerned, there are even some surprises here. There is a correlation between creativity and intelligence, but only up to a point. In other words, if you start out with people whose intelligence is in the superior range or the high average range the correlation between intelligence and creativity, at that point, breaks down.

A number of psychologists, mainly at the Institute for Personality Assessment and Research at the University of California, began to work somewhat more intensively with groups of creative people—artists, scientists, and others (Barron, 1958). They invited them to come to the Institute for a period of days and submit themselves to a whole battery of procedures, tests and examinations. While a fair number of creative people rebelled against "having their heads taken apart," as one poet described it, a substantial number cooperated. The findings, I think, are of interest.

One thing that was studied was the aesthetic preferences of creative people. Given simple line drawings as opposed to rather complicated, messy looking, smudgy drawings, which are preferred? Whereas most people prefer the geometric, symmetrical simple drawings, the creative people tended to regularly select the complex, asymmetrical, disordered, chaotic kinds of drawings. They described them as more interesting, more vital, more dynamic and more challenging. In making mosaic designs, for which the subjects were given colored tiles and a board and told to create their own designs, the normal, non-creative population tended to make symmetrical, simple designs using relatively few colors and balancing the placement of the mosaics, while the more creative people tended to make highly complex patterns involving little symmetry and utilizing many of the colors. In fact, there was a correlation between the number of colors utilized in the creation of some of these mosaic designs and creativity.

When asked to describe ink blot figures the common responses were "smudges and clouds," whereas the more creative people responded in such terms as "magnetized iron filings," "a small boy and his mother hurrying along on a dark windy day trying to get home before it rains." One figure, described commonly as an ape, or a modern painting of a gorilla, was seen by an artist as "a baboon looking at itself in a hand mirror."

What emerges from this is that the highly creative people seem to show a tolerance for the chaotic, the conflicting and the disordered, and a respect for the irrational forces in themselves and in others. They see the irrational as providing a source of novelty. Disorder offers the potentiality for new levels of order.

The highly creative people showed themselves to be especially observant. We all react to our environment in many ways. One way of describing the nature of our reactions is to pose the antagonism between a judging attitude and a perceptual attitude. All our reactions partake of both judgment and perception. The artists lean heavily on the side of the perceptual reaction to their environment as opposed to the judgmental. What is particularly noteworthy is their avoidance of the pre-judgmental attitude. They judge, certainly as we all do, but their primary approach is in terms of a perception of what is really there. Similarly, if we take the perceptual orientation to experience, we can further dichotomize it in terms of what might be called sensual perception as opposed to intuitive perception. Sensual perception is characterized by a kind of descriptive reaction to what is seen, whereas intuitive perception may be characterized as an interest in the meanings of what is seen—an interest in the possibilities as well as the actualities of what is perceived. The highly creative people are the intuitive perceivers. Their interest is in a perception of the larger meanings and inherent possibilities in the world around them.

Creative people are highly independent in their cognitions. They stick to what they see in spite of pressures to conform to other opinions. In one study four people are asked to compare the length of a line to a group of other lines. Three of the four people are cohorts of the experimenter, and are told to give an erroneous judgment of the comparison. The fourth person is the subject to be studied. When the fourth person goes last, he is confronted with the evidence of his senses which is in conflict with the stated judgment of his peers. What does he do? Most of us give in to the community pressure. The highly creative people tend to hold on to their independent cognitions and to rely on their own perceptions. In spite of this pressure they give the right answer.

One can deduce from such a study what pressures the highly creative person is exposed to in everyday living. If a person's perceptions and reactions to the world tend to be original and creative, they tend to be different from everybody else's. The creative person frequently finds himself existing in a minority, sometimes a minority of one. Living a life as a minority of one can have, and often does have, rather severe consequences for one's personal psychological health and adjustment. The highly creative people maintain their reliance on truthful cognitions even at the cost of great personal pain.

In terms of a hierarchy of values, as you might expect, the creative people cluster around the aesthetic and theoretical values, as opposed to the economic, political, social and religious values. Within the area of aesthetic and theoretical values, there may exist a conflict between an emotional and rational orientation, but the creative people seem well equipped to tolerate the conflicting orientation, to reconcile the opposites of their natures and achieve integration of these opposites on a new and more inclusive level.

Creative persons tend to be more open in their feelings and emotions, more sensitively aware of themselves and others. In personality inventories, for example, the more creative tend to describe themselves more critically. They seem to be, at one and the same time, more accepting of themselves and more critical. The experimenters reconcile this by saying that as they experience a greater acceptance, confidence and higher self-esteem, they are freer to be more openly critical, scrutinizing and honest about their perceptions of their own inadequacies or personality characteristics.

One psychologist describes the relationship of conscious and unconscious factors in creative people in this way:

> The truly creative seem to have the capacity to tolerate and override anxiety, to integrate and admit into awareness an unusual depth and intensity of conflicting feeling without being overwhelmed by panic or losing touch with reality. Their ego strength, if you will, can accommodate the chaos of inner experience and be further nurtured by the ability to discover a larger order, even, in paradox and emotional turmoil. Ultimately they seem illuminated and exhilarated by their insights. Their feelings and conflicts become subordinated as only a part of themselves. They strive often with great torment and at times with unusual success to become master of their own unconscious rather than its victim. (Nydes, 1961)

Another writer has described the creative artist as "living on the edge of chaos." Terms like chaos, disorder and complexity pervade the description of the artist's relationship to his world. It is important to be clear about the meaning of chaos and disorder in this context. The artist's preference for the chaotic, of the disordered, does not refer to behavior. Some segments of "beat" society have apparently thought they were emulating the life of the artist by embracing a disorganized existence and an attitude of irresponsibility for the demands of everyday living. Living on the edge of chaos refers rather to the readiness to focus on the unordered, conflicting and complex aspects of one's thoughts, feelings, imagination, intuition and perceptions. The creative person must be hard-working, disciplined, even driven in his application of himself to his work and his responsibilities as artist and human being.

We may now turn to some description of the creative process itself. This comes mostly from the descriptions given by artists and other creative people about the nature of the process that they feel themselves engaged in. Of course, many artists say they know nothing about the creative process; they do not want to take it apart or analyze it. However, if one looks at the autobiographical descriptions written by artists, it is possible to glean a somewhat superficial but nevertheless relevant description of the creative process.

There seem to be three stages in the creative process (Ghiselin, 1955). The first might be described as the stage of preliminary preparation, which may begin in childhood. It is characterized by mastering the accumulated knowledge of one's particular field: observing, explaining, and experimenting, developing technique, skills and sensibility, and refining discrimination. It is a stage which is characterized both by consciousness and willfulness. I consciously and willfully immerse myself in the knowledge and techniques of my craft. The second stage is that of creative inspiration. Its signs are spontaneity, openness, a taking over of the subliminal functions, and a "letting it happen" attitude. The second stage is, I think, where openness to irrational or unconscious processes is crucial. The third state, or stage of artistic elaboration, is again heavily weighted on the side of consciousness. It involves the verification, correction, revision, refinement, aesthetic organization and formalization of the artistic product. One writer said: "Great plays aren't written, they're rewritten," referring clearly to his third stage of artistic elaboration. This is not to imply that conscious processes and unconscious processes ever existed independently of each other. Rather, they are exquisitely merged throughout all functioning and certainly in artistic functioning. The emphasis is on conscious processes in the first and third stages and unconscious processes in the second stage.

I would like to elaborate on the stage of inspiration—particularly that aspect known as "letting it happen" or giving oneself over to the irrational impulses, ideas, fantasies and forces that emerge. One social critic, back in the 1820s, described "letting it happen" as follows:

> If you feel something new, whether thought of sentiment, awake in the root of your being; do not at all bring light or attention to bear on it quickly; protect the birth of the germ by forgetting it; surround it with peace, do not rob it of its darkness; allow it to shape itself and to grow; and do not noise your fortune abroad. Sacred work of nature, every conception should be enveloped in a triple veil of modesty, of silence and of shadow.

This is a rather beautiful admonition against attempting to dive in too quickly and make something familiar, and grasp it, and change it without allowing it to achieve its own form.

The "letting it happen" kind of feeling and orientation is something that another writer sees as crucial in distinguishing what he calls cheap creativity from true creativity. He says, "Creativity is counterfeit when it primarily serves a psychological purpose" (Wyschogrod, 1967). The psychological purpose that he is referring to here is the purpose of finding a meaning in life. The person who attempts to create in order to find meaning is unable to "let it happen" because he is driven by a desperation which shows itself in a frantic attempt to establish his own identity:

> The person who attempts to create in order to find meaning in his life, to convert a pointless existence into one that is no longer pointless, is using creativity to his own end, and that cannot be done . . . we can understand the frenetic tone that now begins to permeate the pursuit of creativity. Where the creator previously could afford a certain attitude of waiting, of letting the creative act happen in its own good time, instead of being forced by the will of man, creation now is a desperate race for survival just because the creator's very being is at stake.

What results is a confusion concerning the relevance of willful action. Although we can will our commitment to a particular creative activity, we can never will the creative moment. The attempt to will the creative moment involves one in the distortion of the inspirational process.

I hope it is clear, although I have been emphasizing the relevance of conscious activity, I am not underemphasizing the importance of the inspirational and unconscious processes involved in creativity. I am merely attempting to put the two into context. Henry Moore, for example, notes that

> . . . though the non-logical instinctive, subconscious part of the mind must play its part in his work, he also has a conscious mind which is not inactive. The artist works with a concentration of his whole personality, the conscious part of it resolves conflicts, organizes memories, and prevents him from trying to walk in two different directions at the same time. (Ghiselin, 1955, p. 73)

Finally, a quote from the poet, John Ciardi, seems to me to capture in graphic language exactly the kind of thing I have been trying to get across:

> In art, good luck happens only to those who have earned it. . . . It is in the wooing, in their devotion to the discipline of love, that they earn their luck. Think of it in terms of a perhaps entirely frivolous figure. The good poet is a student of lighting. He keeps weather charts and he keeps them constantly to hand. He develops a feel

for where the thunderheads are. He also keeps some sort of emotional helicopter ready. As soon as he spots a thunderstorm he is on his way to it. There he instinctively places himself under the tallest tree, makes sure he is soaking wet and standing in a puddle, wraps himself in chains for good measure, and holds up a lightning rod. He won't catch the lightning every time, luck cannot always be with him, but he is ready for whatever luck will come. He has earned it. And he must inevitably have more luck than the dry and stormless souls that live in Faraday cages.

References

Barron, F. (1958). The psychology of imagination. *Scientific American*, 151–165.

Cassirer, E. (1944). *An essay on man.* New Haven, CT: Yale University Press.

Ciardi, J. (19TK). Manner of speaking. *Saturday Review.*

Ghiselin, B. (1955). *The creative process.* New York: New American Library.

Kris, E. (1952). *Psychoanalytic explorations of art.* New York: International Universities Press.

Langer, S. (1948). *Philosophy in a new key.* New York: Penguin Books.

Nydes, J. (1961, September). Personality dimensions of creativity. Symposium conducted at the American Psychological Association annual meeting.

Read, H. (1955). *Icon and idea.* Cambridge, MA: Harvard University Press.

Roe, A. (1946). Artists and their work. *Journal of Personality*, *15*, 1–40.

Wyschogrod, M. (1967). The cult of creativity. *Review of Existential Psychology and Psychiatry*, *7*(1), 30–35.

6

HUMAN NATURE AND PSYCHOTHERAPY
An Existential View (1961)

COMMENTARY BY DONNEL B. STERN

Unlike most contributors to this volume, I did not meet Sabe Basescu until I was in my late 40s. It happened at a meeting at the Westchester Center for the Study of Psychoanalysis and Psychotherapy, one of the places where Basescu taught. (He also served on the board of directors of that institute and had been one of its founders.) I had been invited to deliver a paper, and I arrived to find Basescu waiting there, delighted with the opportunity to meet me. He knew what I had written, which was very gratifying, and was generous and warm in his praise of it. I knew him by name, of course, and I have no doubt that I was even more pleased to meet him than he was to meet me. It was a mutual admiration society, as they say.

I came to New York to study psychoanalysis at the William Alanson White Institute. I knew no one in my new city to begin with, and so for a number of years I did not have deep roots in the analytic community. That was why it took delivering that paper to meet Basescu. During my training there was little or no interchange of any formal sort between the White Institute and the Interpersonal-Humanistic track at the NYU Postdoctoral Program in Psychotherapy and Psychoanalysis, where Basescu taught and supervised. That institutional isolation seems strange to me now, given that we were the two psychoanalytic centers most committed to the interpersonal perspective, and both located in Manhattan, only a few miles from one another. There was contact of a less formal sort between individuals, of course. Some of the senior faculty knew each other well, and had even trained together; some of the younger graduates and candidates knew each other, too, from their years training at various facilities in the area.

It was primarily the faculties of these two training facilities, White and the I-H track of NYU Postdoc, who had created the kind of psychoanalysis I studied and embraced. Many members of both faculties were well-known writers, leaders, and revered teachers and supervisors. Basescu was prominent among them. The only overlapping faculty members, though, as far as I know, were Erwin Singer, who, Basescu tells us in a 1987 paper, was not only his colleague and friend but also once his analyst, and Benjamin Wolstein.

And so when I finally met Basescu I knew that he had been one of those responsible for the possibilities I found in my field. I knew that he was one of the people who had made my opportunities. I was then, and am now, grateful for what he and his generation of interpersonal analysts did. I am proud of their intellectual accomplishments, grateful for the courage it sometimes required of them to persevere in a psychoanalytic world that was often hostile to them, and honored to contribute to this volume.

Basescu's inspirations were existentialist writers, but not only Europeans, and perhaps not even primarily Europeans. Ludwig Binswanger and Jean-Paul Sartre appear in the references of his papers, but so do Isidor Chein, Erik Erikson, Leslie Farber, Rollo May, Carl Rogers, Ernest Schachtel, Paul Tillich, and Irvin Yalom. Like Basescu, most or all of these writers were based in New York during substantial periods of their lives, so I imagine that Basescu knew many of them. It is not a surprise, given what he wrote and taught, that Basescu's scholarship is apparently personal, part of his daily life. I imagine scholarship for him as a kind of engagement with the writers he read. If he actually knew them, so much the better. In my image of him, he would not have wanted to study them from a distance.

"Human Nature and Psychotherapy" was published in 1961, when Basescu was 35 years old. Psychoanalysis was very different in 1961 than it is today. It took me another ten years after Basescu's article appeared to get to graduate school, but I believe that the psychoanalytic world was still enough like the world of 1961 for me to be able to understand firsthand why the kind of corrective supplied by Basescu's article was necessary. Classical psychoanalysis was just beginning to be questioned by some within the field. The structural theory; the analyst's neutrality, anonymity, and authority; and, especially, the power of explanatory interpretation and historical reconstruction were taken so much for granted that, in many quarters, questioning them was enough to bring one under suspicion of being unthoughtful about analytic issues—or, worse, of not being psychoanalytic. Until the 1980s, actually, it was quite common, and entirely acceptable, for classical analysts to toss off the remark, not only in conversation but in print, that interpersonalists, despite what they might think, were not really psychoanalysts. Even more dispiriting and enraging, though, and considerably more common than outright rejection, was the complete lack of notice paid by the mainstream psychoanalytic world to the work of my teachers, who I knew perfectly well had important things to say. We did not belong to the same club, and we knew it.

And so articles such as "Human Nature and Psychotherapy" were terrifically important to us. We cherished them, because they showed the world that we really did have something to say, that our teachers really were accomplishing innovations. The work of Sabe Basescu and his colleagues in the Interpersonal-Humanistic track at NYU, at the White Institute, and in a few other centers encouraged us to believe that we, too, could think and write and teach, and that there would be those who would listen and read. In the end, things have turned out better than we could have dreamed. Psychoanalysis today in the United States, and increasingly elsewhere, is deeply influenced by the ideas that grew from the work of Basescu's generation of interpersonalists.

But Basescu was not just one among a number of faculty members at the NYU Postdoctoral Program. He was the only one who took an explicitly existential point of view about psychoanalysis, and so he brought this view to a large number of candidates and other faculty members who would not have been exposed to it otherwise. In fact, I believe that Basescu was the sole faculty member at either the Postdoctoral Program or White who made a major effort to bring any kind of philosophy to bear on psychoanalysis. I feel a closeness and comradeship with Basescu in this, since I have done the same thing, although with different writings (philosophical hermeneutics). Interpersonal psychoanalysis, in my experience, went through a period in which intellectual activities were not as welcome as they are today. Most of Basescu's career took place during that time. Basescu, though, would have none of it: he was always interested in psychoanalysis as an intellectual discipline.

Now let me turn to the clinical perspective Basescu takes in this paper. It is a perspective rooted in personal responsibility and the conviction that change takes place in the here and now, by virtue of how we engage one another, and not as the result of the abstract explanation of painful feeling and puzzling behavior. Basescu means the paper to be an introduction to the impact of existentialism on psychoanalysis.

His points are basic, but they are very clear. I especially like his brief but lucid descriptions of the nature of existential anxiety and guilt. His description of all the points he makes, even when he is paraphrasing the work of others, has the same quality of authenticity he is talking about. One cannot miss that the way he writes comes from a personal acquaintance with the ideas he addresses.

Basescu accepts the recommendation made by Carl Rogers and others that the therapist should maintain unconditional acceptance of and regard for the patient, but he is quite clear about rejecting anything saccharine or syrupy in defining the therapist's acceptance of the patient. The fact that the analyst is unconditionally accepting of the patient, in other words, "does not mean that the therapist must be uncritically accepting of all the patient's behavior. On the contrary, the therapist may be quite critical, but his criticism must be directed at the self-imposed limitations on being, never at being itself" (p. 154). I appreciate the clarity of Basescu's distinction between the patient's preferences about the best way to live, which in most cases should not be the analyst's concern, and the patient's avoidance of freedoms that might make his life better, something that falls directly in the center of the analyst's interest.

I am more reticent than Basescu sounds here, though, about being critical of "self-imposed limitations on being," because I tend to believe that freedom makes people more effective than they are without it, and it certainly makes life more interesting; for those reasons, I tend to believe that people embrace it unless they have some good reason not to. Of course, it is also true, as Basescu points out, that to accept one's freedom also is liable to raise serious problems, problems that can be avoided by what Fromm called the "escape from freedom" (1941). That is, like all existentialists Basescu recognizes a moral dimension in the refusal to accept one's responsibility to choose. I can hardly disagree with him on that point. But as a clinician, I am usually less inclined to be critical of the turn away from freedom than to be curious about it.

There is no question that the existential emphasis on engagement in the present moment as the source of change, the view championed in this article by Basescu, has had a profoundly beneficial influence on clinical practice, creating aliveness by encouraging us to value the here and now and by discouraging us from conducting treatments for the sole purpose of explaining the patient's problems. But if you accept the possibility of criticizing the patient's choices, as Basescu does seem to, some readers will be led to believe that you might set aside careful inquiry in favor of the attempt to influence the patient. Of course, even this point cannot always be decided in one direction. What analyst worth his salt has not, at times, confronted patients' choices, gently or otherwise?

As is usually the case, then, one cannot make hard-and-fast rules; there are significant exceptions. But generally speaking, criticism of the patient seems problematic to me. When the analyst is critical of the patient, even if the analyst limits his criticism in the way that Basescu recommends, there is the danger that the patient may not feel emotionally safe enough to allow himself the vulnerability to access the experience he needs in order to address the problems that brought him to treatment. As a matter of fact, from the 1970s through the 1980s (and I suspect the same was true in the 1960s, before I arrived), the criticism I most often heard about interpersonal psychoanalysis from other therapists was that interpersonal psychoanalysts were routinely confrontational, and that they were therefore treating all their patients as if they were fully adult, ignoring what was then referred to as their "developmental level." I felt then, and feel now, that these criticisms, while containing a grain of truth, were widely exaggerated. While some interpersonalists valued authenticity and encounter in a way that led them to be more confrontational than their mainstream colleagues, they were also highly skilled clinicians who were hardly going to sacrifice their relationships with their patients to some imagined nirvana of core-to-core contact. The criticism, in other words, stereotyped interpersonalists and minimized the kind of clinical sensitivity and concern for patients that we see in "Human Nature and Psychotherapy."

I have the impression that this criticism is leveled at interpersonalists less frequently than it used to be. I do not know the reasons for this change and cannot even be sure that my impression is correct. But if I am right, it may be because interpersonal and relational analysts are today enough at home with the existential perspective that their definition of authentic encounter with the other has broadened, less frequently demanding a confrontational stance. In any case, today every interpersonal and relational analyst takes for granted as one principle of clinical relatedness Basescu's commitment to the analyst's personal authenticity (e.g., Mitchell, 1993; Hoffman, 1998).

Basescu conveys a surprising degree of clinical wisdom for someone in his 30s. In addressing what he calls the "confusion and misunderstanding about what [the therapist's] participation and presence involve" (p. 154), Basescu takes up questions of self-disclosure and physical contact. "Talking about oneself," he writes, "is very different than being oneself, and is often a substitute for it. Patients are fundamentally concerned with being understood and accepted rather than in satisfying their curiosity about the therapist, in spite of appearances to the contrary" (p. 155). Nicely said, and true. In the following paragraph, he says, "Whether or not the therapist shares his feelings is less important than that he himself know them and be honest about them when he does express them" (p. 155). Again, right on the nose. If the therapist really does know how he feels, he has access to the most significant part of what he needs in order to make a decision about what to do. Basescu goes on to make the point that "it is rare that the therapist's dreams can be directly useful to the patient" (p. 155). Why he bothers to make this particular point is puzzling until one remembers that Edward Tauber, another prominent interpersonalist of that era, had published in 1954 a controversial paper on the use of dreams in which he proposed inviting the patient, when the analyst dreamed about the patient, to help to analyze the countertransferential aspect of the dream. It seems that Basescu disagreed with Tauber.

Basescu next turns to the question of physical contact, wisely observing, "The demand for physical contact by the patient is probably a sign that other ways of communicating have not been effective. It will generally not occur if the patient feels understood" (p. 155). A simple point, but well taken. When I read it I thought about a patient of mine from decades ago, a woman whose demands for sex from me never did abate over the course of a psychotherapy that went on for several years; I wonder whether I failed to understand her in some significant respect, and what difference it might have made if I had asked myself about her demands through Basescu's lens.

A couple of last points about Basescu's clinical work were first suggested to me by Stefanie Solow Glennon, Ph.D., Basescu's wife and herself a faculty member in the NYU Postdoctoral Program. Among other things, Glennon reminded me that Basescu embraced uncertainty and the creative use of himself in his work, including judicious self-revelation. Now, keep in mind that in 1961 self-revelation among psychoanalysts was very much taboo. It still is in conservative circles, but even among today's interpersonalists, the questions of when it is helpful and how to do it remain controversial, as they probably should be. In contemporary interpersonal and relational clinical thinking, even as we open ourselves to considering the analyst's experience, especially his affective experience in the here and now, as part of what can be discussed with the patient (e.g., Bromberg, 1998, 2006; Davies, 1994, 1998; Hoffman, 1998), we maintain the same concern for judiciousness that Basescu had back in 1962 when he cautioned us, in regard to the therapist's feelings, that "it may place undue pressure on the patient to frequently hear about them" (p. 155). For someone such as Basescu, who cared deeply about thinking his way through his psychoanalytic work and was clearly committed to working in a disciplined way, it was courageous to contemplate the possibility of self-revelation. As the times changed and as Basescu himself gained clinical confidence (no one can have the clinical confidence at 35 that he will have at 55), he became more innovative about self-revelation and put less emphasis on caution. This point is evident when one reads his later papers, which appear elsewhere in this book.

As soon as Glennon made the observations I have mentioned, I realized that there exists a prime example of these very attributes of Basescu's work in the one clinical vignette that appears in "Human Nature and Psychotherapy." It is the case, near the end of the article, of the young woman, very upset after her session, who comes back for a second meeting with Basescu on the same day. First of all, we are impressed with Basescu's flexibility in doing this. But many of us probably would do the same thing. More notable, perhaps, is the way Basescu handles the young woman's complaint that he had not understood her earlier in the day, and that she desperately needed him to, if she was to feel better. It would be easy to respond defensively to what must have been at least partly an accusation, but Basescu avoids that course and tells the patient that he sees he really had not understood her earlier in the day, and that he hopes she will help him do that now. In other words, Basescu is able to maintain a sense of uncertainty about the situation and the possibilities of the relatedness with this particular person that allows him to imagine that she is right. Today we are not as likely to assume that the patient's view of the analyst is a transference distortion as analysts were in 1962; in those days, however, this woman's expectation that her therapist would believe she was distorting his participation, and that he would therefore hold her responsible for his own lack of understanding, was entirely reasonable. No doubt it is still reasonable today in more instances than we would like to imagine.

The most impressive moment in this vignette, though, slips by so smoothly that it would be easy to miss how important it must have been to the patient. At the end of the session, she says that "she felt she ought to be the one who says the time is up." Basescu simply agrees. He apparently grasps immediately that she is gently chiding him for his initial lack of understanding, and once again he accepts responsibility for his failure; but he avoids the kind of guilty reaction that would have burdened the patient, and he thereby "survives" (Winnicott, 1971) in just the way we imagine the patient needed him to do. His subdued description of this moment: "We both recognized that this session dealt more with my limitations than hers" (p. 156).

This would be a lovely vignette in any era, but it is remarkable, I think, for the time in which it took place. It shows that Basescu means what he says when he writes, "An encounter implies a profound respect for the worth of the other person, and an interest and concern for him that results in one's being fully present and completely real with him" (p. 154). Or when he tells us this: "To be fully present means to be subjectively real, consistent in the feeling and expression of one's emotions, focused on the here and now, and open to the possibilities of current experience" (p. 155). Such statements could lack specific impact if they were not accompanied by the kind of ballast provided by the vignette.

I have already noted that Basescu cites American writers, or at least writers who lived in the United States. Now I add the claim that Basescu's work is particularly American in both content and sensibility. Oddly enough (oddly, that is, because its inspiration was originally European), the work of the American existential analysts, including, besides Basescu, Leslie Farber (e.g., 1966), Rollo May (e.g., 1953, 1969), and Erich Fromm (e.g., 1941, 1947), often served as a balance to the highly intellectualized ego-psychological psychoanalysis of the Freudians who arrived here from Europe in the diaspora from Europe provoked by World War II and the Holocaust.

What do I mean by "American"? I mean that Basescu was pragmatic, for one thing. His theories, despite the fact that they are rooted in philosophy, are never far removed from clinical reality, so it is not a long jump from his thinking to his conduct. This focus on how the work was done, and an insistence on a fine-grained appreciation of the analyst-patient interaction, was characteristic of the interpersonal writers of Basescu's era, although the others did not write from Basescu's philosophical vantage point. This kind of emphasis resulted in a kind of clarity about what was happening in the analytic relationship that, with the exception of the work of Sándor Ferenczi (e.g., Dupont, 1995), was not even contemplated in most Freudian circles. Basescu's existential approach, with its focus on the here and now and on aspects of the treatment relationship that were quite observable, was very much a part of these developments.

But pragmatism sometimes goes too far. Basescu decries adaptation as a clinical goal, a position we can all agree with in principle—although in practice, of course, we know that we act according to the norms of our cultures more frequently than we realize. Basescu also criticizes insight that does not lead to a change in living, another point it is easy to accept. Yet he then writes that "we must help our patients practice behaving in accordance with the insights they have learned" (p. 149), a statement that sounds uncomfortably similar to the authoritarian and adaptation-based practices he is criticizing.

Another, related aspect of Basescu's paper that seems to me to be typically American is something that Basescu himself would probably call phenomenology, and thus more European than American. I am referring to Basescu's focus on the detailed appreciation of the actual experience of the patient and the analyst. This is another part of clinical conduct that Basescu has in common with other interpersonalists. It is an aspect of what Harry Stack Sullivan (1954) called the detailed inquiry, the careful investigation by the analyst of the events inside the session and in other parts of the patient's life. In keeping his focus on experience and eschewing most abstract theorizing, Basescu takes the same antimetapsychological tack, though perhaps not for the same reasons, that Sullivan and others took in proposing that explanation should take place on the same level as the phenomena to be explained. What Basescu would describe as phenomenology was appreciated by many of his colleagues as an insistence that psychoanalytic sense be more closely related to common sense and operational values than it had been in much of classical theorizing. And so in this way, too, and somewhat ironically, Basescu's work is typically American.

Basescu writes the following near the end of his article: "Much of the material I have discussed has been presented in what many people consider philosophical and unverifiable terms" (p. 157). He seems to believe that his article is going to be hard for readers to assimilate. And yet for any contemporary reader of the article who is even marginally acquainted with psychoanalysis, the article is familiar enough to be virtually a cliché.

Make no mistake, though: "Human Nature and Psychotherapy" was no cliché when it was written. It was innovative stuff. The fact that it seems so obvious to readers today just shows how thoroughly successful Basescu was in conveying his message, and how convincing a message it was. I tend to think that Basescu was right: His article probably really wasn't so easy for people to absorb in 1962. I know I have had analogous experiences with certain psychoanalytic material: The first time I read it, I can hardly grasp its meaning; but 5 or 10 years later I wonder how I could ever have had such difficulty, and the experience of reading is effortless. Most of the material that has been like that for me is now, like Basescu's article, so taken for granted that reading it is treading home ground.

The world changes. What was novel then is familiar now. The message of "Human Nature and Psychotherapy" has become so much a part of our heritage that we do not necessarily recognize now what was once its originality. That is the fate of many of the most successful contributions: to be so influential that their influence disappears into what is.

References

Basescu, S. (1987). Behind the "seens": The inner experience of at least one psychoanalyst. *Psychoanalytic Psychology, 4*, 255–265.

Bromberg, P. M. (1998). *Standing in the spaces: Essays on clinical process, trauma, and dissociation*. Hillsdale, NJ: Analytic Press.

Bromberg, P. M. (2006). *Awakening the dreamer: Clinical journeys*. Hillsdale, NJ: Analytic Press.

Davies, J. M. (1994). Love in the afternoon: A relational reconsideration of desire and dread in the countertransference. *Psychoanalytic Dialogues, 4*, 153–170.

Davies, J. M. (1998). Between the disclosure and foreclosure of erotic transference-countertransference: Can psychoanalysis find a place for adult sexuality? *Psychoanalytic Dialogues, 8*, 747–766.

Dupont, J. (1995). *The clinical diaries of Sándor Ferenczi*. Cambridge, MA: Harvard University Press.

Farber, L. (1966). *The ways of the will*. New York: Basic Books.

Fromm, E. (1941). *Escape from freedom*. New York: Rinehart.

Fromm, E. (1947). *Man for himself*. New York: Rinehart.

Hoffman, I. Z. (1998). *Ritual and spontaneity in the psychoanalytic process: A dialectical-constructivist view*. Hillsdale, NJ: Analytic Press.

May, R. (1953). *Man's search for himself*. New York: Norton.

May, R. (1969). *Love and will*. New York: Norton.

Mitchell, S. A. (1993). *Hope and dread in psychoanalysis*. New York: Basic Books.

Sullivan, H. S. (1954). *The psychiatric interview*. New York: Norton.

Tauber, E. S. (1954). Exploring the therapeutic use of countertransference data. *Psychiatry, 17*, 331–336.

Winnicott, D. W. (1971). The use of an object and relating through identifications. In *Playing and Reality* (pp. 101–111). London: Tavistock.

HUMAN NATURE AND PSYCHOTHERAPY: AN EXISTENTIAL VIEW*

It is rather startling that at least some psychotherapists, representing every psychoanalytic theory, have patients who improve as a direct result of therapy. However, psychotherapeutic practice is not really so varied as the profusion of theory suggests. Rather, the better qualified and more experienced therapists of different theoretical schools are

* Delivered at the 11th Annual Meeting of the Institute in Psychiatry and Neurology, April 26, 1961, this paper originally appeared in print in *Review of Existential Psychology and Psychiatry, 2*(2), 1962, pp. 149–157. Reprinted with permission.

more alike in their work than are good and poor therapists from the same school. How relevant, then, is current theory to practice? And to what extent does a current theory stimulate our thinking about psychotherapeutic work and generate new knowledge? Perhaps, much good therapy is being done despite theoretical considerations rather than because of them.

More and more, therapists themselves question even some of those therapeutic procedures which have been accepted by most schools. They probably question most the effectiveness of psychodynamic interpretations made to the patient.

Sixty years ago people coming for analytic treatment typically suffered from symptom neuroses. Today the problems are more likely to be character disorders and borderline psychoses. With symptom neuroses, the elucidation of psychodynamics and the achievement of insight into the development of the symptoms probably works fairly well. However, with character problems such interpretations often provoke comments from patients like, "I feel I've gained a lot of insight, but I don't know what to do with it," or more simply, "Sounds good, so what?" This can be a very disheartening and deadening experience, for both patient and therapist. One way of rationalizing it comes under the heading of "How to translate insight into action." That is, we must help our patients practice behaving in accordance with the insights they have learned. But this merely confounds one questionable technique by the addition of another. The implied problem with both techniques is how to bridge the gap between a fragmented, intellectualized procedure and a desired experiential result. In fact, the larger question, of which the value of interpretation is a part, is, what transpires in psychotherapy that is really therapeutic?

A second major question concerns the goals of psychotherapy (May, 1960a). The implied goal of any therapy based on a homeostatic theory of motivation, such as the Freudian, is a reduction of tension. Indeed, the expressed goal of much therapy is the state of reduced personal and social tension known as adjustment. But adjustment fosters conformity. How then do we theoretically justify, and practically implement the more highly valued goals of individuality, creativity and self-fulfillment?

Precisely these issues, the discrepancy between theory and practice, the inadequacy of many therapeutic procedures, and the limitations of conventional goals, have led to the developing interest in the existential viewpoint. There is an obvious need to broaden our understanding of man and to provide a theoretical framework upon which effective therapy can be consistently based.

Scientific attempts to understand human behavior have been largely concerned with the communalities between other animal species and man, and therefore, with the simplest, most unusual aspects of human functioning. It is only very recently that some thinkers have come to realize the limitations inherent in such an approach and have turned their attention to what is unique about man, to his complexities. It is what distinguishes man's behavior that is most relevant to his human-ness, and it is in terms of his unique humanness that his biological functions must be understood.

Man lives in a radically new dimension of reality. He is immersed in the world of nature up to his neck, subject to all its laws and forces. However, he has the capacities for self consciousness and meaning-ful use of symbols. These introduce a psychological freedom into his behavior that makes its explanation in reductionistic terms impossible. That is, although man is subject to the laws of physics, chemistry and biology, these laws do not account for all the phenomena of his exis-tence. This is man's "finite freedom" (Tillich, 1952, p. 52). Embedded up to his neck in nature, he nevertheless must lift his head and must use it. In doing so, he, on the other hand, develops all that we know as human culture, and on the other hand, experiences existential anxiety.

Awareness of one's being in the natural world demands an immedi-ate awareness of possible and eventual non-being. What lives is born, grows, and dies, often unexpectedly, tragically and arbitrarily. Physical death is the most obvious instance of non-being. The evolutionary evi-dence that "man stands no better chance for future survival than his distant cousin, the tapeworm" (Simpson, 1959) dramatizes the transito-riness and lack of necessity of individual existence, and even that of the species. But there is non-being in life as well as in death, the non-being of meaninglessness. With neither a fixed nature to unfold instinctually, nor a clear cut transcendentally imposed destiny, man becomes what he makes of himself. He is continually confronted with the absolute neces-sity of making choices based on the fundamental option of affirming his being or denying it. As Rollo May (1960b) writes, "Consciousness itself implies always the possibility of turning against one's self, deny-ing one's self. The tragic nature of human existence inheres in the fact that consciousness itself involves the possibility and temptation at every instant of killing itself" (p. 695). It is the awareness of this possibil-ity and the struggle against this temptation that characterize natural, basic, existential anxiety. It takes courage to make of oneself what one chooses to be, but the alternative is psychological death and despair.

In assuming the responsibilities of self affirmation, man can only more or less fulfill his potentialities, but never completely. He is not an isolated consciousness, but a field or region of being (Barrett, 1958), a responding being limited by the historical conditions relevant to the particular time and place of his existence, and the constitutional and genetic determinants of his personality. The awareness that at any given moment one is potentially more than one actually is, gives rise to the experience of existential guilt.

Existential guilt and existential anxiety are unavoidable conditions of being. One can only avoid the anxiety of non-being by avoiding being itself. It is in such an attempt that pathological anxiety and neurosis arise. The fundamental neurotic process is an attempted denial of the full range of responsibility and sense of being in order to preserve the central core (May et al., 1968). But even the neurotic exercises his freedom, however constricted its expression may be. His affirmation is of a reduced self (Tillich, 1952). It is as if he had given up the fight for the whole of his territory fearing complete defeat and were clinging to only a part. He clings tenaciously, though, because any further withdrawal bring him closer to a complete loss of self, the very state that initially precipitated the withdrawal. This is the neurotic's dilemma and why there is rarely a successful neurotic adjustment.

But as Rollo May (1960b) has pointed out, neurosis is very much an attempted adjustment and therein lies its fault. Neurosis may be seen as the sum total of those aspects of an individual's life style that are determined by the need to preserve the center of his being in the face of threat. Whether it be by means of symptoms, character patterns or defenses, or psychotic distortions, every one of us sacrifices a greater or lesser part of his potential world of being in order to preserve at least the central identity of a self. We forfeit some aspect of our psychological freedom to transcend the immediate situation and experience the possible. We restrict some part of our potential for growth and development. We all, to some extent, give up a dynamic, boundless, but uncertain future and adjust to a limited, static, but known past. This is a characteristic of the human predicament and therefore makes a sharp distinction between normal and neurotic possible. We are all more or less neurotic in the sense I have described.

It is when the neurotic adjustment breaks down that a person may seek psychotherapeutic help. The identity of the self is again threatened in spite of the limitations on the affirmation and extension of one's existence. But it is generally not the therapeutic task to help reinstate some level of adjustment. To do so would be to forfeit the creative opportunity afforded the patient by the therapeutic relationship. One may have to settle for this limited goal in some cases of severe psychotic pathology, but it is not the goal of choice. On the contrary, the aim of psychotherapy is to make the patient more fully aware of his being. To continue with a previous analogy, rather than again defend a limited portion of his territory against the next expected assault, the patient must be helped back onto the path of authentic growth, a path that cannot be described in terms of adjustment. Nor is it a path free of anxiety. In fact, the change is from being entangled in pathological anxiety to confronting directly existential anxiety.

Certainly, it is essential to understand the significance of symptoms, repressions, defenses and the like in terms of their historical development, but their full dynamic meaning can only be comprehended in an ontological context. That is, they must be experienced as the method chosen by the person to affirm or deny his potentialities. From this point of view, one can account for the observation that historical or causal interpretations of psychodynamics do not affect the changes we have expected. They are always an invitation to step outside the immediately experienced present and view oneself from the perspective of the past. There are very specific consequences of this, some of them highly desirable. For example, interpretations, even if they are incorrect, as a good many probably are, can be reassuring by alleviating guilt and anxiety, and by offering hope for the future. No matter what the specific content of the interpretation, the therapist is in effect telling the patient not to judge himself too harshly. He is saying that the patient's personality has been influenced by his experiences with others and that he has been acted upon by forces beyond his control. Furthermore, in realizing that the present has developed out of the past, the patient can experience himself in the time dimension, and can anticipate a future in which he can realize some of his aspirations. On the other hand however, interpretations may induce the patient to think *about* his behavior rather than experience himself. In any case, an interpretation of psychodynamics is an abstraction, a bit of factual knowledge about someone. Imparted to a patient, it remains knowledge about someone even if the someone is oneself. It becomes existential knowledge, that is, essential and meaningful, only when it is experienced in the world in which one creates.

A new patient of mine, in talking about a therapeutic experience he had just terminated, told me the following:

> Dr. S made interpretations that made sense. They evoked something in me. I understood them but I didn't feel them. They didn't help me open up with what I really felt. Everything seemed so obvious to him that I began to doubt his ability to really understand me, to know me. I don't really understand what this relationship was all about, what it means to me. I had a desire to say, "You talk about feeling, but do you really feel?" My sessions in which I really produced something were totally frustrating. His interpretations cut me off.

This was not in response to any questions of mine, nor had this person known me long enough to pick up my theoretical biases, but he is obviously very sensitive, intelligent and highly articulate. These remarks followed a very agitated description of a hallucinatory episode he experienced the previous night. He awoke feeling that space was becoming solid and that he had razor blades on his eyelids. In great panic, he fought off the urge to jump out of the window. After reporting this, he asked what it meant. In response to my sole comment that he seemed very much afraid to hear what it might mean, he poured forth his fears of insanity and institutionalization. Then followed the previously quoted remarks.

What he said illuminates the concepts of existential truth and knowledge. Existential truth is neither the truth of abstract propositions nor the objective facts of reality. It is concerned with the nature of a person's relation to objective fact or subjective reality, their meaning to the individual. Existential truth exists only as a person produces it in action, only as it is lived. Similarly, existential knowledge is not familiarity with facts about someone or something, but rather direct experience through meaningful participation (Heineman, 1953). The facts may become existential in the matrix of a vital relationship, at which point they contribute to widening the scope of the experience. However, until that time they turn up mainly on final exams, television quiz shows and in case reports. To explain human behavior, it must first be understood in terms of its meaning to the experiencing person, in a sense by participating in his world. The attempt to fit observations of an individual into a preconceived conceptual framework, whether it be physiological or Freudian, runs the risk of serious distortion.

Paul Tillich (1961) has written:

> A person becomes a person in the encounter with other persons, and in no other way. This interdependence of man and man in the process of becoming human is a judgment against a psychotherapeutic method in which the patient is a mere object for the analyst as a subject. The inevitable reaction then is that the patient tries in return to make the analyst into an object for himself as subject. This kind of acting and reacting has a depersonalizing effect on both the analyst and the patient. (p. 15)

The concept of encounter does not refer simply to an interpersonal relationship. It refers rather to the unique form of relatedness in which each of two people participates with his full being in the world of the other, without treating the other as an object subordinated to some purpose of one's own. An encounter implies a profound respect for the worth of the other person, and an interest and concern for him that results in one's being fully present and completely real with him. Tillich is correct in his criticism of the classical analytic procedure as preventing such an encounter but his conception of the patient's contribution is, I think, oversimplified.

Every person, to the extent that he is neurotic, constructs his world in such a way that he deals with the people in it as objects. He attempts to manipulate others to meet his own needs. In so doing, he elicits the following kinds of reaction from others. They may lend themselves to the neurotic manipulation, filling in their own neurotic patterns so that each achieves some gratification from the other as an object. Or, they may tolerate the presence of the neurotic without participating in any substantial way in his world. Or, they may reject him more or less completely by removing themselves, by hostile criticism or by retaliatory measures. When the neurotic adjustment fails, and the person becomes a patient, he attempts again to reconstruct his very same world, this time with the therapist as an object to fulfill his needs.

This provides the setting for what is unique about the therapeutic relationship to unfold. Firstly, the therapist participates in the patient's world as it is constructed within the confines of the analytic office. He is not merely a tolerant observer and an intellectual analyzer, but a human being sharing in the experience of another human being. Secondly, the therapist has an unconditional acceptance of, and regard for, the patient. That is, the patient's worth as a human being is not a function of his desirability, pleasantness, adequacy or capacity to fulfill the needs of the therapist. This does not mean that the therapist must be uncritically accepting of all the patient's behavior. On the contrary, the therapist may be quite critical, but his criticism must be directed at the self imposed limitations on being, never at being itself. (I shall never forget my utter surprise at what a patient told me in the session following one in which I expressed criticism and anger very openly. She said, "In the last session, for the first time, I really felt you like me.") Thirdly, and perhaps most important of all, the therapist is fully present to the patient, and it is by virtue of the therapist's full presence that the patient is unable to reconstruct his neurotic world.

There is a great deal of confusion and misunderstanding about what participation and presence involve. Questions arise as to whether the therapist should tell the patient about himself, the details of his life, his dreams and his feelings, and to what extent he should engage in any kind of physical contact, from hand shaking to embracing, with the patient. While it is impossible to make rules covering all contingencies, some principles may be clarified. Talking about oneself is very different from being oneself, and is often a substitute for it. Patients are fundamentally concerned with being understood and accepted rather than in satisfying their curiosity about the therapist, in spite of appearances to the contrary. In fact, there is some experimental evidence that indicated there is no correlation between improvement in therapy and the therapist's making himself known to the patient. In addition, this is something less experienced therapists do more often than the more experienced ones (Rogers, 1961).

Although it is essential for the therapist to continually clarify his feelings to himself, it may place undue pressure on the patient to frequently hear about them. Whether or not the therapist shares his own feelings is less important than that he himself know them and be honest about them when he does express them. His dreams about a patient may be exceedingly useful to him but are likely to involve his own neurotic reactions to a patient rather than simply insights about the patient. Therefore, it is rare that the therapist's dreams can be directly useful to a patient.

The demand for physical contact by the patient is probably a sign that other ways of communicating have not been effective. It will generally not occur if the patient feels understood. Since there are so many complicating overtones to physical contact, and since it tends to narrow rather than broaden the opportunity for living out symbolically the possibilities of experience, it is not therapeutically desirable.

To be fully present means to be subjectively real, consistent in the feeling and expression of one's emotions, focused on the here and now, and open to the possibilities of current experience. Such a state of presence makes it impossible for the therapist to be treated as an object, and the patient must contend with this fact. It is as if the therapist were saying, "I'm here with you in this world of you and me. I'm here as a real person, not as an object or thing." When the patient realizes this, he may terminate the relationship. As a patient said to me, "I've made my compromise and although I'm not really happy, things go okay most of the time. Changing means opening up a lot of things that might make me uncomfortable and scared. I'm not sure I want to do it." This is a legitimate choice, one any individual can only make for himself, but one that exacts its price. The price with this patient is ulcers and periods of physical illness. Most of the time the choice is not made that consciously.

Man chooses his destiny within the limits of his finiteness and the opportunities of his freedom, but choose he must. If the patient chooses to contend with the therapist's realness he must be committed to change, in a sense willing to take a chance by participating in a new and unfamiliar world. He then again experiences the failure of his neurotic adjustment but this time with a difference, namely, it occurs within the context of the therapeutic relationship. His neurotic manipulations of the therapist are not successful but the therapist does not react as others have done. That is, the therapist neither abandons the patient nor retaliates against him, but maintains his presence with the patient. His attempt to construct his world with the therapist in the pattern of the past fails, and he experiences the feelings of despair which characterize the loss of one's world. It is this condition that is probably meant by "therapeutic psychosis." The more extensive the loss, the more profound the despair, and the greater the opportunity for creative change. This loss precipitates the existential crisis in therapy, the point at which the patient is confronted with his own responsibility in perpetuating his life style. He must embark on a new mode of being, on the making of a new world in which he is more authentically human and deals with others as equally so. Although it is a time of despair, it is also a liberating experience. What one is responsible for maintaining, one can change. This is not so if an individual is the helpless victim of circumstance, passively reacting to impinging personalities. Numerous insights into the fact that "my mother didn't love me" are not worth a tinker's dam until they include what I did about it.

Admittedly, I have described the therapeutic process in its essence. This process, as all human processes, is subject to all kinds of existential limitations. No therapist is completely free from neurotic restrictions of his own. Therefore, the therapist's participation, unconditional acceptance and presence in the therapeutic relationship are always more or less operative.

A highly perceptive and potentially quite disturbed young woman called me a few hours after leaving a session in which I was not "with it." She asked for another appointment that same day. When she returned she was very agitated and she said, "You don't understand me. If you don't understand me I'm all alone and I can't take it. If you would understand me I wouldn't break down. I feel the only thing I have to do is reach you and everything will be okay." When I said I hadn't understood her earlier that day, and I wanted her to help me to, she experienced immediate relief and said she felt "better already." She told me she expected me to blame her lack of clarity for my difficulty in understanding. At the end of the hour she said she felt she ought to be the one who says time is up and I agreed. We both recognized that this session dealt more with my limitations than hers.

The process of psychotherapy is further limited in that no patient is ever completely willing or able to fully commit himself to change.

Even a radically new mode of being includes some neurotic patterns from the past or newly developed ones. However, the extent to which change takes place, the extent to which the therapeutic goal of greater awareness of being is achieved, will be a function of the extent to which the particular therapeutic relationship approximates the essential one.

Much of the material I have discussed has been presented in what many people consider philosophical and unverifiable terms. However, there are an increasing number of psychoanalytic psychotherapists whose observations are consistent with this approach to the understanding of the therapeutic process and who find in it a meaningful framework for continued exploration. Furthermore, there is a growing body of controlled studies which illuminate the process of psychotherapy and support some of the contentions of this approach. Carl Rogers (1961), for example, has recently reported very interesting findings of studies conducted by his students. He writes:

> The facts seem to suggest that personality change is initiated by attitudes which exist in the therapist, rather than primarily by his knowledge, his theories, or his techniques. . . . There is a strong probability of an effective helping relationship if the therapist is congruent, his words match his feelings; if the therapist liked and accepts the client, unconditionally; and if the therapist understands the feelings of the client as they seem to the client, communicating this understanding. (pp. 29, 41)

Certainly the therapist's knowledge and his techniques are not superfluous, but neither are they sufficient to effect change nor account for his contribution to the therapeutic process. What part they do play is yet to be defined. At this point we know more about the contribution of the therapist's attitudes than that of his knowledge or techniques.

Existentialism as philosophy is not a systematic theory nor are its proponents system builders. It is essentially an attempt "to gather all the elements of human realities into a total picture of man" (Barrett, 1958, p. 19).

Existential psychotherapy is not a new and different kind of psychotherapy. It, too, is an attempt to gather all that we know about the conditions of psychological freedom and the development of authentic being, and apply it correctively where freedom and being have been perverted. The measure of its success lies in its capacity to help us meaningfully integrate our clinical and experimental observations, and in its stimulation to our thinking about that most difficult of all subjects . . . man.

References

Barrett, W. (1958). *Irrational man.* New York: Doubleday & Co.

Heineman, F. (1953). *Existentialism and the modern predicament.* New York: Harper Torchbooks.

May, R. (1960a). Existential analysis and the American scene. In *Topical problems of psychotherapy.* New York: Basel.

May, R. (1960b). Existential bases of psychotherapy. *American Journal of Orthopsychiatry, 30*(4).

May, R., et al. (1958). *Existence.* New York: Basic Books.

Rogers, C. (1961). The process equation of psychotherapy. *American Journal of Psychotherapy, 15*(1), 27–45.

Simpson, G. (1959, December 30). Address to the American Association for the Advancement of Science. *New York Times.*

Tillich, P. (1952). *The courage to be.* New Haven, CT: Yale University Press.

Tillich, P. (1961). Existentialism and psychotherapy. *Review of Existential Psychology and Psychiatry, 1*(1).

7

TOOLS OF THE TRADE
The Use of the Self in Psychotherapy (1990)

COMMENTARY BY ELLIOT ADLER

The clinical issue that Sabe is addressing in this paper is the challenge of being natural, spontaneous, and emotionally authentic within an intimate yet professionally bounded therapeutic relationship. More specifically, he is concerned with exploring how and when an analyst can express his spontaneous feelings, thoughts, and judgments—about his patient or about himself—in a way that furthers the therapeutic aims. Yet every paper on technique, no matter how narrowly conceived, implies a broader conception of therapeutic action and speaks to more fundamental issues such as the essential nature of transference and its relation to the psychoanalytic situation. Sabe clearly recognizes this and explicitly anchors his technical recommendations in a theoretical tradition that give his ideas weight in the endless rhetorical dialectic of our professional literature. And though his paper is written about the use of self in psychotherapy, where his ideas would be less controversial, it is evident that Sabe wants his vision to be relevant for all forms of psychoanalytic treatment. As his title suggests, he considers this use of self as a basic tool of our trade and argues that this understanding poses a fundamental challenge to a more traditional (i.e., Freudian) model that holds analytic neutrality as an essential ideal of technique.

This article was published in 1990, a time when interpersonal thinking was beginning to receive more respectful attention in the mainstream psychoanalytic literature, and when analysts of all schools were engaging in direct competitive dialogue and mutual influence more frequently than had been true in the past. The politics of the period are evident in a less aggressive argumentative tone explicitly softened by the conciliatory declaration that some controversial technical issues typically framed in dichotomous terms are more reasonably viewed as matters of degree and proportion. This stance makes it possible for analysts of divergent orientations to engage in more fruitful discussion and perhaps even to be influenced by new ways of thinking and working. This is, however, more difficult than it might seem. Serious discussions of technique between practitioners immersed in alternative traditions don't usually take into account the extent to which another's concepts have become imbued with layers of connotative distinction and affective loading. Ideas and attitudes intersect in complex patterns of meaning in the mind of each analyst to form a larger gestalt that is not easily penetrated. It is laborious to tease apart and think through the real distinctions and differences that compose alternative analytic identities and visions. Thus, although we may employ a similar vocabulary, we run the risk of speaking past one another without comprehension, or of reducing the other's vision to a one dimensional cliché. I am especially concerned in this discussion to try as much as possible to avoid this pitfall, because Sabe is a respected colleague and personal friend, as well as a vigorous advocate of an alternative psychoanalytic orientation.

As co-author with Janet Bachant of a series of papers that eventuated in a general text, *Working in Depth: Framework and Flexibility in the Analytic Relationship* (1998), I have thought carefully about the challenges that intersubjective, interpersonal, and relational ways of thinking and working pose to the classical psychoanalytic tradition that primarily informed my own development. In that work, we attempted to forge an inclusive framework that capitalizes on the virtues of a variety of contemporary models, without discarding what we consider of enduring power and value in the classical tradition. It is this contemporary perspective that I will be bringing to my consideration of Sabe's contributions in this paper. In my discussion, I will first speak to general issues of analytic neutrality as it pertains to the boundaries of analytic relatedness, and then look closely at the most detailed clinical vignette that Sabe presents to illustrate his technical concepts.Neutrality is one of those broad technical concepts in psychoanalysis that organize and orient an analyst's attitude and behavior toward the very complex task at hand. As such, it can never be an altogether precise or static concept; rather, it necessarily evolves as each generation of analysts adapts their theory and practice to meet the unique clinical challenges they must master. The term first appeared in Freud's (1915/1966b) technical papers as a warning against emotional overinvolvement with one's patients. To be neutral as opposed to passionate was a brake upon the seductive and destructive enticements of psychoanalytic intimacy. It was also in the service of maintaining interpretive objectivity, a position from which the analyst could hope to reflect what was true about his patient rather than project a vision biased by the analyst's countertransferential love or hate. Freud had a fervent wish that psychoanalysis would be accepted as a scientific project free of the dismissive assumption that its results were a tainted product of suggestion and emotional manipulation (Makari, 2008). In retrospect, it is easy to see that at times he went too far in circumscribing the boundaries of the analyst's involvement, as in his infamous surgical metaphor (Freud, 1912/1966a). Yet we shouldn't forget that these lessons about the limits of psychoanalytic intimacy that we take for granted and that are now enshrined in our professional code of ethics were not self-evident to the pioneering generation of psychoanalysts engaged in inventing a new profession. At a later time in the history of psychoanalysis, with the ascendance of the structural model (Freud, 1923/1961), neutrality took on a different though related meaning. For ego psychologists it came to stand for adopting an appropriate psychological distance from passionate internal conflict, the loving and hating and desiring parts of the patient's internal world that together constituted a neurotic equilibrium (A. Freud, 1936). The analyst who understood that the patient was beset by both archaic desire and conscience and bound by the adaptive demands of an implacable external reality would not make the mistake of pressuring the patient in one direction or the other. Instead, he would concentrate on illuminating the balance of internal forces that overwhelmed the patient's integrative capacity. By guarding against the temptation to impose the analyst's own morality or his personal adaptive solutions to life's numerous challenges, neutrality served to maintain interpretive balance and to safeguard the patient's autonomy. Sabe's brief against neutrality centers on its constraining influence on analytic spontaneity and authenticity, essential values that he sees as integral to the therapist's expressive humanity in the therapeutic encounter. He would like more room "to disclose values, feelings, judgments, and personal experiences." He recognizes, however, that this technical argument is significantly enhanced when grounded in a particular two-person model of transference, one in which the actualities of the analyst's personality and behavior constitute the adaptive context in which a patient's transference projections and reactions arise as plausible interpretations of that behavior. He contrasts this to a one-person model in which the patient's experience of the analyst is viewed as distortion-grounded "whole cloth" in prestructured intrapsychic dynamics. It is important for him to prioritize this two-person view of transference (Gill, 1984), because if the analyst's actual person is the essential stimulus to transference, there is powerful theoretical justification for a technique that embraces self-disclosure as a tactical response to dissipating and resolving transference. Indeed, if one subscribes to a view of transference as reactive rather than enactive of repressed longings and conflicted desires, then the traditional analytic stance of neutrality loses much of its conceptual force. There are alternatives to this either/or polarization, however. Janet Bachant and I (1997) have proposed that transference is most usefully understood as a multidimensional phenomenon, one that manifests itself in myriad ways in the psychoanalytic relationship.

> We think of transference as ongoing activity, a constant feature of mental life, something the individual does to generate an expedient way of meeting the world. Yet this activity continues the influence of unconscious fantasizing—itself an expression of conflict—by contributing to the organization of the multiple forces that converge in every interaction. (1998, p. 68)

Though we found it cogent to differentiate two broad dimensions of transference, which we called the "adaptive" and the "archaic," in practice these conceptual distinctions are almost impossible to tease apart. Our description encompasses both the active "filtering system" Sabe metaphorically describes and the wellspring of unconscious fantasy, infantile desire, and intrapsychic conflict that are so central to the classical understanding. Patients both interpret the actuality of current reality in light of the past and use that reality to reanimate the past in the context of the present reality. This more inclusive view eliminates the necessity to choose between two incompatible models, though it complicates the one-sided technical implications that follow from either view alone. In effect, the analyst must constantly balance the twin requirements of being responsively present, yet sufficiently restrained and evocative, in order to achieve the most effective psychoanalytic interaction. The therapist's freedom would be constrained not by arbitrary and restrictive rules but by a profound comprehension of the complexities of the analytic task. In my opinion, it is only after the analyst has thoroughly understood and internalized the necessary boundaries of analytic relatedness that he or she is free to engage in a fully spontaneous and creative exercise of this demanding art. This inclusive view of transference also demands some revision of the traditional concept of neutrality. Rather than discard it entirely, as Sabe seems inclined to do, Janet and I thought it preferable to update it in keeping with the interactive and intersubjective perspectives on transference that are at the forefront of contemporary psychoanalytic advances.

Neutrality is the technical name for a very complex attitude toward the patient's inner life and experience that imbues the analyst's listening in the analytic situation with a unique qualitative dimension. . . . In this interactive sense it is better thought of as defining a specific quality of responsive presence, rather than as the "blank screen" or mirroring function some have described. . . . Neutrality defines the boundaries, the edges of the interaction between patient and analyst where meaning takes shape. (Adler & Bachant, 1996, p. 1032)

From our perspective, neutrality is best thought of as a central structuring dimension of the analyst's professional subjectivity and stands in a complementary relation to the patient's role of spontaneous self-expression. Yet the classical emphasis on restraint is still important:

Inherent in this dimension of neutrality is awareness that a patient's conscious feelings, fantasies, wishes and intentions, however poignantly expressed or authentically experienced, are seldom simply one way or another. In effect, that which is currently manifest is not the whole story, and to fully acknowledge what is, means to leave room for what is yet to surface. Perforce, the neutral listener is required to be patient listener, only reluctantly concluding that he or she has heard as much as is likely to be learned about any particular topic at any particular time. (p. 1033–1034)

Since transference in the analytic situation is a bidirectional phenomenon, this last caution applies equally to the analyst and to the patient. Spontaneous self-disclosure will be restrained by an understanding that actions taken in the name of authenticity may prove deceptively ambiguous and complex. Before I turn to the clinical vignette, I need to explore the question of the analyst's self-disclosure further. Within the inclusive view of transference and a contemporary understanding of neutrality that I have very briefly sketched above, it makes perfect sense that at times an analyst can reveal his emotional experience of the patient or of the interaction with that patient as part of an ongoing interpretive dialogue. There are some forms of transference-countertransference engagement and enactment that cannot be addressed without the analyst being explicit about his emotional involvement or response.* It is a type of intervention that must be

---

* I believe this is the kind of self-disclosure that Sabe considers to be least controversial.

employed judiciously, for the analyst's subjectivity inevitably has much greater force and impact upon the patient than the patient's has upon the analyst. I do not mean that the analyst is or should be immune to the patient's opinions and feelings about himself or herself. I simply mean that one should never confuse—nor encourage one's patients to confuse—analytic relatedness with a relationship of equals. Friends or colleagues or lovers may explore and resolve interpersonal conflict and strive to resolve difference through open, uninhibited encounters with each other. Yet in analysis, even things we say that seem quite innocuous to us turn out to have enormous unanticipated weight for the patient. Often we only hear about these meanings and their effects months or perhaps years later. Sabe is right to challenge the principle of absolute anonymity, that is, the withholding of all factual details of the analyst's life, such as whether he is married, summers in the Hamptons, or has seen a particular movie or television show. It might be pointed out that many influential analysts within the classical tradition share his doubts (e.g., Stone, 1961). I prefer a principle of "evocative ambiguity," rather than anonymity, one that allows the patient room to represent us as they need to, rather than as we might prefer them to. This receptive attitude toward transference is one of the central dimensions of neutrality as Janet and I conceive it. As far as possible, the patient gets to initiate the sequence and substance of the themes that will be engaged, developed, and worked through in the analytic relationship. Loewald's (1975) analogy of the theater director helping to focus, refine, and stage a largely unconscious drama of which the patient is the author captures this attitude precisely. Though we may be drawn into the drama, it is the patient's initiative and fantasy that constitute the central action. Absolute anonymity serves little purpose in this regard and may cause iatrogenic harm by creating a stilted and stifling therapeutic atmosphere where drama gets suppressed. I believe such rigid postures are relics of an antiquated model of therapeutic action that authorized intentional frustration and abstinence as a way of instituting a regressive transference neurosis. After all, the patient who knows that the therapist is married is still free to imagine that the marriage is an unhappy one, if he or she needs to. The demographic details do not truly impede the patient's freedom to realize the dramatic potential of his or her transference. And I agree with Sabe that virtually everything an analyst does or doesn't do may provide the patient with material for transferential elaboration and creative enactment. In every analysis some things about the analyst will be revealed to the patient without our telling them and other things will be discovered by the patient. In this Internet age, the curious patient has means to dissolve the analyst's incognito with the click of a mouse.

However, there is a significant distinction between these inadvertent revelations and inevitable discoveries and the analyst's sharing aspects of his personal life or experience outside the analytic relationship as an intentional therapeutic strategy.* Exposing emotionally revealing information about one's inner life, history, or problems, whether as a technique to encourage the patient to be more revealing and less inhibited or as a way of influencing the patient's deeper attitudes toward him- or herself or his or her problems, seems to me essentially misguided. The analyst's self-disclosure is always extremely stimulating to a patient in ways that provoke, rather than evoke transferential reactivity. The potential risk that the analyst will use this license to consciously or unconsciously manipulate the patient's transference experience outweighs any substantive advantage that I can see arising from the technique. In analysis my primary goal is to create and safeguard an analytic situation that is conducive to the most radical expressive freedom for the patient. My expressive freedom is always subsidiary to and guided by that larger purpose. I want my patients to feel safe enough to spontaneously reveal everything that they think and feel and remember, and I want them to discover things about themselves that they have no conscious awareness of. This is the unique opportunity of an analysis conceived around the reciprocal roles of analytic neutrality and free association: to know oneself profoundly in the presence of another who does not judge or demand. From this perspective, when an analyst chooses to reveal his personal concerns, human weaknesses, or fantasies, it will necessarily be a heavily censored, selective version of their truth. This is not the kind of openness or spontaneity that I would wish to model or encourage. Yet for the analyst to be less selective, to be authentically, spontaneously himself, would violate the fundamental prerequisite of emotional safety that is a precondition for the patient's deeper self-revelation and understanding to unfold (Schafer, 1983).† Nor do I believe it fundamentally reassures a patient to learn that his or her analyst is neurotically human after all. What reassures a patient is the belief that his or her analyst knows a way to help the patient work free of the recurrent anxiety, depression, and self-destructiveness that encumbers the patient's life. Reading through the vignettes—anecdotes, really—Sabe provides to illustrate his ideas, I am struck with the fact that he shows himself to be on the whole a much more conservative and

---

* Ironically, Sabe makes a similar argument to the patient who requests that he provide her with copies of his writing. If she seeks out his work, it's one thing, but for him to provide it for her violates a boundary that he feels impelled to defend and justify.

† Indeed, any analyst who attempted to do more would soon start behaving as defensively and resistantly as his patient—a sure recipe for therapeutic disaster.

restrained analyst than some of the bolder rhetoric he cites might suggest. He is at pains to warn of the potential dangers and countertransferential abuses of self-disclosure, even as he concludes that analytic restraint is a greater danger. I will consider the most extensive clinical example he describes because it presents enough process to formulate an independent view of what transpired. Sabe quotes his intervention to a female patient—herself an experienced analyst—who was talking about how heavily her self-doubts weigh upon her. We analysts all have doubts about our work, he tells her, but "for you it's life and death, for me there'll be other chances." What separates this from a more traditional interpretation is that Sabe offers a view into his own experience of being an analyst, as a contrasting model to the anxious and depressive attitude of his patient. He doesn't explain why he felt it necessary to add this personal spin to what sounded like an acute summary of his patient's tormented work life. If he simply intended to be reassuring and to suggest an alternative way of feeling and thinking, he could have achieved this goal without explicitly bringing himself into the picture. In the following session, the patient reports a "nice" dream from the night of the previous session. She was dressing herself in a new, more comfortable style (in less somber colors) that made her "very happy." She adds the spontaneous reflection that in real life she is ambivalent about calling attention to herself. The patient proceeds to interpret her own dream as a response to Sabe's "saying something about himself" in the previous session. She viewed this sharing something about himself as a "caring" action. She went on to contrast his personal sharing with memories of her parents' lack of involvement. Analytic anonymity, she complains, only duplicates her depriving familial background.

By suggesting that this excerpt has relevance to the broader issue of neutrality, I assume Sabe wants to illustrate how his personal interpretive form had a beneficial effect on the patient and the analytic atmosphere. That he presents this as evidence for the value of analytic self-disclosure ("if I show my true colors, she feels freer to show hers"), suggests that he is taking her reaction as a response to a more authentic act of caring than would have been implicit in a conventional interpretive form. But how compelling is this evidence? Certainly he must realize that another patient could have had an aversive reaction to the very same interpretive style, experiencing it as intrusive or arrogant or exhibitionistic rather than caring. Inevitably, her response to his interpretation was transferentially mediated. In this instance she apparently experienced his act as one of sharing and caring, perhaps because it confirmed a set of wishful fantasies that she brought to the encounter, if not the therapy itself. Is she seeking a corrective emotional experience rather than an exploration of her depressive anxieties? Did this "well-trained and experienced analyst" know something about Sabe's way of working before she chose him as her analyst? And I wrote "apparently" above because it's hard for me to ignore the idea that this patient's "nice," "happy," "colorful" dream in which she is putting together a new outfit that is more like those of the women she admires expresses manic and exhibitionistic elements stimulated by these (or similar) gratifying fantasies. In this light, her identification with Sabe may be primarily defensive, rather than adaptive, as he implies. Is her testimonial to analytic self-disclosure a way of displaying colors she believes Sabe will respect and find attractive? Does she wish that her "life-and-death" anxieties will be ameliorated by simply changing her analytic style? None of this is either good or bad in itself; it simply points to the complexity of any interpretive dialogue in which the conscious and unconscious transferential fantasies and wishes of the patient are perpetually stimulated—and in this instance, perhaps overstimulated—by the therapist's interventions. Ironically, the patient herself frames our technical debate most elegantly, putting her finger on the heart of the larger question at issue. She says to Sabe approvingly, "Your anonymity is not background but a constant stimulus. It's not freeing. It's provocative." Exactly.

I'm aware that my discussion does no more than help to sharpen some differences that arise from alternative visions of the analytic situation. To do full justice to these differences, I would have to include more extensive discussions of the role of free association as a means of confirming interpretive hypotheses versus the effectiveness of an active detailed enquiry, the place and meaning of the good object in therapeutic action, the role of the real relationship, the distinction between psychotherapy and psychoanalysis, and alternative views of the unconscious and dream interpretation. All of these issues have a direct bearing on why Sabe might view his interaction with his patient one way and I another. Of necessity, I have focused more narrowly upon the question of analytic self-disclosure as it relates to the principle of neutrality and to an understanding of the complexity of transference.

References

Adler, E., & Bachant, J. L. (1996). Free association and analytic neutrality: The basic structure of the analytic situation. *Journal of the American Psychoanalytic Association, 44*, 1021–1046.

Adler, E., & Bachant, J. L. (1998). *Working in depth: A clinician's guide to framework and flexibility in the analytic relationship.* Northvale, NJ: Jason Aronson.

Bachant, J. L., & Adler, E. (1997). Transference: Co-constructed or brought to the analytic relationship? *Journal of the American Psychoanalytic Association, 45*, 1097–1120.

Freud, A. (1936). *The ego and the mechanisms of defense.* New York: International Universities Press.

Freud, S. (1961). The ego and the id. In J. Strachey (Ed. & Trans.), *The standard edition of the complete psychological works of Sigmund Freud* (Vol. 19, pp. 1–59). London: Hogarth Press. (Original work published 1923)

Freud, S. (1966a). Recommendations to physicians practicing psychoanalysis. In J. Strachey (Ed. & Trans.), *The standard edition of the complete psychological works of Sigmund Freud* (Vol. 12, pp. 109–120). London: Hogarth Press. (Original work published 1912)

Freud, S. (1966b). Observations on transference-love. In J. Strachey (Ed. & Trans.), *The standard edition of the complete psychological works of Sigmund Freud* (Vol. 12, pp. 157–171). London: Hogarth Press. (Original work published 1915)

Gill, M. (1983). The interpersonal paradigm and the degree of the therapist's involvement. *Contemporary Psychoanalysis, 19*(2), 200–237.

Loewald, H. (1975). Psychoanalysis as an art and the fantasy character of the psychoanalytic situation. In *Papers on psychoanalysis* (pp. 352–371). New Haven: Yale University Press.

Makari, G. (2008). *Revolution in mind.* New York: Harper.

Schafer, R. (1983). *The analytic attitude.* New York: Basic Books.

Stone, L. (1961). *The psychoanalytic situation: An examination of its development and essential nature.* Madison: International Universities Press.

COMMENTARY BY BARRY FARBER

Sabe Basescu's 1990 paper on the use of the self in psychotherapy was remarkably prescient in its acknowledgment of the inevitability and clinical value of therapist disclosures. While nowadays therapists of virtually every theoretical persuasion—including those adhering to CBT models—agree that therapist openness and disclosure are integral aspects of the therapeutic enterprise, valuable if for no other reason than their ability to facilitate the all-important therapeutic alliance, at the time that Basescu published this paper and its companion piece, "Show and Tell: Reflections on the Analyst's Self-Disclosure" (1990a), there was considerable debate in the analytic community regarding the advisability of disclosing aspects of oneself to one's patients. This practice was widely seen as violating the classical analytic principles of neutrality, abstinence, and anonymity. Freud's position (if not actual practice) was unambiguous: "The doctor should be opaque to his patients, and like a mirror, should show them nothing but what is shown to him" (1912/1966, p. 117).

especially his or her willingness to know and be known, more than technique per se, that contributes to the effectiveness of the work. In the balance of this chapter, I will examine the extent to which his advocacy of specific forms of disclosure is consistent with the research on the use of this class of therapist behavior. To this end, I will rely heavily on two sources: my own recent (2006) book on self-disclosure and Norcross's (2002) edited volume that reviewed the research on aspects of the therapy relationship that appear to "work." While Basescu himself, like many analytically and existentially oriented colleagues, might eschew the need for an empirical analysis of the deeply personal work of a psychoanalytic treatment, the field continues to move inexorably in the direction of empiricism. Newly minted therapists, trained in clinical programs that have been mandated by the American Psychological Association to design curricula that include information about empirically supported treatments and evidence-based practice, are far more likely than their predecessors to be guided in their clinical work, at least in part, by research findings. If we are (thankfully) no longer asking the question of whether psychotherapy is effective—research has proven conclusively that it is—we are now more than ever asking questions about which specific interventions yield what types of outcomes for which individuals under which circumstances.

Psychodynamic therapy has been a relatively late entrant into the field of psychotherapy research, in part because its tenets are far less amenable to the kind of manualization that randomized clinical trials dictate and in part because many practitioners have traditionally been reluctant to subject their work to quantitative methods of empirical scrutiny, believing that this approach to understanding the workings and effective ingredients of psychodynamic therapy cannot capture the idiographic and complex nature of this type of therapeutic work. Nevertheless, research on both the process and outcomes of psychodynamic therapy has increased substantially in recent years (e.g., Fonagy, Roth, & Higgitt, 2005; Westen, 1998). Moreover, there is now a solid body of research on the use of therapist disclosures (e.g., Hill & Knox, 2002) that can inform a discussion of whether Basescu's paper offers empirically supported suggestions.

Research on self-disclosure in psychotherapy is for the most part a relatively recent (post-1990s) phenomenon, but empirical investigations of the nature and processes of self-disclosure in everyday life have a longer history, one that can be traced back to the work of Sidney Jourard in the 1960s. Jourard, much like Basescu, was interested in existential questions, especially the nature of interpersonal knowledge. As part of his own existential quest, Jourard began studying lapses in understanding between people, a phenomenon he believed was at the root of the problems he observed in families and societies. Not surprisingly, his research was influenced by the work of many interpersonalists, including Fromm and Horney, who believed that human beings are essentially social creatures who nevertheless have a tendency to hide from or misrepresent themselves to others. In one of his many attempts to investigate disclosure, Jourard (1971b) asked his friends a seemingly straightforward question: "What do you know about me?" He reported that he barely recognized himself from these answers and that his friends hardly seemed to know him. Jourard came to believe that self-disclosure was central to a person's mental health and a prerequisite for satisfying relationships with others. In fact, he suggested that not only was mental health contingent upon self-disclosure but that mental illness resulted from its absence. One of Jourard's continued points of emphasis—one noted by Basescu in the paper under discussion here—was that disclosure was abetted by reciprocity (i.e., individuals tend to disclose to the extent that they are disclosed to).

The research on therapist disclosure per se builds upon Jourard's foundation, though it has been beset by a host of methodological problems. Indeed, synthesizing the research on the prevalence, nature, and consequences of therapist disclosure is confounded by the diverse range of opinions as to how this phenomenon should be defined, categorized, and measured. Nevertheless, despite the dizzying array of definitions, purposeful verbal therapist self-disclosure can be divided into two primary categories: *factual disclosures* that include a therapist's disclosure of facts or information about him or herself and *self-involving disclosures*, also known as "immediacy" or countertransferential disclosures, that involve the therapist's articulation of his or her immediate or past feelings or experiences in response to a patient's feelings or experiences. This latter category may be further divided into responses directly related to patients' statements, expressions of the therapist's emotional responses, or reactions to the patient in general. According to Matthews (1988), 35% of therapist disclosures consist of factual information about their own lives, while the balance consists of either feelings therapists had experienced in their own lives (46%) or feelings currently experienced toward patients (19%).

Which type of self-disclosure does Basescu most subscribe to? He notes in this article that "what the analyst says about his or her reactions to what transpires in the relationship . . . is predominant in importance, in relevance to the therapeutic work, and in frequency of occurrence" (p. 162). That is, Basescu's emphasis falls squarely within the category of self-involving disclosures and, more specifically, of the subtype that involves articulating one's personal feelings or thoughts in response to something that has occurred in the room: "Your looking at me had a whimsical quality that struck me funny" (p. 162); "I feel like I'm listening to a lecture" (p. 162). In this regard, a survey of former patients in psychoanalysis indicated that this group believed that therapist disclosures of feelings were associated with their improvement, while factual therapist disclosures were not (Curtis, Field, Knaan-Kostman, & Mannix, 2004).

Some of Basescu's examples in this article are a combination of his own experiences and his reactions to experiences of his patient—for example, his response to a therapist he was treating who was fearful of making clinical mistakes: "For you it's life and death, for me there'll be other chances" (p. 158). Or, in trying to assuage a patient's sense of frustration at the length of her own therapy, he shared the following: "I was in analysis for 8 years and that was only the first time." In addition, based on at least one of his examples—"I observed that she never expressed interest in any aspect of my life, such as where I went on vacation or if I enjoyed it" (p. 163)—it appears as if he would be willing to share relatively mundane facts of his life as well. It is clear, though, that while Basescu's generally open stance toward disclosure allows for the expression of both factual and self-involving material, his strong predilection is toward statements that allow him to be disclosing of his own experiences while commenting on an aspect of the client's presentation about which he or she is essentially unaware.

Using another classification system, Hill, Mahalik, and Thompson (1989) found that reassuring disclosures (those that reinforce or legitimize patient experience) were rated as most helpful by clients and therapists. In addition, disclosures categorized as both reassuring and involving (communicating the therapist's feelings or thoughts about the client) were rated as helpful by clients and therapists. Basescu's disclosures seem of the latter variety—that is, both reassuring and involving (e.g., "I was in analysis for 8 years and that was only the first time")—and, consistent with Hill et al.'s research, highly valued by him and his patients.

Hill et al. (1988) found that disclosures account for only 1% of total therapist responses but that this behavior elicits the highest client helpfulness rating. Moreover, they found that therapist disclosures lead to the highest level of client experiencing, significantly greater than other therapeutic interventions such as approval and reflection. Although one gets the sense from reading his articles that Basescu's work involves a higher proportion of disclosures than is typical of most therapists, this is of course impossible to determine without clinical transcripts. But what seems virtually certain, even in the absence of such data, is that Basesu's disclosures greatly intensified his patients' level of experiencing. The patient to whom he said, "For you it's life or death, for me there'll be other chances," felt "relieved," acknowledged how "meaningful" his words were, and sensed his caring for her. Other patients were clearly moved by his openness and felt closer to him and/or more involved in the treatment, more available to engage in "experiential exploration of more than meets the eye" (p. 162).

Interestingly, too, in Hill et al.'s (1988) study, therapist ratings of the helpfulness of disclosures were lower than that of patients. Perhaps this finding is due to the fact that these data were collected more than 20 years ago, a time when therapists may have been more reluctant to acknowledge the benign influence of their disclosures. But the finding may also be valid, pointing to the possibility that many therapists were and perhaps still are unaware of the power that their personal style exerts in the treatment. Basescu was not of this ilk. He was well aware of the clinical benefits of being genuine, authentic, and disclosing; perhaps even more remarkably, he was willing to unabashedly state the case for this approach to his colleagues in a rather divided psychoanalytic community.

Lane, Farber, and Geller (2001) asked therapists to rate disclosures in terms of their effectiveness in furthering treatment aims. Among those disclosures ranked highest on this list were therapists' feelings of respect or admiration for their patients, emotional reactions to patients, reactions to patients' expressive style, acknowledgment of feelings similar to those of patients, apologies for mistakes, and strategies for coping with stress. Basescu would likely endorse several of these items; in particular, his examples suggest that he believed the following kinds of disclosures were particularly helpful: expressing his emotional reactions to his patients ("I went on to say that I did cut him off because I was not going to have that kind of vacation and felt somewhat deprived about it"), expressing his experience of a patient's expressive style ("I have the feeling of being buttered up"), and acknowledging feelings similar to those of a patient (Patient: "I hate my rockiness." Basescu: "Don't we all"). His overarching theme was that we further the treatment by sharing with our patients our sense of who they are and how they come across to us. Although he doesn't address this explicitly, his examples imply that this goal is far better served through the therapist's immediate experiential feedback than through explications of the nature of transference.

Lane et al. (2001) also investigated therapists' perceived reasons for disclosing. The three most common reasons cited were strengthening the therapeutic alliance, normalizing patients' experiences, and providing the patient with alternative ways of thinking. Knox and Hill (2003) added an additional reason: that it abets patient disclosures. Here again, Basescu's clinical intuition and insights match those of the empirical literature. He valued the ability of his disclosure to have a positive effect on the alliance; "[It] allows for the development of intimacy and trust" (p. 162); "[It] enhances the spirit of collaboration" (p. 162). He also understood how some disclosures helped normalize a patient's sense of self: "When working with someone who feels so separate and distant from the rest of the human race, I might say something about myself that bridges that feeling of distance." And, as noted earlier, he fully appreciated the reciprocity that often accompanies disclosures: "Answering questions directly helps clarify for both of us what's happening. It often has the additional consequence of enabling further exploration of the patient's experience" (p. 162). Arguably, though, Basescu's most salient reason to disclose is that it enables patients to understand themselves better. His patient's response to Basescu's observation that the patient "had a whimsical quality" to his stare was, "Thanks. That helps me know something about myself." "Disclosing these reactions," he noted, "conveys to the other person the kind of impact he or she is having" (p. 162).

Studies have found mixed result regarding the effects of therapist disclosure. Some studies (e.g., Ramsdell & Ramsdell, 1993) have shown that former clients feel that their therapists' disclosures had a positive impact on their treatment, while other studies (e.g., Audet & Everall, 2003) have found that some clients believe that disclosures decreased their ability to trust their therapists. It may well be that as Hill et al. (1989) suggest, the more frequent the occurrence of therapist disclosures, the lower the probability of positive impact; that is, "less may well be more" (Farber, 2006). One frequently cited reason for possible negative effects of therapist disclosure is patient awareness that at least some disclosures seem too narcissistically motivated (Lane et al., 2001). When patients sense that their therapist's sharing is more for the therapist's needs than their own, their reactions are, not surprisingly, negative. In a related vein, too-frequent therapist disclosures may create the perception that the therapist's issues are too much a part of the therapeutic discourse. "The research indicates that most therapists appropriately assume that their primary task is to focus on the needs of their clients—not their own needs to appear or feel smart, useful, or friendly" (Farber, 2006, p. 140).

Basescu, of course, understood these facts. His stance was that when analyst disclosure is in the service of "eliciting sympathy, warding off criticism or anger, or manipulating a feeling of intimacy" (p. 161), it is likely to be destructive to the relationship. "Inappropriate self-disclosures," he added, "are those compulsively driven by the analyst's personal needs or responses to the patient's intimidating manipulations" (p. 163). As noted earlier, he was also well aware of the tension between helpful disclosures and those that burdened the patient with what contemporary youth might well call "TMI" (too much information). "The analyst's self-disclosure," he noted, "is an intervention that can cut both ways" (p. 164). When Basescu wrote of "the mutuality of relevant self-revelation" (p. 162), I suspect that he was alluding to what is an empirically demonstrated phenomenon: that most therapists have adopted a flexible attitude toward self-disclosure, varying their practice according to the clinical needs of the moment (Johnson & Farber, 1996).

Basescu's message to therapists in this paper centered on the central role of disclosure within the therapeutic enterprise, especially their "being fully present, available, and freely responsive" (p. 163). It is good to know that this is not only the advice of an extremely well-respected colleague but also consistent with emerging empirical data on the use of the self in clinical practice.

References

Aron, L. (1996). *A meeting of minds: Mutuality in psychoanalysis.* Hillsdale, NJ: Analytic Press.

Audet, C., & Everall, R. D. (2003). Counselor self-disclosure: Client-informed implications for practice. *Counseling and Psychotherapy Research, 3,* 223–231.

Basescu, S. (1977). Anxieties in the analyst: An autobiographical account. In K. A. Frank (Ed.), *The human dimension in psychoanalytic practice* (pp. 153–163). New York: Grune & Stratton.

Basescu, S. (1990a). Show and tell: Reflections on the analyst's self-disclosure. In G. Stricker & M. Fisher (Eds.), *Self-disclosure in the therapeutic relationship* (pp. 47–59). New York: Plenum.

Basescu, S. (1990b). Tools of the trade: The use of the self in psychotherapy. *Group, 14,* 157–165.

Beutler, L. E., & Mitchell, R. (1981). Differential psychotherapy outcome among depressed and impulsive patients as a function of analytic and experiential treatment procedures. *Psychiatry: Journal for the Study of Interpersonal Processes, 44,* 297–306.

Curtis, R., Field, C., Knaan-Kostman, I., & Mannix, K. (2004). What 75 psychoanalysts found helpful and hurtful in their own analyses. *Psychoanalytic Psychology, 21,* 183–202.

Edwards, C. E., & Murdock, N. L. (1994). Characteristics of therapist self-disclosure in the counseling process. *Journal of Counseling and Development, 72,* 384–389.

Farber, B. A. (2006). *Self-disclosure in psychotherapy.* New York: Guilford.

Fonagy, P., Roth, A., & Higgitt, A. (2005). Psychodynamic psychotherapies: Evidence-based practice and clinical wisdom. *Bulletin of the Menninger Clinic, 69,* 1–58.

Freud, S. (1966). Recommendations to physicians practicing psychoanalysis. In J. Strachey (Ed. & Trans.), *The standard edition of the complete psychological works of Sigmund Freud* (Vol. 12, pp. 109–120). London: Hogarth Press. (Original work published 1912)

Hill, C. E., Helms, J. E., Tichenor, V., Spiegel, S. B., O'Grady, K. E., & Perry, E. S. (1988). Effects of therapist response modes in brief psychotherapy. *Journal of Counseling Psychology, 35,* 222–233.

Hill, C. E. & Knox, S. (2002). Self-disclosure. In J. Norcross (Ed.), *Psychotherapy relationships that work: Therapist contributions and responsiveness to patients* (pp. 255–265). New York: Oxford University Press.

Hill, C. E., Mahalik, J. R., & Thompson, B. J. (1989). Therapist self-disclosure. *Psychotherapy: Theory, Research, and Practice, 26,* 290–295.

Johnston, S., & Farber, B. A. (1996). The maintenance of boundaries in psychotherapeutic practice. *Psychotherapy: Theory, Research, Practice, Training, 33,* 391–402.

Jourard, S. M. (1971a). *Self-disclosure: An experimental analysis of the transparent self.* New York: Wiley.

Jourard, S. M. (1971b). *The transparent self: Self-disclosure and well-being.* Princeton, NJ: Van Nostrand.

Knox, S., & Hill, C. E. (2003). Therapist self-disclosure: Research-based suggestions for practitioners. *Journal of Clinical Psychology/In Session, 59,* 529–539.

Lane, J. S., Farber, B. A., & Geller, J. D. (2001, June). *What therapists do and do not disclose to their patients.* Paper presented at the annual conference of the Society for Psychotherapy Research, Montevideo, Uruguay.

Mathews, B. (1988). The role of therapist self-disclosure in psychotherapy: A survey of therapists. *American Journal of Psychotherapy, 42,* 521–531.

Norcross, J. (Ed.) (2002). *Psychotherapy relationships that work: Therapist contributions and responsiveness to patients.* New York: Oxford University Press.

Ramsdell, P. S., & Ramsdell, E. R. (1993). Dual relationships: Client perceptions of the effect of client counselor relationship on the therapeutic process. *Clinical Social Work Journal, 21,* 195–212.

Renik, O. (1995). The ideal of the anonymous analyst and the problem of self-disclosure. *Psychoanalytic Quarterly, 62,* 553–571.

Rogers, C. R., Gendlin, E. T., Kiesler, D. J., & Truax, C. B. (Eds.). (1967). *The therapeutic relationship and its impact: A study of psychotherapy with schizophrenics.* Madison: University of Wisconsin Press.

Simon, J. C. (1990). Criteria for therapist self-disclosure. In G. Stricker & M. Fisher (Eds.), *Self-disclosure in the therapeutic relationship* (pp. 207–225). New York: Plenum Press.

Westen, D. (1998). The scientific legacy of Sigmund Freud: Toward a psychodynamically informed psychological science. *Psychological Bulletin, 124,* 333–371.

COMMENTARY BY NEIL SKOLNICK

Approximately 25 years ago I was an analysand of Sabe Basescu's. When George Goldstein invited me to discuss Sabe's paper "Tools of the Trade: The Use of Self in Psychotherapy" for this project, I understood that I was being asked to participate partially because I am indeed a former analysand and now a colleague of Sabe's. I was honored to accept and immediately filled with both delight and trepidation. I felt delight because it gave me yet another opportunity to express heartfelt appreciation and gratitude to someone who, as my analyst, helped me rescript my life up to, including, and following, my early adulthood. My trepidation was more complex. First, I wanted to do his paper justice. Simply put—and Sabe, if nothing else, is a master of the simply put—it would be a sorry expression of gratitude to write a crummy discussion, period. Also, I had to wrestle with the question of to what degree I should be self-revealing about my analysis. I was dealing with a dilemma within a dilemma, that of self-revelation. Is not part of his paper addressed to the question of self-revelation? Taking Sabe's advice from his paper, I decided it would be foolish to let it all hang out. Instead, I opted for a "natural, unstudied and real" (p. 157) approach to discussing his paper, an approach that was first and foremost human. In my discussion, I weave back and forth between scholarly criticism and my own personal relationship with Sabe.

Yikes. How do I honor someone whose life path was significantly altered by the misfortune of a freakish bicycle accident, one that brought two entirely separate lives together in place and time for one horrific moment and left one of them with a brain injury? How do I write a paper honoring my analyst and his ideas that does justice to the complexities of our relationship, the good, the bad, and the otherwise, as an analysand, a colleague, and more recently, a friend? How do I craft a paper that by definition will open the door to the privacy of my analysis, of my singular observations of, and inimitable relationship with, a man who participated in the shaping of my adult life out of the rather unformed, unintegrated ingredients of my youth? Paying homage to someone from this vantage point needs to be both appropriately personal but also to transmit the unique attributes of this person that will have meaning to not just those who know him but also those who do not.

The hubris that led me to accept this task is intimately related to an older grandiosity that I possessed when I entered this field. This grandiosity was a necessity for motivation when "leap before you look" was my rule of the day. I needed it when diving into clinical work with no experience to anchor me. But it was also grandiosity in need of correction by the person I am writing about. I am writing about Sabe, my analyst, Sabe, the academician and teacher, and Sabe, who, many years after I lay on his analytic couch, was becoming my friend when this accident occurred.

So ostensibly, I have accepted the task of discussing a scholarly paper. But no one reading this will be fooled by such a misleading premise. I am writing about Sabe, myself, and our relationship. These layers weave unabashedly in and out of the scholarly intent and content of my discussion. I hope I will get something across to you, the reader, that transcends what you learn about Sabe the scholar. Maybe this is self-evident.

The Message Is in the Mode

While reading the paper I could not fail to notice, first and foremost, how much of Sabe's style as an analyst is reflected in his stylistic cadence as a writer. Pithy, in the best sense of the word, is the quality that comes frequently to me when I think of Sabe. His paper is laced with pithy statements. Whether he is expounding upon the use of self theoretically or quoting a clinical intervention, he is remarkably to the point in what he says and how he says it. I have memories of his discerning the meaning of a complex interaction that went right to the heart of the issue in just a few well-chosen words. Consider his comments on the issue of patient questions. "At times I feel prompted to express something I'm thinking or feeling in a session, but I almost always respond to a patient's questioning about it. *If I am asked, I generally answer*" (p. 162, italics added). How similar is this to the response he gives to a patient who repeatedly asks why he will not refer her to a paper he has written: "Well, let's see if I can be clear about it. It's because I don't want to participate in or reinforce something that I don't know the meaning of. *My job is to analyze the meaning, not to collude with it*" (p. 162, italics added)? Similarly, no lengthy explanations were forthcoming in my analysis. He was the master of the parsimonious interpretation. I recall his attempting to get me to see a less than virtuous quality of mine in a seemingly empathic comment I had been making about a family member. My comment had been something like, "It was difficult to see her so helpless and childlike." To which he replied, "I hear that, but you appear to be enjoying it as well." After a brief silent moment of indignation, I realized he was right on target.

My appreciation of this aspect of his style evolved. At first, I was annoyed and disappointed at the brief comments my neurotic musings evoked. No lengthy interpretations were in the offing for me. However, I learned to appreciate how much space they actually opened up—space to explore together the multitude of meanings that were being constructed both about my inner life and about my relationship with him. His interpretations, because they were brief and somewhat enigmatic, usually prompted further questioning. In an endeavor that does not purport to give answers, what could be better than increased questioning?

His sparse comments are consistent with the furnishings of his office. A few pieces of Danish modern, a simple couch, a simpler chair, a piece of driftwood, and a framed photo of Martha's Vineyard graced his office, carved from a two-car garage on a quiet suburban street near the Long Island Sound. I remember my disappointment when I started analysis. Where were the trappings of the Vienna-born profession? Freud's office, embellished with his multitude of collections and Oriental rugs, seemed to have morphed into the sparse trappings of Dag Hammarskjöld's UN office. "Less is more" proclaimed the esthetic of the times in which Sabe entered the field. My appreciation of the sparse décor increased along with my appreciation of his sparse but pithy interpretive manner. I alternatively envied it, idealized it, and admired it. I ultimately identified with Sabe's style of analyzing, though my office remained as cluttered as a well-appointed Viennese spread. We could be different.

But that I did identify with moments of his style is very much to the point I have spoken about previously (Skolnick, 2005) when I claimed that *dynamic identification* with an analyst is one of the mutagenic variables embedded in a relational analysis. By dynamic identification, I mean that our patients not only identify with us in a wholesale concordant fashion but also take in the whole relationship with its complementary identifications and interactions. A patient identifies with both the analyst being a certain way with him (i.e., pithy) and with oneself as the patient contextualized in the relationship, in my case being with someone who is addressing me with a pithy style. Analytic style was but one arena in which my analyst's use of self had a profound impact on my professional and personal identity as it continued and continues to live on in me with the inevitable distortions of memory and intervening experience. Twenty-some years after termination, I still can have the experience that I am channeling Sabe's voice. I endeavor to construct my interventions to be short and to the point. If my interpretation starts to become long, convoluted, and unwieldy, I know that I'm not fully affectively connected to, or am not certain of, what I'm trying to say. Parenthetically, I have chuckled to myself when cautioning students that if they think they are talking too much, they probably are.

As a footnote to the issue of his writing style and how it embodies his personal style, I must make note of his lack of jargon in both. Instead of jargon, what comes across is the use of careful thought and expression with everyday language. Sometimes jargon can be employed as a smokescreen for a lack of understanding or human connection. Sabe typically expresses himself in colloquial, unpretentious, no-nonsense words. This mode of relating is an extension of his belief that the analyst as a human being is, "being natural, unstudied, and real" (p. 157). I applaud and revere this manner of being an analyst. Basescu states that self-disclosing analysts make for self-disclosing patients. I would add that real, authentic analysts ultimately make for real, authentic patients.

Analysts' Use of Self

Basescu's discussion on the use of self focuses partly on the related issues of self-disclosure, anonymity, and neutrality. He adds his own idiom to the ongoing debates regarding each of these issues. Self-disclosure, anonymity, and neutrality have been hotly debated almost since the birth of psychoanalysis. His contentions hark back to the nascent use of self in Ferenczi's experiments and later in Fairbairn's focus on the central importance of the analyst-patient relationship to the entire endeavor of an analysis. Listen to Fairbairn writing in his 1958 paper on technique:

> It becomes obvious, therefore, that, from a therapeutic standpoint, interpretation is not enough; and it would appear to follow that the relationship existing between the patient and the analyst in the psychoanalytical situation serves purposes additional to that of providing a setting for the interpretation of transference phenomena . . . and, if this view is correct, the actual relationship existing between the patient and the analyst as persons must be regarded as in itself constituting a therapeutic factor of prime importance. (p. 377)

Now listen to the resonances of Fairbairn in Basescu:

> The patient–therapist relationship is the most immediate and experientially cogent arena in which to explore the patterns of interpersonal relatedness and the role that each person plays in actively creating and maintaining these patterns. . . . The truthfulness with which the participants can explore and acknowledge what it is that is going on between them empowers the relationship to be an agent for change. (p. 158)

There are important differences between Fairbairn's object relational approach and Basescu's interpersonal approach that go beyond the scope of this discussion. Briefly, Fairbairn's use of relationship is to provide the patient with an emotional experience denied to him or her in childhood; by contrast, while the interpersonal approach also advocates for the provision of a different kind of relationship, its version is a relationship that is predicated on participating in and observing the relationship as it is happening in the here and now. Both approaches do indeed situate the locus of change in the analyst/patient relationship. Neither drive nor traditional transference interpretations, while at times useful, carry as much mutagenic value.

Basescu's arguments, particularly on the topic of self-disclosure and neutrality, also very much presage what relational theorists are pronouncing (rediscovering?) in the current literature. He presents a largely interpersonal stance on the related issues of neutrality and anonymity.* In another paper from the same year (Basescu, 1990a), as well as in the paper (1990b) being discussed, Basescu claims in no uncertain terms, "The increasing recognition and acknowledgement that the analytic relationship is a fully human encounter between two more alike than different, fallible human beings, implies that neutrality may be primarily a technical fiction, more honored in the breach, rather than an analytic attribute" (p. 159). There are numerous ways in which the analyst reveals his or her personal values, attributes, likes and dislikes, feelings, judgments, and personal experiences, both deliberately and inadvertently. Of the many ways an analyst can reveal himself, Basescu states it is often a matter of degree and that all analysts employ different levels of anonymity, which span complete anonymity to outright disclosure. He also states that probably all analysts engage in varying types of self-disclosure at one time or another. Eschewing the possibility of anonymity in the psychoanalytic encounter has been independently suggested by analysts subsequently writing from a relational perspective (Aron, 1996; Davies, 2004).

Where's the Unconscious? Use of Projective Identification

The lion's share of arguments about contemporary ideas of anonymity, neutrality, and self-disclosure, Basescu argues, are predicated on a revised view of transference. His definition of transference and countertransference privileges a two-person, interactional model. He restates the time-worn interpersonal question "What's going on around here?" (Levenson, 1983) as "The transference is regarded as the patient's attempt to arrive at a plausible understanding of the analytic relationship and is more or less influenced by the analyst's behavior" (p. 157). By honestly exploring this question, the analytic relationship is empowered as a vehicle for change. I could not agree with him more. However, relational theories of intersubjectivity (Ogden, 1994; Benjamin, 1995; Stolorow, 1994; etc.) emphasize that the two-way interaction between analyst and patient extends beyond conscious interaction, and consider the unconscious interaction to be of significant import in the

---

* For Basescu, anonymity represents by and large the way in which therapist neutrality has been operationalized.

transference-countertransference equation. To partially respond to Levenson's query about what's going on around here, I would answer, "More than meets the eye." Unconscious factors in the bidirectional and mutually influential analytic relationship greatly increase the complexity and comprehensive quality of the question of transference.

Basescu makes a point of bifurcating the issue of self-disclosure into those disclosures the analyst intentionally makes to the patient and those disclosures that are inadvertent. He does not appear to entertain, even under the rubric of inadvertent self-disclosure, the possibility of unconscious communication in the process. Absent is any consideration of unconscious communication as a use of self, either from the therapist to the patient or from the patient to the therapist. But if we accept his characterization of psychoanalysis as a human endeavor by two people who are more alike than not, then the analyst and the patient are unconsciously communicating pieces of themselves to each other continuously. Consider what happens when a patient is communicating via a projective identification, a special form of unconscious communication. From my own informal survey, there appears to be a consensus amongst interpersonal analysts that projective identification is not a valid or useful concept, some preferring empathy instead. One of the sticking points is the language with which Klein defined the term. For her, projective identification referred to an unconscious fantasy in which the infant places an unbearable piece of his or her psyche into the mother. However, if one regards the Kleinian concept of fantasy as the psychic equivalent of Chomsky's "deep structure" (1968) in language development, as Ogden (1982) has suggested, it might become more feasible to imagine that the fantasy of placing part of one's psyche into another represents a predisposition of the infant for later empathy. As Irma Pick (1985) puts it, "If there is a mouth that seeks a breast as an inborn potential, there is, I believe, a psychological equivalent, i.e. a state of mind which seeks another state of mind" (p. 35). Whether the process is conceived as a placing into or merely as communicating an unconscious piece of self to another, projective identification can be understood as representing a deep psychological potential for knowing that others can have minds that are like ours, minds that contain thoughts, experiences, motives, and feelings that are similar to our own. These other minds then would be capable of knowing our mind and our subjectivity. It is not much of a stretch to posit that the fantasy of projective identification provides the infant with a predisposition to the later experience of knowing and being known that we call empathy. Put another way, projective identification can be seen as a forerunner, if not facilitator, of the breakdown of the solipsistic, omnipotent mind of the infant, paving the way for an infant to discover another's subjectivity as separate from, but able to communicate with, one's own mind.

No doubt Klein's fantastical, dynamic use of language is untenable to interpersonal theory. Interpersonal theory at times eschews both the idea of an unconscious and the concept of self. As is well known, Sullivan considered the self an illusion. Ogden (1982) presents a model of projective identification that bridges interpersonal and intrapsychic models of mind. He posits that projective identification is a process that is both intrasubjective and interpersonal. His model of projective identification privileges a two-step process in which a circumscribed piece of unconscious self, typically disruptive to self-coherence, is split off and then, through the employment of nonverbal, inchoate interpersonal pressure, is communicated to another.

Acknowledgment of the process of projective identification would be tantamount to acknowledging yet another use of the analyst's self in the psychotherapy endeavor. Not only do patients unknowingly and unconsciously communicate important unconscious material to the therapist, but the therapist unconsciously and unknowingly can communicate unconscious aspects of their selves to the patients.

Consider first the therapist-to-patient direction of unconscious projective identification. In this way patients come to know our anxieties, fears, biases, likes, and dislikes. If we remain unaware of what we are communicating unconsciously via projective identification, a patient, mystified by the communication, might engage us in a struggle we now refer to as an enactment. One way out of the enactment is for therapists to comb their own unconscious in order to both recognize and work through an issue of their own, an issue that can be, in its unprocessed form, contributing to the enactment. In a previous article (Skolnick, 2005), I describe an enactment of the therapist's sadistic impulses communicated to a patient through a projective identification. The situation is resolved when the therapist recognizes and works through his own sadism, allowing the patient to acknowledge, explore, and work through her own split-off and projected sadism. The analyst's use of himself in this situation involves a recognition, acknowledgment, and working through of his own projective identification in a manner that frees the patient to do the same with his own disavowed self.

Likewise, it becomes important for the analyst to be able to recognize when a patient is communicating something to the analyst by means of a projective identification. Often, these communications are experienced at first take by the analyst as uncanny, difficult to decipher, and affectively charged. This type of experience requires further use of the therapist's self in several ways. When having such an experience, the analyst needs to employ empathic and cognitive processes in order to be aware of, contain, and make use of the projective identification. If not, the analyst is more likely to respond in a complementary fashion and may retaliate or enact a similar type of defensive, self-protective maneuver. But if the analyst is able to recognize that a patient's communication is tweaking a similar organization in the analyst's internal world, it enables the analyst to contain the patient's projective identification in a fashion that makes it increasingly tolerable for the patient to reintroject the projection and integrate it into her own self-organization.

Imagine a patient who has been emotionally abused by a parent in such a way that the patient harbors, in his unconscious, unbearable feelings of ineffectiveness and helplessness. The patient, largely unaware of these unconscious feelings of inefficacy, might engage the analyst in an interpersonal encounter that renders the analyst feeling useless and incompetent. The analyst who does not recognize her feelings as a communication from the patient's split-off feelings of inefficacy runs the risk of either helpless, impotent resignation or angry retaliation. If the analyst can recognize her feelings of helplessness and uselessness as a communication from the patient—a projective identification, if you will—the analyst can use these feelings to fashion an intervention. In addition, a patient's projective identifications are usually attracted by disowned or painful parts of our own selves. These pieces of our own psychic organization function like lightning rods that attract another's projective identifications. In the above example, not only does the patient project his own uselessness onto the therapist, but also the therapist must have similar realms in her own psyche to receive the projections. It then becomes incumbent upon the therapist to acknowledge these painful places if the therapist is to be able to recognize the projective identification. If not, the therapist is likely to miss the patient's communication and retaliate defensively.

Basescu does not include in his toolbox working with unconscious projective identifications. He comes closest to acknowledging this use of self when he cites Singer's (1968) claim that analysts may, at times, be reluctant to make correct interpretations. Singer's quote is worth repeating here:

> The more to the point and the more penetrating the interpretation, the more obvious it will be that the therapist is talking and understanding from the depth of his own personal life. . . . It takes one to know one, and in his correct interpretation the therapist reveals that he is one. (p. 369)

How does it take one to know one? It is my contention that one source of knowledge about another person results from an unconscious communication whereby one subject (the patient) seeks out, discovers, and tweaks another subject's (the analyst's) unconscious. It is incumbent upon us to know not only our interpersonal selves but also the sounds of our own unconscious or preconscious selves. I would add unconscious communication, in the form of projective identification, to Basescu's list of tools of the trade.

Come Together

Previously (Skolnick & Warshaw, 1992) I noted that those writing from a relational perspective include theorists coming from diverse psychoanalytic backgrounds, including British object relations, interpersonal, self psychology, and contemporary Kleinian psychoanalytic schools. Relational theory has also been informed by gender studies, mother-infant research, and developmental and attachment theory and research. What joins these diverse schools under one relational umbrella is the belief that the fundamental building blocks of mental life are to be found in human relationships. I have always, and still, consider the so-called relational school a work in progress. I see it as a dialogue amongst non-Freudian psychologies in which important similarities and differences are being sharpened and outlined. More recently, I've become aware that psychoanalysts who are writing from a relational perspective but who come from different theoretical traditions are inexorably moving closer together. Commonalities are being cited between such unlikely bedfellows as contemporary Kleinians and interpersonal theorists (Nachmani, 2009; Pantone, 2009). Frankel (1998) notes similarities between those identified as relational theorists and those from the interpersonal school. To be sure, important differences exist between the different schools, realms of unbridgeable divergence that cannot be reconciled. Reading Basescu's paper, it became eminently clear that there are tongues among interpersonal and relational theorists that do not speak with confusion. Basescu's tools of the trade can be remarkably similar to the tools utilized by those, including myself, who work from a relational vantage point.

Conclusion

So there I was, many years after completing my analysis, and finishing teaching a class of analytic candidates at the Westchester Center, a psychoanalytic training institute that meets in a northern suburb of New York City. It was late in the evening, and as I was leaving, exhausted from a long day of patients, meetings and teaching, this question came to mind: "Who else would deign to teach a course that meets weekly 8:30–10 p.m.? I love to teach, and I know a lot of people love to teach. But how many would teach at this hour? After such a long day?" I exited the room and immediately ran into Sabe. He was teaching in an adjacent classroom. "Ah!" I said to myself, and as I did, the image of Sabe and me conducting classes at the same time a few feet apart in adjoining rooms came to my mind. I chuckled. I knew perfectly well that I started teaching during the time I was in analysis with Sabe. I also knew I never had the ambition to teach until I went into analysis. And there we were, a score or so years later, teaching within a few feet of each other at this late hour. Do you imagine Sabe Basescu's use of self influenced my life? In this case, was there not a concordant identification with the analyst? I'll let you, the reader, decide.

References

Aron, L. (1996). *A meeting of minds: Mutuality in psychoanalysis.* Hillsdale, NJ: Analytic Press.

Basescu, S. (1990a). Show and tell: Reflections on the analyst's self-disclosure. In G. Stricker & M. Fisher (Eds.), *Self-disclosure in the therapeutic relationship* (pp. 47–59). New York: Plenum.

Basescu, S. (1990b). Tools of the trade: The use of the self in psychotherapy. *Group, 14,* 157–165.

Benjamin, J. (1995). *Like subjects, love objects: Essays on recognition and sexual difference.* New Haven, CT: Yale University Press.

Bromberg, P. (1994). "Speak! That I may see you": Some reflections on dissociation, reality, and psychic listening. *Psychoanalytic Dialogues, 4,* 517–547.

Chomsky, N. (1986). *Language and mind.* New York: Harcourt, Brace, & World.

Davies, J. M. (2004). Whose bad objects are we anyway? Repetition and our elusive love affair with evil. *Psychoanalytic Dialogues, 14,* 711–733.

Fairbairn, W. R. D. (1958). On the nature and aims of psychoanalytical treatment. *International Journal of Psychoanalysis, 29,* 374–385.

Frankel, J. B. (1998). Are interpersonal psychoanalysis and relational psychoanalysis the same? *Contemporary Psychoanalysis, 34,* 485–500.

Levensor, E. A. (1983). *The ambiguity of change: An inquiry into the nature of psychoanalytic reality.* New York: Basic Books.

Nachmani, G. (2009). Hatred and devaluation of the other: A post-Kleinian and interpersonal perspective. Paper presented at Division 39 of the APA, San Antonio, TX.

Ogden, T. (1982). *Projective identification: Psychotherapeutic technique.* New York: Jason Aronson.

Ogden, T. (1986). *The matrix of the mind: Object relations and the psychoanalytic dialogue.* Northvale, NJ: Jason Aronson.

Ogden, T. (1994). *Subjects of analysis.* Northvale, N.J.: Jason Aronson.

Pantone, P. (2009). Who's afraid of Melanie Klein? Paper presented at Division 39 of the APA, San Antonio, TX.

Pick, I. B. (1985). Working through in the countertransference. In E. B. Spillius (Ed.), *Melanie Klein today* (Vol. 2, pp. 29–40). London: Routledge.

Singer, E. (1968). The reluctance to interpret. In E. Hammer (Ed.), *Uses of interpretation in treatment.* New York: Grune & Stratton.

Skolnick, N. J. (2005). What's a good object to do? *Psychoanalytic Dialogues, 16,* 1–29.

Skolnick, N. J., & Warshaw, S. C. (1992). *Relational perspectives in psychoanalysis.* Hillsdale, NJ: Analytic Press.

COMMENTARY BY GEORGE WHITSON

I met Sabe Basescu in the early 1980s. Over the years my involvement with Sabe encompassed class work, committee collaboration, papers presented (both his and mine), small group discussions, dinners out, and an occasional tennis game. Even though it's been a number of years since we've had any substantial contact, many of Sabe's attitudes and perspectives still resonate with me. This is especially true in the area of the impact of the analyst's personality in the therapeutic process. Over the years I have often applied concepts learned from Sabe in my clinical work and especially with candidates in training. To truly appreciate the power of Sabe Basescu's so-called self-centered papers, I suggest that you assign the first in the series, "Anxieties in the Analyst" (1977), to any class or supervisee. The sense of immediate recognition and relief that others feel those same anxieties is often palpable.

My first meaningful involvement with Sabe was when I was a student affiliated with the interpersonal track at the NYU Postdoctoral Program. During those years the interpersonal track was a heterogeneous group loosely bound together by a common belief in the importance of lived experience and the two-person nature of clinical work. The track included classical Sullivanians, those deeply influenced by Fromm, existential humanists, and those identified with the British object relations school. Students set up their own curriculum and chose instructors from across the metapsychological spectrum. It was an exciting time to be in analytic training. I had the opportunity to participate in didactic and clinical seminars with seminal thinkers such as Benjamin Wolstein, Edgar Levenson, and Joseph Barnett. The full range of interpersonal theory was well represented by an articulate faculty who could debate with intensity and passion. These years also served as a critical developmental period for what was to become the relational position. For example, Manny Ghent offered a course that blended classical interpersonal theory with British object relations theory and foreshadowed his break with the interpersonal track. And then there was Sabert Basescu. In some ways his was a lone voice in his solitary representation of the existential and phenomenological positions. While clearly identified as an existentialist, Sabe taught his seminar from an atheoretical perspective, focusing on thorny issues in clinical practice, ranging from fee and billing policies to patient crises and self-disclosure.

My clearest memory from that seminar was how present Sabe was. He exuded an air of confidence, patience, and focus. While Sabe was respectful of our comments, he always moved the discussion to the immediacy of our experience. It quickly became clear that patient history, theoretical perspectives, and diagnostic thinking were irrelevant in this course. He showed little interest in how we came to our perspectives or if they lined up with his position. The interchange of student viewpoints, Sabe's attitudes, and the unfolding dynamics of the class all had a sense of immediacy. These conversations were never embedded in technical language. There were moments of anxiety, but remarkably, I remember little self-consciousness. This accepting tone left us with the confidence to begin to speak from our own subjective perspectives rather than paraphrasing theoretical constructs.

Rereading "Tools of the Trade: The Use of the Self in Psychotherapy" for the first time in many years, I am reminded of my time with Sabe, and struck by how well the article captured the experience of being with him. Sabe's willingness to present his theoretical and clinical views from such an exposed personal stance reflects his guiding principle that the unique personality of the analyst is a central variable in the outcome of the therapy. To keep within the spirit of personal exposure that mark Sabe's "self-centered" papers, I will try to weave into my discussion of the article examples from my early years with Sabe as teacher and mentor. I view Sabe's paper not only as reflective of his personal decisions concerning self-disclosure but also as an invitation to apply it to our own clinical work.

Theoretically, Sabe worked from an existential/phenomenological center. With the exception of Hoffman's (1998) articles focusing on meaning, mortality, and death anxiety and Yalom's writing (1980), existentialism rarely figures within contemporary analytic dialogue. At the same time, existentialism's basic tenets of an agentic self, free will, and the relevance of immediate experience remain at the heart of current issues of clinical practice. This timeliness makes Sabe's reflections all the more relevant today.

While Sabe's existential position maintains dimensions of both a defined theoretical stance and a prescribed clinical approach, it would be more accurate to consider it an encompassing attitude through which he approached both critical thinking and clinical practice. Sabe's existential orientation also reflects qualities of traditional interpersonal theory. Levenson (2000) identifies the two parameters of investigation that most identify the interpersonal position. He states: "There is some variety of detailed inquiry into the patient's life (past, present, real, fantasized). Second, there is close attention to the nuances of the patient–therapist interactional field. The therapist is considered a co-participant in the creation of that field" (p. 119). Clearly Basescu's work emphasizes Levenson's second criterion. Sabe describes it as "being fully present, available and freely responsive to the ongoing interpersonal interactions" (p. 163). With his emphasis on immediate experience, Sabe's conceptualizations have much in common with the tradition of Fromm (1947) and Wolstein (1983), the latter a contemporary and colleague.

Given the growth of multiple interpersonal and relational positions that emphasize the coparticipatory nature of analytic work, a two-dimensional categorization limits and obscures the many differences that exist within this broad spectrum. A comprehensive interpersonal schema, utilizing contemporary analytic concepts, was developed by Fiscalini (2004) to try to delineate differences within the interpersonal/relational position. Fiscalini has divided interpersonal analysts into four broad categories. The first group he labeled "traditional interpersonalists," which includes traditional Sullivanians with their emphasis on "detailed inquiry" in their work. The second group, the "eclectic integrationists" or "relationalists," are seen by Fiscalini as trying to meld multiple metapsychological positions such as object relations, self psychology, and ego psychology with the interpersonal view. The remaining two groups are the "radical empiricists" and the "radical preservationists." Those theorists have extended the notion of participant observation to a model of coparticipation created by both participants. The radical empiricists, among whom I include Sabe Basescu, are differentiated from the radical preservationists by their "emphasis on the curative role of experience rather than that of formulative hermeneutics" (p. 56). In addition, Fiscalini states that the radical empiricists "bring a clinical focus to bear on the intrapersonal" (p. 56). Fiscalini's emphasis on the intrapersonal (1988) echoes the qualities of Sabe's agentic self. This knowable, more permanent self, which is central to existentialism, is in many ways analogous to Wolstein's psychic center of the psychoanalytic self (1983) and Fiscalini's intrapersonal self (1988). Both Wolstein and Basescu were pioneers of the coparticipant model, with its emphasis on lived experience rather than historical reconstruction. This wing of the interpersonal movement shares an emphasis on what Fiscalini succinctly captures as "formation not just formulation of new experience" (p. 202).

In a clear and brief review, Sabe moves the reader through some of the most contentious metapsychological arguments of the 1980s. Is transference a distortion or reflective of the "real relationship"? Should we conceptualize it as a one- or two-person model? Is therapist anonymity desirable or even possible? What do we mean by neutrality? Is neutrality a desirable analytic attitude or is it an undesirable anachronism, as when Sabe describes it as "operationalized in anonymity" (p. 158)? Students of the history of psychoanalytic theory are well acquainted with these discussions. For the sake of brevity I will simply note that I share with Sabe the notion that therapist authenticity dictates and supersedes technical issues such as neutrality and that authenticity is at the heart of the efficacy of the therapeutic relationship.

Sabe's passion was the study of the intricacies of the phenomenology of clinical interaction. "Tools of the Trade" focuses on the use of the self: its benefits, consequences, and dangers. Two immutable beliefs underlie his clinical orientation: the coconstructed nature of the therapeutic relationship and the impact of the therapist's unique personality in the work. These two concepts are intertwined, as one inevitably influences the other. Sabe states his underlying belief early: "The therapist's unique person and personality are always impacting on the therapeutic relationship, and it behooves the analyst to recognize them as such" (p. 158).

Sabe's discussion of self-disclosure is enriched by an understanding of his conceptualization of the therapeutic relationship. At its center, the mutative power of the relationship depends on the ability of both participants to create and maintain an authentic relationship. Sabe summarizes it clearly: "The truthfulness with which the participants can explore and acknowledge what it is that is going on between them empowers the relationship to be an agent for change" (p. 158). While many of Sabe's perspectives on the therapeutic relationship would be familiar to interpersonal and relational analysts, there are two points worth highlighting. For an existentialist, the concept of agency has particular meaning. It introduces the concept of will and the responsibility of both participants to take ownership of the choices they make in the work. Agency implies two proactive selves mutually influencing each other, but more than just a sum of their interpersonal dimensions. Sabe's therapeutic relationship is not curative in itself, and it certainly isn't a corrective emotional experience. The relationship is a mechanism by which change can happen.

Once Sabe develops his case that neutrality is more fictional than real, he directs our attention to the various ways and reasons analysts self-disclose. He first addresses the broad area of inadvertent self-disclosures. In his penchant for brevity Sabe only summarizes manifestations of self-disclosure rather than teasing out the nuances intrinsic to each.

> There are further, perhaps more profound, ways in which analysts reveal themselves inadvertently. The questions asked and not asked, the content focused upon, the connections made, the fleeting and not so fleeting emotions invariably displayed, the facts remembered and the facts forgotten—all convey information about the analysts interests, values, theories, anxieties and emotions. (p. 159)

In this single paragraph Sabe conveys many of the rich and complex ways that analysts may be seen. Let me offer a personal example that captures an inadvertent self-disclosure and which I hope conveys a sense of what it was like to work with Sabe.

During our seminar discussion of self-disclosure, class members were presenting their own personal examples; I described an interaction with a patient who was also a psychologist. She referred to a session that she had cancelled a few weeks earlier. I had filled the hour with another patient, and so, given my billing policy, had not needed to charge her. She said, quite suddenly and with a tone of disdain, "I would never have paid you for that, and if you insisted I'd have quit." Her response was unexpected, out of rhythm with how I knew her. It was also discordant with my experience of the tone of our relationship. I remembered being left speechless, feeling blindsided and embarrassed. After a few moments another student asked what my self-disclosure had been. I realized I didn't know, and I couldn't understand why I had volunteered this example. Sabe suggested simply, "It was the look on your face." Exactly right. I didn't flush because I was startled by the tone of her comment. I felt I had misread the nature of our relationship, and my face had revealed my embarrassment at being caught so unaware—"the fleeting and not so fleeting emotions invariably displayed" (p. 159). In a few words, Sabe captured the essence of my experience and reflected it back: succinctly, right to the core of the issue, and with little elaboration. Sabe's clarification alerted me to my self-consciousness, but I was left to develop its meaning on my own. For Sabe the moment was often enough.

In my own work, I am more likely to embed these powerful here-and-now moments in our shared therapeutic life or within the larger context of what we have been exploring. The same is true with embedding experience in the patient's personal history. Sabe doesn't report linking immediate experience with his patient's history. His concern seems to be that focusing on a patient's history may lead to a dilution of the patient's immediate experience and/or the reification of the patient as a victim of his or her experience. My belief is that here-and-now experience, left freestanding, may not sufficiently contextualize it in ways that would allow for more nuance and subtlety in the patient's experience of self.

I find this especially true with patients who have histories of early abuse and trauma and who dissociate. To embed powerful clarifying moments in actual life experience can provide a framework for otherwise chaotic self states and allow for the development of a narrative of coherent meaning. It may also provide a framework to locate the patient in the present and as an agent for constructing a future.

One form of inadvertent self-disclosure not addressed directly by Sabe occurs when personal metaphors emerge or shift in relation to changes in the therapist's life. In clinical supervision, I have noted changes in a candidate's choice of language or metaphor that have revealed personal data. A female analyst utilized increasing references to signs of patient growth, new construction, and a healthy emerging self. She later revealed that she was pregnant. A male analyst referred to a patient's terror about never ridding himself of his "toxic" mother. At other times he utilized phrasing such as "encapsulated" and "growths within." He had recently been diagnosed with cancer. While both supervisees had been aware of their physical condition, they had been unaware of the ways in which it permeated their language. Once we discussed these metaphoric shifts, both therapists found previously unnoticed artifacts of their unacknowledged situations contained within patient communications including dream content. Regardless of a therapist's awareness of his or her communications, the patient often apprehends these shifts. To this point, Sabe states that "patients attempt to arrive at a plausible understanding of the analytic relationship" (p. 157). We must be vigilant about the impact of dissonant messages to patients when inadvertent self-disclosures differ from the therapist's conscious self-presentation. A significant discrepancy has the potential to have an impact upon the patient's sense of safety within the relationship.

Sabe's review of inadvertent disclosures is followed by a discussion of conscious, deliberate self-revelations. Here he changes his discussion to the first person singular. In wonderfully clear language Sabe describes what led him to self-disclose: facts, feelings, or attitudes. Sabe's choices are personally descriptive rather than prescriptive. In my work with candidates, I often suggest that students monitor their self-disclosures over time, not just noticing the what and why of their decision to disclose but paying particular attention to their felt state at the time of each disclosure. As Sabe has noted, deliberate self-revelations may feel "driven, compelled or manipulated" (p. 160). Sabe is emphasizing pressures within each unique treatment. I would add that the choice and timing of deliberate self-revelations reflect characterological dimensions of the analyst. In accepting psychoanalysis as co-constructed, Sabe's thinking anticipates by more than a decade the idea that these influences are bidirectional.

Sabe's guiding credo is to address anything that appears to have the potential to endanger the authenticity of the work. The broad dictum includes a variety of life changes or personal issues that impinge on the work. I recently was reminded of this during the final week of writing this article, when I was really pushing to finish it. A patient referenced a point I made in a previous session and realized that I had no idea what she was referring to. She gave me more and more information to help me remember. With each additional hint there was increased stress in her voice. I decided to tell her that I had been preoccupied with finishing this paper for the past two weeks and had thought about little else. She was relieved and said, "Thanks, otherwise I would really think I was crazy." In essence I said, "It's me, not you." This freed her to go on with what she had wanted to explore. Sabe reminds us that regardless of what we disclose, it is our primary responsibility to monitor the impact of our comments and remain curious about our motivations for disclosing.

A particular concern of mine arises when the examinations of our motivations stay anchored to particular exchanges with particular patients. My experience is that choices that seem spontaneous are often more reflective of the analyst's character. One way to operationalize our curiosity is to expand specific self-disclosures in our larger worldview. Ghent (1989), speaking to the larger issue of the analyst's personal credo, says that this credo is

> basically a belief system, that the analyst lives and works by (and there is no assurance that the analyst has full conscious access to the system under which he or she is really operating)—[and that it] makes a very significant difference as to how one hears, what one hears, how one assembles what is heard, and how one conducts oneself in the analytic setting. (p. 170)

We also must be alert to the subtle, often unattended ways in which therapists attempt to influence patients' attitudes. This often happens to manage patient anger or disappointment, but not infrequently to generate positive feeling as well as narcissistic admiration. Hirsch (2007) has noted, for example, that many of these unattended behaviors are in the service of our economic security.

Our current financial crisis presents us with great anxiety for both patients and therapists. During this period, clinicians are managing their own economic woes from risky market investments to loss of value in their assets. Sabe's caution about staying authentic in the work is particularly relevant to the acknowledgment of this economic anxiety. There is increased economic pressure for therapists to keep their patients in treatment. Sabe's comments on inadvertent self-disclosure would encourage all of us to remember that our patients intuit our reactions. It behooves us to capture the extent of our own anxiety so that we do not manipulate patients to continue in treatment. Sabe states: "The mutuality of relevant self-revelation works against the mystification of experience in the relationship and allows for the development of intimacy and trust" (p. 162).

As analysts, we still can demonstrate an ambivalent relationship with finding our own voice independent of where and how we trained. Some of us may speak mainly in the voice of our analyst or supervisor. Others feel safer staying within the metaphors of our belief systems. Given our coparticipant model, if we are going to ask ourselves to have the courage to speak in our own voice, it is clear we need to continue to foster ways to help articulate our unique self and speak from that personal place.

Looking back on my time as a candidate at NYU, I appreciate the diversity and complexity of both the theoretical and the clinical perspectives I experienced. But with Sabe, these safe and important constructs retreated to the background, leaving me with access to my own voice. For that I will always be grateful.

References

Basescu, S. (1977). Anxieties in the analyst: An autobiographical account. In K. A. Frank (Ed.), *The human dimension in psychoanalytic practice* (pp. 153–163). New York: Grune & Stratton.

Fiscalini, J. (1988). Curative experience in the analytic relationship. *Contemporary Psychoanalysis, 24*, 125–141.

Fromm, E. (1947). *Man for himself.* New York: Harper & Row.

Ghent, E. (1989). Credo: The dialectics of one-person and two-person psychologies. *Contemporary Psychoanalysis, 25*, 169–211.

Hirsch, I. (2007). *Coasting in the countertransference: Conflicts of self interest between analyst and patient.* New York: Analytic Press.

Hoffman, I. Z. (1998). *Ritual and spontaneity in the psychoanalytic process: A dialectical-constructivist view.* Hillsdale, NJ: Analytic Press.

Levenson, E. A. (2000). An interpersonal perspective on dreams: Commentary on paper by Hazel Ipp. *Psychoanalytic Dialogues, 10*, 119–125.
Wolstein, B. (1983). The pluralism of perspectives on countertransference. *Contemporary Psychoanalysis, 19*, 506–521.
Yalom, I. (1980). *Existential psychotherapy*. New York: Basic Books.

TOOLS OF THE TRADE: THE USE OF THE SELF IN PSYCHOTHERAPY*

The public image of the typical psychoanalyst has always been given expression in many jokes and satirical comments such as, "He always answers a question with a question," or "I knew he was alive because I could hear him breathing." That image has been consistent with the classical analytic role of the blank screen which discloses no personal facts, reveals no emotions, but simply mirrors the projections of the patient. But there has been an evolution in the conception of the role of the therapist from mirror to participant observer to human being or, as Michels (1986) puts it, "from authority to collaborator" (p. 288). Each succeeding role does not displace the former, as in the Kuhnian (1962) sense of a succeeding paradigm overthrowing a former one, but rather exists alongside of the others. That is, most analysts seem to function in each role at some time with the same patient and to varying degrees with different patients. Of course, the analyst's theoretical allegiance might be expected to govern the predominance of one role over others. In any case, each succeeding role does involve a greater degree of involvement on the part of the analyst than the former one.

It is the meaning of analyst as human being that I will deal with in the presentation. It does not mean "letting it all hang out" or other aspects of what might be called "wild analysis." Nor does it mean obliterating the boundaries of a professional relationship. It does mean being attentive, interested, caring, respectful, and empathic. It also means being natural, unstudied, and real. But more than that, it presumes a specific conception of transference and countertransference.

Is transference a one-person or two-person affair (Gill, 1984)? Those who hold to the one-person model see the patient's distorting perceptions of the analyst as coming whole cloth from the patient's past experience as structured by his or her intrapsychic dynamics.

Those who hold to the two-person model see transference as interactional. That is, transference is regarded as the patient's attempt to arrive at

* This paper originally appeared in *Group, 14*(3), 1990, pp. 157–165. Reprinted with permission of Springer Science and Business Media.

a plausible understanding of the analytic relationship and is more or less influenced by the analyst's behavior. The concern is less with the patient's distortions and more with constriction in modes of understanding.

In other words, the therapist's unique person and personality are always impacting on the therapeutic relationship, and it behooves the therapist to recognize them as such. Similarly, the therapist's countertransference is not simply an undesirable interference; rather, it refers to the therapist's total responsiveness to the other person in the therapeutic relationship. In that sense, countertransference can never be avoided, it can only be denied—and in its denial it becomes problematic and obstructionistic. In its acknowledgment, however, it becomes the therapist's single more useful clue to understanding what it is like to be in the world of the other.

The patient–therapist relationship is the most immediate and experientially cogent area in which to explore the patterns of interpersonal relatedness and the role that each person plays in actively creating and maintaining these patterns. What is unique about psychoanalysis, as opposed to other therapies, is the focus of this relationship, the nature and structure of which colors the way all other experiences are dealt with in the analysis. That is, it acts like a filter system through which other experiences are seen and processed. The exploration of this filter system itself is the primary work of psychoanalysis.

The direct person-to-person encounter between patient and analyst "creates a history together, experienced as relevant engagement and characterized by wholeness and complexity" (Held-Weiss, 1986, p. 3). The truthfulness with which the participants can explore and acknowledge what it is that is going on between them empowers the relationship to be an agent for change.

The patient and therapist are "a complex two-person system whose actions and reactions to one another are of coequal importance and concern" (Strupp, 1989, p. 719). This view of the therapist's role requires reexamination of some traditionally conceived attributes of the therapist's functioning, namely, neutrality, anonymity, and self-disclosure.

Psychoanalysis, as a nondescriptive discipline, has traditionally maintained the importance of the therapist's neutrality. The means by which neutrality has usually been operationalized is therapist anonymity. By avoiding disclosure of values, feelings, judgments, and personal experiences, the therapist is presumed to convey neutrality.

But what is really conveyed? Here is an excerpt from a session. The patient, a well-trained and experienced analyst, was speaking of her work and describing how she is plagued by self-doubts—thoughts of not doing enough for her patients or not doing something right. I said that I thought the problem was not so much the self-doubting questions—we all have those—but the consequences. "For you it's life and death, for me there'll be other chances."

In the following session she said she had a dream that night.

A nice dream. I was dressing in a different style—a checked blouse, blue and aqua, more comfortable and stylish. It made me very happy. It was such a happy dream. I was dressing more like women I admire—effortlessly. I just found things in my closet and realized they could go together. It was a color I like but never wear. I tend to wear somber tones. I don't like to . . . I'm ambivalent about calling attention to myself.

She spontaneously went on to say,

I feel the dream is related to the last session. It was revealing when you said last time that for you the consequences aren't dire. You said something about yourself. That's meaningful to me. I feel you care about me. For me, anonymity of my therapist duplicates my background with my parents. I never knew anything about my parents' experience of themselves. I remember being thrilled once that my mother colored in my coloring book. I have only one or two memories of my father revealing something about himself. Your anonymity is not background but a constant stimulus. It's not freeing. It's provocative.

Whatever the other messages conveyed in this, one seems to be that if I show my true colors, she feels freer to show hers. This is consistent with Jourard's (1971) research findings that the best way to foster self-disclosure is to model it: "Intimate self-disclosure begets intimate self-disclosure" (p. 17). Greenberg (1986) makes the point that personal revelations may enhance or detract from neutrality. There is no fixed relationship between the two. He goes on to write: "The analyst who maintains a posture of aloofness—that is the analyst who has confused the behavior of anonymity with the goal of neutrality—offers the patient no context within which to appreciate the nature of his transference" (p. 95).

But there is even a further question as to the desirability of the neutral stance itself, especially when it doesn't reflect the true state of the analyst's feelings—and how often it is that we analysts feel truly neutral? Wachtel (1986) writes, "For some patients, the stance of neutrality can contribute to their tendency to invalidate their own perceptions and even to doubt their own sanity" (p. 66). The increasing recognition and acknowledgement that the analytic relationship is a fully human encounter between two more alike than different, fallible human beings, implies that neutrality may be primarily a technical fiction, more honored in the breach, rather than an analytic attribute. However, what is indisputably an analytic attribute is the striving to analyze and understand deviations from neutrality, which may or may not be countertransferential, and to deal with them openly in the context of the therapeutic relationship. Ehrenberg (1982) writes,

> What defines an analytic relationship is that our impact, whether the result of deliberate interventions or the result of inadvertent aspects of our participation, must be explicitly clarified. . . . The hallmark of an analytic relationship is that it is essential that there be no covert manipulation and that the patient be cognizant of whatever critical transactions have occurred as well as the impact. (p. 540)

It is by virtue of this openness that the essential attributes of analytic neutrality is maintained, namely, that control of the patient remains in the patient's hands, not in the analyst's.

It is obvious that anonymity as such is always a matter of degree. Analysts show themselves all the time in their dress, in their office surroundings, in their manner of speaking, in the way they establish time and money ground rules, and in the myriad ways of being that are publicly observable. One person knew when my eyeglass prescription changed. Another took me to task for the horrible painting I had on my office wall. (Since I was a part-time tenant in someone else's office at the time, I was sorely tempted to disclaim any responsibility for the painting that I didn't like either.) Somebody was pleased that I didn't wear a tie. Somebody else assumed I was going to a bar mitzvah when I did wear one. (It was actually a funeral.) My books have been criticized. My plants have been taken to mean that I'm good at making people grow. My cough meant I was getting a cold. My eyes showed that I was tired. My car proved I didn't know much about cars, and the loud voice on the other end of the phone indicated I was a hen-pecked husband, not all of such conclusions are accurate, but some are, and some are more accurate than I initially gave them credit for being.

There are further, perhaps more profound, ways in which analysts reveal themselves inadvertently. The questions asked and not asked, the content focused upon, the connections made, the fleeting and not so fleeting emotions invariably displayed, the facts remembered and the facts forgotten—all convey information about the analyst's interests, values, theories, anxieties, and emotions. Singer (1968) claims that analysts are, at times, reluctant to make correct interpretations:

The more to the point and the more penetrating the interpretation, the more obvious it will be that the therapist is talking and
understanding from the depth of his own psychological life. . . . It
takes one to know one, and in his correct interpretation the therapist reveals that he is one. (p. 369)

Patients come to know their analysts through the shared experience
of the therapeutic relationship. The quality of that subjective knowing
is not simply dependent upon knowing objective facts of the analyst's
personal life. Singer (1977) maintains that patients' readiness to know
their analysts, that is, to make use of the experience that is always available to them, is a measure of their psychological health.

So much for the kind of self-revelation that takes place whether we
wish it or not. There is also what we choose to disclose deliberately and
intentionally, although it may also be experienced as driven, compelled,
or manipulated. What analysts tell their patients about themselves runs
the full range of personal facts, opinions, feelings, reactions, associations, memories, experiences, fantasies, and dreams. Very few analysts
tell all, but some "wild" analysts do. It is a safe bet, however, that all
analysts tell something. The motivations, circumstances, and rationales
vary tremendously, as do the therapeutic consequences.

For example, Masud Khan (1986) informed his patients of his brother's death. He writes,

Analysts rarely speak about events in their personal life that affect
their work mutatively. The death of my brother had changed my
whole outlook on life, and I know my patients would sense it; so I
told them as much. It is not a question of transference or countertransference, but actually real, lived life that makes out fatedness
or destiny, and about which we are often somewhat devious, both
with ourselves and others. (p. 664)

Similarly, Singer (1971) reports that when his wife became seriously
ill, requiring him to frequently cancel appointments, he told his patients
the reason.

One analytic candidate I was supervising learned suddenly that she
had a cancerous growth and had to have a mastectomy. In discussing
how best to inform her patients, she decided she would tell them in general terms that she would be out for some weeks for surgery but she did
not feel comfortable being more specific than that. However, when she
returned to work after the surgery and was confronted by her patients'
fantasies, especially the fantasies that were correct or near-correct, she

was unable to contain her own distress and burst into tears. At that point she told them the fuller story.

Some years ago I had a back condition that left me unable to sit, although I could stand or lie down comfortably enough. I chose to continue working and informed the people I was seeing that I would have to use the couch myself for about one month. I could discern no disruptive impact on the work and have since talked with a number of other analysts who have had similar experiences with similar results.

In none of these situations, or a host of others like them, have I heard of destructive consequences for the analysis. One might anticipate that the analyst's misfortune or infirmity would mobilize sadistic, vengeful or hostile impulses, but a common theme seems to be the desire to be helpful. The asymmetrical structure of the analytic relationship, with the patient expected to be needy and the analyst helpful, can induce a humiliating sense of uselessness in the patient, without the opportunity for reality-oriented and constructive relatedness (see Singer, 1971). A woman dreamed that when she came for her session, she found me on the couch with a fever and she put a cool, damp washcloth on my forehead. We both understood the dream to mean that she wanted to be helpful to me as I was to her.

One moral to be drawn from these experiences is that when the analyst's life impacts upon his or her work, it is in service of clarifying the patient's attempts to make sense out of the relationship to acknowledge the facts of life. However, there are dangers in such disclosures, having less to do with the patient's ability to handle the facts and more to do with the analyst's motives in disclosing them. If the analyst is exploiting the patient by eliciting sympathy, warding off criticism or anger, or manipulating a feeling of intimacy, the disclosures are likely to be destructively double-binding.

Other occasions on which I have found it useful to tell of events in my life have to do with my feeling that some messages are better conveyed through recounting experiences than by saying what you mean. That is, in order to convey that I understand something that has been told to me, I might briefly tell of a similar experience that I've had. Or when working with someone who feels so separate and different from the rest of the human race, I might say something about myself that bridges that feeling of distance. One woman said, "I had a bad weekend. Other people are stable. I'm so up and down, I hate my rockiness." I said, "Don't we all?" She: "You too?" I: "Does that surprise you?" She: "Well, I guess not. You're human too." I understood that to mean she also felt human, at least for the moment. On another occasion she expressed her anguish that something was so wrong with her because her therapy took so long. I said I was in analysis for 8 years, and that was only the first time. She said she felt better knowing that I didn't feel she was taking too long and wasn't fed up with her. I am aware that she may have meant something was wrong with me because her therapy took so long, and that's an issue we have also dealt with.

There are those inevitable times when the analyst's personal issues intrude upon the work and disrupt the patient's understanding of what's happening. The most likely outcome is for the patient to assume the blame and experience self-contempt. At such times it is essential that the analyst acknowledge the intrusion. Ehrenberg (1984) puts it: "No matter how entangled analysts find themselves they must be able to reestablish the analytic integrity of the relationship. The process of doing so actually becomes the medium of the analytic work, and may involve making the analyst's reactions explicit to engage the patient in a collaborative way" (p. 563).

Prior to my taking a brief out-of-town trip, a man who knew where I was going wished me a good time and began to tell me of interesting things to do there. I somewhat brusquely replied that I'd been there before. In the session following my return he was angry and had been upset for hours after the previous session, feeling rejected by me, as if something were wrong with him. Although these were characteristic reactions of his, I suggested that there might be other possible explanations. I went on to say that I did cut him off because I was not going to have that kind of vacation and felt somewhat deprived about it. He said it helped to know that. I said that he was always ready to see something wrong with himself; sometimes there were things wrong with others.

Michels (1983) claims,

> The primary data of psychoanalysis are neither what happens in childhood nor what happens in adult life, and not even the cause-effect relationship between them; the primary data are what the patient says in the analyst's present, how the analyst responds, and how the patient can make constructive use of the experiential and dialectical process. (p. 61)

This points to what I think is the predominant area of analysts' self-disclosure, namely, what the analyst says about his or her reactions to what transpires in the relationship between the two people. It is predominant in importance, in relevance to the therapeutic work, and in frequency of occurrence. It is also probably the least controversial area of analysts' self-disclosure.

The mutuality of relevant self-revelation works against the mystification of experience in the relationship and allows for the development of intimacy and trust. In that context, unattended-to or anxiety-laden aspects of relatedness can be acknowledged and clarified, and resistance overcome. Wolf (1983) claims that

> since in essence, resistance is nothing but fear of being traumatically injured again, the decisive event of its analysis is the moment when the analysand has gained courage from these self-revelations of the analyst to know that the analyst does not need to feed on the patient to achieve cohesion and harmony. (p. 500)

At times I feel prompted to express something I'm thinking or feeling in a session, but I almost always respond to a patient's questioning me about it. If I am asked, I generally answer. For example, a man, himself a therapist, previously told me that he looks to see if I am glad to see him. This time, as he scrutinizes me when I come into the waiting room, something strikes me funny, and I can't stop myself from broadly smiling as he enters the office. He asks me why I'm smiling, and I tell him it's because he's scrutinizing me. He says, "That's no answer. I realize you don't have to answer me." I say, "Your looking at me had a whimsical quality that struck me funny." He says, "That's an answer. Thanks. That helps me know something about myself." When I asked him what it helped him know he told me that oftentimes people don't take him seriously and that perhaps he doesn't present himself as serious.

A woman who is familiar with psychotherapeutic literature but not in the profession herself asked me if I would give her a reprint or reference for anything I've written. I told her I didn't care what she read but I didn't want to give her what she asked for. She asked why not, saying that she could get it on her own and this would simply save her some trouble. That made sense to me, but I still didn't feel right about doing it, although I wasn't clear why. She pressed for a reason and I said, "Well, let's see if I can be clear about it. It's because I don't want to participate in or reinforce something that I don't know the meaning of. My job is to analyze the meaning, not to collude with it." She said, "I understand that," and then told me she wanted something of mine to have while I was away on vacation. That then was what we dealt with.

I generally find that the process of answering questions about what is going on with me at the moment helps clarify for both of us what's happening. It often has the additional consequence of enabling further exploration of the patient's experience. It conveys a respectful attitude toward the other and enhances the spirit of collaboration.

Another class of personal reactions that I tend to readily express are those that are discrepant with what seems to be going on. I've said things like, "You're smiling while you tell me this, but I feel sad.

I wonder why," or "I feel like I'm listening to a lecture," or "I have the feeling of being buttered up." I think it is fairly common for analysts to rely on their own reactive emotional sensibilities for clues to understanding the less obvious aspects of what is enacted. Disclosing these feeling reactions invites an experiential exploration of more than meets the eye. It also conveys to the other person the kind of impact he or she is having.

Vulnerable people tend to defend themselves against humiliation in ways that often bring about the very hurts they are trying to avoid. The therapeutic relationship affords a unique opportunity to experience these defensive patterns and their consequences in a context that allows for learning, not simply blind repetition. I saw a woman who was in therapy with me, a therapist herself, at a professional meeting. From her look and manner I gathered she would be more comfortable if I kept my distance, which I did. In the session following she told me how hurt she was that I was so unfriendly, as if I were letting her know that she should make no mistake about the boundaries of our relationship. I told her how I had felt warned away by her appearance and thought I was complying with her wishes. This led to our discussing other aspects of the same pattern. I observed that she never expressed interest in any aspect of my life, such as where I went on vacation or if I enjoyed it. She explained that she was fearful of my seeing her as intrusive and slapping her down for it. Her stance was that of rigid avoidance to forestall rejection. Her impact was that of indifference.

In thinking about the way I say things to people in therapy sessions, I realize that sometimes I know in advance what I'm going to say and sometimes I don't. I may formulate something or mull it over momentarily before I say it or it may just come out. A woman said to me critically that she never knew what to expect from me. I said, "That makes two of us," and that just came out. Two weeks later she said my remark stuck with her and she realized that unless you're rigid, you don't always know what you're going to say.

This bears upon the issue of the therapist's spontaneity. I think that when I'm working effectively I am functioning spontaneously—and that does not refer to whether or not I mull over things before I say them. It refers to freely functioning in the mode appropriate to being the analyst in a psychoanalytic relationship. One's way of being is influenced by the nature of the relationship, as in a marriage or in a friendship, or in a classroom or social gathering. The different structures elicit different modes of being and different behaviors. The differences are a function of varying meanings, purposes, and intentions. The manifestations of spontaneity vary as well.

While there clearly may be detrimental consequences to the analyst's self-disclosures under the best of circumstances, I think most problems are not caused by the analyst's true spontaneity but the lack of it. That is, inappropriate self-disclosures are those compulsively driven by the analyst's personal needs or responses to the patient's intimidating manipulations. If the analyst is operating out of countertransferential reactions like needing to impress the patient, or being defensive, seductive, hostile, controlling, fearful, or placating, personal revelations are likely to be intrusive, diverting, burdensome, inhibiting, or otherwise countertherapeutic. Saying whatever comes to mind may be the mark of thoughtless impulsivity. Being fully present, available, and freely responsive to the ongoing interpersonal interactions are to my mind the hallmarks of spontaneity.

The fact that the distinctions are often difficult to make has led many analysts to warn against self-disclosures. Gill (1983), for example, is concerned that the analyst's subjective experience may be defensive and that revealing it may result in shutting off further inquiry into the patient's experience. He is wary about changing the patient's analysis into mutual analysis. He emphasizes the importance of the analyst being especially alert to the patient's experience of any of the analyst's revelations—a point with which I would strongly concur.

On the other hand, there are those such as Coltart (1986), who writes, "If we are too protective of our self-presentation and of what we consider grimly to be the sacred rules of True Psychoanalysis, then we may suffocate something in the patient, in ourselves, and in the process" (p. 197). Or Symington (1986), who, in referring to owning and expressing his feelings reactions to the patient, writes, "Again when I acted from personal freedom rather than follow some specific technical regulation . . . then therapeutic shifts occurred. . . . My contention is that the inner act of freedom in the analyst causes a therapeutic shift in the patient and new insight, new learning and development in the analyst" (p. 260).

Clearly, the analyst's self-disclosure is an intervention that can cut both ways. However, we can no longer use what was always a mythologically conceived position of anonymity as a way out. We are who we are and it will out. Wolstein (1987) puts it, "Every psychoanalyst must seek a perspective and create a technique that allow the deeply private gift of talent to show itself; the inner voice gives a psychoanalyst the uniqueness of self and the wholeness of personality" (p. 348). It behooves each of us, in keeping with our professional responsibility to our patients, to do what we can to insure that the use we make of our selves is primarily in the service of the therapeutic enterprise, and not simply an act of self-indulgence.

One final word. In recent years I have written a number of self-centered papers on my work as an analyst: on the anxieties of the analyst (1977), the inner experience of the analyst (1987), and now this one. Therefore, it was heartening for me to read that in research on therapy outcomes, eight times as much outcome variance was accounted for by therapist differences as by treatment differences. Luborsky (1987) concluded, "The study of forms of treatment may be drastically less enlightening than the study of therapists, yet there are phenomenally more studies of the former" (p. 58). This confirms for me that the tools of the trade are not primarily found in theories and techniques but in the use of the self.

References

Basescu, S. (1977). Anxieties in the analyst: An autobiographical account. In K. A. Frank (Ed.), *The human dimension in psychoanalytic practice* (pp. 153–163). New York: Grune & Stratton.

Basescu, S. (1987). Behind the "seens": The inner experience of at least one psychoanalyst. *Psychoanalytic Psychology, 4*, 255–265.

Coltart, N. (1986). "Slouching towards Bethlehem . . ." or thinking the unthinkable in psychoanalysis. In G. Kohon (Ed.), *The British school of psychoanalysis: The independent tradition.* New Haven, CT: Yale University Press.

Ehrenberg, D. (1982). Psychoanalytic engagement: The transaction as primary data. *Contemporary Psychoanalysis, 18*(4), 535–555.

Ehrenberg, D. (1984). Psychoanalytic engagement II: Affective considerations. *Contemporary Psychoanalysis, 20*(4), 560–582.

Gill, M. (1984). Psychoanalysis and psychotherapy: A revision. *International Review of Psychoanalysis, 11*, 161–179.

Greenberg, J. (1986). The problem of analytic neutrality. *Contemporary Psychoanalysis, 22*(1), 87–106.

Held-Weiss, R. (1986). A note on spontaneity in the analyst. *Contemporary Psychoanalysis, 22*(1), 2–4.

Jourard, S. M. (1971). *Self-disclosure: An experimental analysis of the transparent self.* New York: Wiley.

Khan, M. R. (1986). Outrageousness, complaining and authenticity. *Contemporary Psychoanalysis, 22*(4), 629–651.

Kuhn, T. (1962). *The structure of scientific revolutions.* Chicago: University of Chicago Press.

Luborsky, L. (1987). Research can affect clinical practices : A happy turnaround. *Clinical Psychologist, 40*(3), 53–61.

Michels, R. (1983). Contemporary views of interpretation in psychoanalysis. In L. Grinspoon (Ed.), *Psychiatry update, VII.* Washington, DC: American Psychiatric Press.

Michels, R. (1986). How psychoanalysis changes. *Journal of the American Academy of Psychoanalysis, 14*(3), 285–295.

Singer, E. (1968). The reluctance to interpret. In E. Hammer (Ed.), *Uses of interpretation in treatment*. New York: Grune & Stratton.

Singer, E. (1971). The patient aids the analyst. In B. Landis & E. Tauber (Eds.), *In the name of life*. New York: Holt, Rinehart, & Winston.

Singer, E. (1977). The fiction of analytic anonymity. In K. A. Frank (Ed.), *The human dimension in psychoanalytic practice*. New York: Grune & Stratton.

Strupp, H. (1989). Psychotherapy: Can the practitioner learn from the researcher? *American Psychologist*, 44(4), 717–724.

Symington, N. (1986). The analyst's act of freedom as an agent of therapeutic change. In G. Kohon (Ed.), *The British school of psychoanalysis: The independent tradition*. New Haven, CT: Yale University Press.

Wachtel, P. (1986). On the limits of therapeutic neutrality. In A. Goldberg (Ed.), *The future of psychoanalysis: Essays in honor of Kohut*. New York: International Universities Press.

Wolstein, B. (1987). Experience, interpretation, self knowledge. *Contemporary Psychoanalysis*, 23(2), 329–349.

AFTERWORD

Stefanie Solow Glennon

When Helen Golden called and told me of her plan, with George Goldstein, to put together a *festschrift* for Sabe and asked if I would be interested in writing something for the book, I was thrilled by their idea and honored to be asked to contribute. I also made some suggestions as to whom I thought Sabe would want included in the book. Each of the people we asked readily accepted.

What I had not anticipated was that rereading (and in some cases reading for the first time) papers by Sabe would be so painful. As I immersed myself in his extraordinary and prescient body of work, I fell in love all over again, but this time with a kind of awe and respect that intimate, day-to-day life can preclude. I suppose that what I'm suggesting is that a degree of idealization has emerged in me from renewed exposure to these remarkable papers. Yet I am so grateful for the experience in spite of the exacerbation of pain over the loss of this creative mind, the part of him that is gone.

After reading Irwin Hoffman's beautiful discussion of Sabe's most well-known paper, "Anxieties in the Analyst: An Autobiographical Account," I picked up Irwin's book, *Ritual and Spontaneity in the Psychoanalytic Process*, which Sabe had loved and put on his reading list for his classes. As I opened the cover, I found a photocopy of a letter Sabe had written to Irwin, the one Irwin makes reference to in his discussion. I have no memory of having photocopied the letter, and if Sabe did so, I have no memory of having put it in Irwin's book. But I must have because there it was, in my copy of the book, and I would like to share it with you.

On February 14, 2002 (about a year and a half before our marriage), in longhand, Sabe wrote:

Dear Dr. Hoffman,

Stefanie Glennon told me she mentioned to you how much I appreciated reading *Ritual and Spontaneity* and that I would include it in the reading list for my classes. She also told me how much you appreciated getting feedback to counter the feeling that something one writes just disappears into the void. So let me elaborate.

Although I've read many of the articles in your book as they appeared over the years, it was a pleasure to reread them. In addition, the whole is greater than the sum of its parts, in that the book conveys a sense of the development of your thinking over time, as well as the comprehensiveness of your approach.

Your openness, clarity, expressiveness and readiness to examine all sides makes the journey through the material interesting, stimulating, inviting and *fun*. Thanks for all that!

Since I so much sense a kindred spirit in you, I've taken the liberty of enclosing 2 articles I wrote some 15 & 25 years ago which gave me a good time in the writing.

I look forward to meeting you some time not too far off. Stefanie says she's going to take care of that.

Most sincerely,

Sabe

They did meet a number of times, and they did very much enjoy each other's company, which was a great pleasure for me.

In going through Sabe's papers after his accident, I found a letter he had written to the editor of the *New York Times* in 1961 (when he was 35 years old) that again made me weak in the knees. His brilliance, his profundity, and his vision have been confirmed not only by the current relational/existential turn in psychoanalysis but also by the world in which we still find ourselves.

He was at heart a philosopher, but one who didn't talk very much, certainly didn't expound. He loved ideas, but was more tuned in to the phenomenological nuances of human interactions. Then, almost as an eruption, a comment would emerge with no preamble that would limn magnificently what was going on in our life together, in the world at large, in the extended family, or about individuals with whom we had spent time. I often thought this must be how he was as an analyst:

listening, watching, intensely focused yet relaxed, and then spouting a concise, frequently humorous Sabe-take on what was going on or had gone on.

Here is the *New York Times* letter. Note that he does not include either his profession, in which he was already prominent, or his Ph.D.

Our Concern for Survival

The condition of anxiety impels men to act. Any action is more tolerable than paralyzing helplessness in the face of undefined and overwhelming catastrophe. We live in a world in which the threat of final catastrophe is thumped into us with each heartbeat, and the feeling of impotence irresistibly mounts.

Inaction is intolerable, so we act. We build fall-out shelters. We take concrete steps with concrete blocks to ward off the invisible lethal rays.

But perhaps the fall-out shelter craze has more to do with an attempt to counteract the anxiety of personal impotence than with counteracting the lethal rays. It is a questionable protection against the latter and a downright self-destructive antidote to the former.

With fall-out shelters we console ourselves that we have at least done something, that we have done all we can. But what are we really doing?

We are constructing monuments to the new era of civilization, the era in which the submersion of man is completed—his body joining his spirit underground. We accept the assumption of our helplessness to influence our world and concern ourselves with mere survival as statistical ciphers in a skyless hole.

Are we really unable to affect the course of events? The psychological danger of the fall-out shelter mentality is that it saps us of the energy and the conviction to try. Even under the best of circumstances it is harder to be more human than less human. The tools of humanity make it so. The pen hasn't changed much in two hundred years, but now it has to be mightier than the bomb.

Sabert Basescu
Larchmont, NY, Nov. 7, 1961

I want to express the great sadness I feel about the loss of Helen. I met Helen and Howard Golden through Sabe in 2002. They had been friends for many years. Helen and Ellie Basescu, Sabe's wife of 50 years who passed away in 2001, had gone to college together, and I was the newcomer. Yet Helen and I connected immediately and began a separate relationship. When Howard, her husband of I think more than 50 years, died, we uninhibitedly talked about our experiences with mourning. (My husband of 28 years had passed away in 1998.) We read each other's papers and spoke with an openness that belied the newness of our friendship.

Helen's great appreciation and love of Sabe made her someone to whom I could speak after his accident, and she never tired of hearing the details of what was going on with him. I didn't have to worry that I was going over that line of being too much.

She visited him frequently, even after she was diagnosed with lung cancer, and she and I had long, intimate telephone conversations up until shortly before the end. What a remarkable woman. I miss her every day. She would have been so proud of how this book has evolved; she did not get to read the wonderful papers it contains.

For those of you who might be reading this *festschrift* not having known Sabert Basescu, I want to let you know that the accident referred to above occurred when he was riding his bike in Central Park in Manhattan on May 2, 2006, when he was almost 80 years old. At that time he was completely healthy, fully functioning, seeing patients, writing, teaching, supervising, and doing some form of strenuous exercise every day. We were told by the police that he was in a crowded lane on a beautiful spring evening, braked suddenly to avoid hitting a jogger, and went over the handlebars. He sustained a traumatic brain injury and, though much improved at the present time, will never be cognitively what he was. It is truly a tragedy that has hit a wide circle of people. I have received countless e-mails and calls from people whose life he has touched, all of whom are devastated by the loss of him.

I am so grateful for and moved by the articles that have been written by our eminent authors, each of whom has added a unique dimension to Sabe's work. I only wish the book could have come out while he was still whole.

BIBLIOGRAPHY OF WORKS BY SABERT BASESCU

(1960). Existentialism. *NYSPA Proceedings (23rd Annual Meeting)*, 38–39.

(1962). Human nature and psychotherapy. *Review of Existential Psychology and Psychiatry*, 2(2), 149–158.

(1963). Existential therapy. In A. Deutsch & H. Fishman (Eds.), *Encyclopedia of mental health* (Vol. 2, pp. 583–595). New York: Franklin Watts.

(1964). Phenomenology and existential analysis. In E. Abt & B. Riess (Eds.), *Progress in clinical psychology* (Vol. 6, pp. 67–68). New York: Grune & Stratton.

(1964). [Review of the book *Research in psychotherapy*]. *American Journal of Orthopsychiatry*, 34(1), 173–174.

(1965). The threat of suicide in psychotherapy. *American Journal of Psychotherapy*, 19(1), 9–105.

(1968). Creativity and the dimensions of consciousness. *Humanitas*, 4(2), 133–144.

(1968, with Rollo May). Existential psychology. In D. Sills (Ed.), *International encyclopedia of the social sciences* (Vol. 13, pp. 76–84). Macmillan/Free Press.

(1971). Existence and experience. In G. Goldman & D. Milman (Eds.), *Innovations in psychotherapy* (pp. 94–102). New York: Charles S. Thomas.

(1974). The concept of freedom. *Contemporary Psychoanalysis*, 10(2), 231–238.

(1977). Anxieties in the analyst: An autobiographical account. In K. A. Frank (Ed.), *The human dimension in psychoanalytic practice* (pp. 154–164). New York: Grune & Stratton.

(1978). In search of my self. *Contemporary Psychoanalysis*, 14(4), 548–553.

(1979). Existential psychotherapy. In G. Goldman & D. Milman (Eds.), *Therapists at work* (pp. 31–58). Dubuque, IA: Kendall/Hunt.

(1980). [Review of the book *Masochism and the emerging ego: Selected papers of Esther Menaker*]. *Psychoanalytic Review*, 67(4).

(1981). [Review of the book *Existential psychotherapy*]. *Contemporary Psychology*, 26(7).

(1984). Discussion of psychoanalysis in groups: Creativity in diegophrenia. *Group*, 8(1), 27–28.

(1984). [Review of the book *The analytic attitude*]. *Contemporary Psychology*, 29(1).

(1987). Behind the "seens": The inner experience of at least one psychoanalyst. *Psychoanalytic Psychology*, 4(3), 255–265.

(1988). The therapeutic process. *Contemporary Psychoanalysis*, 24(1), 121–125.

(1989). [Review of the book *The Freudian metaphor*]. *Contemporary Psychology*, 34(4).

(1990). Tools of the trade: The use of the self in psychotherapy. *Group*, 14(3), 157–165.

(1990). Show and tell: Reflections on the analystís self-disclosure. In G. Stricker & M. Fisher (Eds.), *Self-disclosure in the therapeutic relationship* (pp. 47–60). New York: Plenum.

(1990). Personal analysis. In M. Meisels & E. Shapiro (Eds.), *Tradition and innovation in psychoanalytic education* (pp. 131–134). Hillsdale, NJ: Lawrence Erlbaum.

(1995). Battered, bothered, and bewildered: Daily life of the therapist. Unpublished manuscript.

INDEX